Cuba and the Tempest

ENVISIONING CUBA • Louis A. Pérez Jr., editor

the Tempest

EDUARDO GONZÁLEZ

Literature & Cinema in the Time of Diaspora

THE UNIVERSITY OF NORTH CAROLINA PRESS · CHAPEL HILL

Designed by Eric M. Brooks

Set in Quadraat and Schmutz by Tseng Information Systems, Inc.

The paper in this book meets the guidelines for permanence
and durability of the Committee on Production Guidelines
for Book Longevity of the Council on Library Resources.

Publication of this book was supported by a grant from
The Johns Hopkins University.

Library of Congress Cataloging-in-Publication Data
González, Eduardo, 1943–
Cuba and the tempest: literature and cinema
in the time of diaspora / Eduardo González
    p. cm. — (Envisioning Cuba)
Includes bibliographical references and index.
ISBN-13: 978-0-8078-3015-4 (cloth: alk. paper)
ISBN-10: 0-8078-3015-1 (cloth: alk. paper)
ISBN-13: 978-0-8078-5683-3 (pbk.: alk. paper)
ISBN-10: 0-8078-5683-5 (pbk.: alk. paper)
1. Cuban literature—20th century—History and criticism.
2. Exiles' writings, Cuban—History and criticism. 3. Cabrera Infante,
G. (Guillermo), 1929– —Criticism and interpretation. 4. Benitez Rojo,
Antonio, 1931– —Criticism and interpretation. 5. Padura, Leonardo—
Criticism and interpretation. I. Title. II. Series.
PQ7378.G66 2006
860.9'9206914097291—dc22   2005031385

cloth   10 09 08 07 06   5 4 3 2 1
paper   10 09 08 07 06   5 4 3 2 1

For FIFI *and our grandchildren,*

JOHN T. IRWIN *in Baltimore,*

BEATRIZ MAGGI *in Havana,* &

ANTONIO BENÍTEZ ROJO

(in memoriam)

My purpose is to tell of bodies which have been

transformed into shapes of a different kind.

    OVID, *Metamorphoses*

Everyone senses that the work escapes, that it is

something else than its history, the sum of its sources,

influences, or models.

[Tout le monde sent bien que le oeuvre échappe, qu'elle

est autre chose que son histoire même, la somme de ses

sources, de ses influences ou de ses modèles.]

    ROLAND BARTHES, *On Racine/Sur Racine*

contents

acknowledgments

This book is entirely owed to the writers it deals with and to each of the works of literature, cinema, and philosophy it examines in the effort not to improve or outsmart them but to join their energies, their potential lives in other readers' minds. It is in this sense a naive book, made a bit wiser, one hopes, by the help of uncynical irony and plain sympathy, a perspective in which it trusts to engage the reader.

A special word of thanks is due to Charles Hatfield, in whom the old possum ruminates fables of ashes turned into honey and then into smoke; to Regina Galasso, in the light of whose eyes Sappho is mirrored trembling; to Giulia Sissa for her style and wisdom in hymeneal matters; and to Barbara Zecchi and José Monleón for their immensurable warmth.

Elaine Maisner and Louis Pérez (and those who read the manuscript) rewarded with their encouragement and trust my own faith in a project too long in the making and unmaking through various reincarnations. Steve Nichols fueled my energies with high-octane bluntness. Jerry Christensen led me to Coleridge's poem "Limbo" and provided (without much trying) inspiration with *Romanticism and the End of History*, of such force in fact that his book goes unlisted in the bibliography. I am most grateful to Paula Wald and Julie Bush for transforming the text into a book.

Cuba and the Tempest is dedicated to the memory of Antonio Benítez Rojo. It is also dedicated to my wife, Fifi, and our grandchildren, Emily, Anna, Luke, Nicolás, and Elías, and to John Irwin here in Baltimore and Beatriz Maggi in Havana.

abbreviations

The following abbreviations are used throughout this book for frequently cited works.

AA Lewis Carroll, *The Annotated Alice*, Martin Gardner, ed. (New York, 1960)

AAI Fray Ramón Pané, *An Account of the Antiquities of the Indians* (Durham, 1999); page references followed by those from *Relación acerca de las antigüedades de los indios*

AP Thomas Gregor, *Anxious Pleasures: The Sexual Lives of an Amazonian People* (Chicago, 1985)

ArP Walter Benjamin, *The Arcades Project* (Cambridge, Mass., 1999)

Atn Guillermo Cabrera Infante, *Arcadia todas las noches* (Madrid, 1995)

Bde Joan Corominas, *Breve diccionario etimológico de la lengua castellana* (Madrid, 1967)

Cc Fernando Ortiz, *Contrapunteo cubano del tabaco y el azúcar*, Enrico Mario Santí, ed. (Madrid, 2002)

CC Fernando Ortiz, *Cuban Counterpoint: Tobacco and Sugar* (Durham, 1995); page references followed by those from *Contrapunteo cubano*

Conf Thomas De Quincey, *Confessions of an English Opium Eater and Other Writings*, Grevel Lindop, ed. (Oxford, 1985)

Cro Guillermo Cabrera Infante, "Cronología a la manera de Laurence Sterne . . . o no," *La Gaceta del Fondo de Cultura Económica* (Oct. 1998): 12–18

Cs Guillermo Cabrera Infante, *Cine o sardina* (Madrid, 1997)

CS Calvert Casey, *The Collected Stories* (Durham, 1998)

DJ Lord Byron, *Don Juan*, T. G. Steffan, E. Steffan, and W. W. Pratt, eds. (London, 1986)

DN Friedrich A. Kittler, *Discourse Networks: 1800/1900* (Stanford, 1990)

EH Friedrich Nietzsche, *Ecce Homo*, R. J. Hollingdale, trans., Michael Tanner, ed. (London, 1992)

G Barry Paris, *Garbo: A Biography* (New York, 1994)

GB Sir George James Frazer, *The Golden Bough: A Study in Magic and Religion* (London, 1994)

GCI	Raymond D. Souza, *Guillermo Cabrera Infante: Two Islands, Many Worlds* (Austin, 1996)
Gg	Guillermo Cabrera Infante, "Del gofio al golfo," *Jornadas de Estudios Canarias-Americas* 1.4 (1984)
HAH	Friedrich Nietzsche, *Human, All Too Human: A Book for Free Spirits*, R. J. Hollingdale, trans. (Cambridge, 1996)
HC	Norberto Fuentes, *Hemingway in Cuba* (New York, 1984)
HFR	Robin Wood, *Hitchcock's Films Revisited* (New York, 1989)
HID	Guillermo Cabrera Infante, *La Habana Para un Infante Difunto* (Barcelona, 1979)
HM	Peter Conrad, *The Hitchcock Murders* (New York, 2000)
Hu	Fernando Ortiz, *El huracán: Su mitología y sus símbolos* (Mexico, 1949)
II	Guillermo Cabrera Infante, *Infante's Inferno* (New York, 1984)
IS	Ernest Hemingway, *Islands in the Stream* (New York, 1997)
JMH	Leonardo Padura Fuentes, *José María Heredia: La patria y la vida* (Havana, 2003)
LS	Bruce Fink, *The Lacanian Subject: Between Language and Jouissance* (Princeton, 1995)
LV	Sigmund Freud, *Leonardo da Vinci and a Memory of His Childhood* (New York, 1989)
M	Leonardo Padura Fuentes, *Máscaras* (Madrid, 1997)
MC	Guillermo Cabrera Infante, *Mea Cuba* (Barcelona, 1992); page references followed by those from the English translation (New York, 1994)
Mor	Edgar Allan Poe, "Morella," in *Tales and Sketches: Vol. 1, 1831–1842*, Thomas Ollive Mabbott, ed. (Urbana, Ill., 2000)
MS	John T. Irwin, *The Mystery to a Solution: Poe, Borges, and the Analytic Detective Story* (Baltimore, 1994)
NS	J. D. Salinger, *Nine Stories* (Boston, 1991)
Ody	Homer, *The Odyssey of Homer*, Richmond Lattimore, trans. (New York, 1965)
OED	*The Oxford English Dictionary*, 2nd ed., J. A. Simpson and E. C. S. Weiner, eds. (Oxford, 1989)
Ol	José Martí, *Obra literaria*, Cintio Vitier, ed. (Caracas, 1978)
OMS	Ernest Hemingway, *The Old Man and the Sea* (New York, 1995)
OTM	Claude Lévi-Strauss, *The Origins of Table Manners: Introduction to a Science of Mythology: 3* (New York, 1978)

OXX   Guillermo Cabrera Infante, *Un oficio del siglo XX* (Barcelona, 1973)

PBn   Lino Novás Calvo, *Pedro Blanco, el negrero: Biografía novelada*, in *Obra literaria*, Jesús Díaz, ed. (Havana, 1990)

Po   Leonardo Padura Fuentes, *Paisaje de otoño* (Madrid, 1998)

POu   Issac Deutscher, *The Prophet Outcast: Trotsky, 1929–1940* (New York, 1963)

Pp   Leonardo Padura Fuentes, *Pasado perfecto* (Madrid, 2000)

QC   Susanna Åkerman, *Queen Christina of Sweden and Her Circle: The Transformation of a Seventeenth-Century Philosophical Libertine* (Leiden, 1991)

R   Fray Ramón Pané, *Relación acerca de las antigüedades de los indios* (Mexico, 1974)

RI   Antonio Benítez Rojo, *The Repeating Island: The Caribbean and the Postmodern Perspective* (Durham, 1996)

Sl   Alejo Carpentier, *El siglo de las luces* (Madrid, 1989)

SM   Norman M. Klein, *Seven Minutes: The Life and Death of the American Animated Cartoon* (New York, 1998)

SW   José Martí, *José Martí: Selected Writings*, Esther Allen, ed. and trans. (New York, 2002)

Symp   Plato, *The Symposium*, R. E. Allen, ed. (New Haven, 1991)

TSZ   Friedrich Nietzsche, *Thus Spoke Zarathustra: A Book for Everyone and No One*, R. J. Hollingdale, trans. (London, 1969)

TTT   Guillermo Cabrera Infante, *Tres Tristes Tigres* (Barcelona, 1967)

TV   Sigmund Freud, "The Taboo of Virginity (Contributions to the Psychology of Love III," in *The Complete Psychological Works of Sigmund Freud*, vol. 11 (London, 1962)

V   Charles Barr, *Vertigo* (London, 2000)

VC   Leonardo Padura Fuentes, *Vientos de Cuaresma* (Madrid, 2001)

Vt   Guillermo Cabrera Infante, "La voz de la tortuga," in *Todo está hecho con espejos: Cuentos completos* (Madrid, 1999)

Cuba and the Tempest

Life after Cuba

SOUL AND SOIL

"The territory is German, the Earth is Greek . . ." *and both are Cuban*—should, perchance, the phrase end, in recognition of the sovereign idiocies and exactions which inform and rule over brands of nationalism everywhere there is (or should be) a nation? A nation as embattled and hard-fought upon its soil and scattered soul as the one set upon that island (also spelled Island), in recent decades renamed Archipelago? The French authors of the above sentence (the notorious nomadic bandits of Empire and road warriors of tenure track known as Gilles Deleuze and Félix Guattari) go on to write: "And this disjunction is precisely what determines the status of the romantic artist, it is that she or he no longer confronts the gaping of chaos but the pull of the Ground (Fond)" (1987, 339). This is hardly the place in which to grapple any further with the dualities established by the authors in dealing with the European Romantic geographies impacted by the Napoleonic aftermath of the French revolution and the multiple births of nationalism. ("Romantic" is used hereafter whenever Romanticism's historical roots in Europe are implied.)

A translation of the scattered European geographies and conditions reads: *Cuba: the Territory is for sale; the Earth, the Ground, the Soil, never.* For it seems that colonies (as in Cuba's own former case) were made to be sold, as even nations are when fallen into territorial status through sheer malfeasance or geopolitical stress. Or (as again in Cuba's case) a born-again nation can confer upon itself the contingent status of *territorio libre de América* (free territory of the Americas) when driven by policies aimed at setting other nations free, just as it sees itself, in doctrinal standards and by eventual insurgent guerrilla infiltration and revolutionary rule.

Moreover, if *German* and *Greek* are made strictly contemporaneous with the 1830s post-Romantic period of concern to Deleuze and Guattari, the *Cuban* in Cuba would suddenly resemble the Germanic and Grecian nation labels at the height of the Communist nation's anti-imperialist militancy during the revolutionary 1960s. *Greek* as in Lord Byron (who in 1824 wretchedly died Greek—as in 1967 Che died Bolivian), together with José

María Heredia (who in 1821 wrote a poem to the insurgent Greek patriots in whom he mirrored his own struggle to free Cuba from Spain). But also *German, All Too German*, in the sense in which issues of belated nation-building and empire haunt the phrase, just as such issues resonate in the history of Spain's last colony, but not as loudly as when the fall of a certain Wall in 1989 ruined the partnership in modes of hard State rule between Cuba and the German Democratic Republic at the undoing of Ronald Reagan's christened *Evil Empire*.

Though political in whichever way it may strike the reader, this is not a book about politics, just as it is not concerned with Cuba as a nation but mainly with the lives and afterlives in various ways touched by the nation-bound or after-birth condition of being Cuban at home and abroad: being incurably Cuban; coming after Cuba; running after Her; after Her and from Her; in signs, syllables, icons, figures.

ISLANDS IN FLIGHT

Thus, as if on the run or in flight, this book endeavors, though never through mere resistance, to *escape* disciplinary and cultural allegiances to Cuba, just as if what Roland Barthes means here by *oeuvre* or literary *work* meant something like the object of study known as *Cuba*: "Everyone senses that the work *escapes*, that it is *something else* than its history, the sum of its sources, influences, or models: a hard, irreducible core, in the undefined mass of events, conditions, collective mentalities; that is why we never possess a history of literature, but only a history of littérateurs" (1964, 155). (Well, if not exactly about *littérateurs* themselves, this work in the form of a book is certainly about what is written and escapes—escapes as it is read and as such released in the myriad afterlives of the various acts of authorship it questions in their interrelated works.)

In the best book yet written about Cuba at large and dispersed beyond its territory and cultures, Antonio Benítez Rojo found in *La isla que se repite* (1989) or *The Repeating Island* (1992) the release point for a fugue of orchestral narrations about becoming hyper-cosmopolitan through a process set against the grain of reiterative insularity.[1] The fifth and pivotal chapter of this book—"Antonio's Island (The Long Goodbye)"—engages the central gesture made by *The Repeating Island* as *obra* or work in the tradition of Romantic authorship, the grand gesture achieved by Benítez Rojo against nihilism in his sequence of hyphenated essays about islands-repeated-and-in-flight. His suite of essays sets itself against the nihilism that—often as postmodernist cant—takes all that escapes into contingent or unscripted dialogue (as works of all sorts are reread and reinvented) as if such revisions and reworkings implied that anything goes; that chaos rules to the benefit of random moral and political choices.

What is developed here by means of the literary precedents of *Tempest* and *Odyssey* in their joint *Romantic* occasion of authorship—synthesized in Byron's aboriginal postmodernist *Don Juan*—is meant in response to that earlier gesture by Benítez Rojo; Prospero's gesture to Caliban to *allow the island to repeat itself* by working through *its own escape from itself*: an island from its own flight a fugitive, *isla a su vuelo fugitiva* (as Harold Bloom was once heard to mumble).

THREE ODYSSEYS AND A TEMPEST

This book is divided into three parts set in thematic sequence between an introduction and a conclusion. The three-part sequence examines and recreates, through closely observed and intersecting interpretations, the European and postcolonial drama of Romantic literary authorship, in overt or covert reference to the nation of Cuba, encountered in the writings of two exiled authors, Guillermo Cabrera Infante (1929) and Antonio Benítez Rojo (1931), and one who still lives and works at home, Leonardo Padura Fuentes (1955). As it sets out to relate the works of these and other authors from other nations and related literary traditions and philosophies, the book recognizes the *intertextual* character of the various readings it pursues, even as it finds such a label redundant, insofar as acts and works of literature are taken here as if they originated under the spell of someone else's authorship—and were in such fashion *interwoven* with significant others. Although, so taken, the power of author over interpreter often emanates from arts other than literature (such as film, painting, politics), a first-degree instance of specific authorship design in literary agency informs the readings and the writing that have clashed and rubbed faces and fates in the making of this book.

There should be no mistake about the book's bias when it comes to its principal authors and their respective authorships: Plato is literary; Hitchcock and Almodóvar are literary—but so, too, are Homer, Shakespeare, Byron, Poe, Lewis Carroll, Freud, Nietzsche, Martí, Joyce . . . and (the) Cubans themselves.

The main aspects of Romantic authorship are found repeated in three interlocked odyssey parts.

"Part 1: The Star Husband" defines and dramatizes the question of Romantic authorship in face-off between Guillermo Cabrera Infante's *Defunct Infant* fictional *persona* and Thomas De Quincey's split conception concerning a *literature of knowledge* and a *literature of power*. The split *persona* of the manic-melancholic writer all-at-once *Defunct* and *Infant* is given illustration in the mirror of De Quincey's two-headed conception of Romantic readership.[2] *Infancy*—as in *Infante*—lends *power*, gives birth, nurtures, and poisons the author's personal trove of memories, images which to a large extent remain embedded in his defining issues of national kinship and familial exile. *Defunctness*—as in *Difunto*—frames those negotiations of *knowledge* through which *power* takes shape in the arts and ruses of writing for effects, writing at the risk of allowing such showy effects to downgrade into sheer gamesmanship the sublime force of what is read, written, heard, and felt.

In this first part, the interplay between *Infancy* and *Defunctness* unfolds through the combined reading of Cabrera Infante's pastiche folktale "La voz de la tortuga [The voice of the turtle]" and a dinner-speech act of his published as "Del gofio al golfo [From gruel to gulf]." Native Cuban grounds for the murder tale (involving the non-murder murder mystery of man by beast) are revisited through a return-to-the-scene-of-the-crime odyssey emanating from the "Gofio" speech, given at Tenerife, in which the murder-suicide of the author's paternal grandmother by her husband, his Canarian father's father, is disclosed to the audience. In what amounts to a literary homage to his Cuban-Canarian ancestors, the exiled author recounts to the Tenerife audience the grandparents' murder and suicide as it had occurred on Cuban native grounds thus seeded (as in Diaspora) with Canarian blood. The speaker as revised by the writer combines the story with the exquisite character assassination of his own father, whom he exposes as a Communist and closet womanizer, allied sinful conditions he has himself long forsworn.

The pastiche folktale of the bridegroom who dies while mounting a sea turtle by wrongful means is brought back home in the setting of Arawak stories about human origins, food squalor, the scarcity of women, and the birth of turtles from a hero's swollen back. The recycling of a literary turtle tale (grounded in *Alice in Wonderland*) through folklore and myth constitutes the first instance of Romantic authorship in the book, Romantic in the manner in which male heroic acts might be said to triumph on condition of their being in bondage to their own representation of female power, grasped in lethal conspiracy with sublime love. Rather than relying on abstract theories of myth-making in the works of Claude Lévi-Strauss, the Romantic authorship of heroic character so depicted is further illustrated in concrete reference to the adventures and misadventures of a serial (five wives) Amazonian monogamist and Star Husband, a figure borrowed from the pages of the French anthropologist's moral treatise (*The Origins of Table Manners*) on the social accommodation to the beauties and blemishes of young women when viewed as prospective wives and mothers.

"Part 2: No Wedding without Funeral" traces the second odyssey through the tenement and movie-house episodes serialized in *La Habana Para un Infante Difunto*. Tales of sex in the movies and at the movies are rendered in analytic kinship with Hitchcock's *Spellbound* and Freud's *Totem and Taboo*. The exploits of the infant moviegoer, sex hunter, film reviewer, and smitten and cheating-cheated lover migrate from improvised habitats for carnal predation, incidentally attached to the silver screen, toward the sublime realm of Orphic cinephilia in Hitchcock's *Vertigo* and Almodóvar's *Hable con ella*, or *Talk to Her*.

Exiled Orpheus comes home alone to a bygone Havana in which, as Odysseus, and with help from Edgar Allan Poe, he dies, home alone at last, the death of a chess-playing automaton from Romantic Germany, once upon a time unsheltered from his lair of stage tricks in a Baltimore back alley.

"Part 3: Cuban Afterlives" examines the third and final odyssey in the four afterlives of a Havana police detective who, in the year of 1989 as it never was, inspects in the daily rounds of his city's battered flesh the clues of catastrophe and stubborn hope he must face in the post-revolutionary decline of civility in 1990s Havana. Inspecting 1989 as reinvented in 1989 as it never was is preceded by a portrait of Friedrich Nietzsche and José Martí joined in Romantic penmanship as brothers of the fraternal kind, fraternal as thus virtual, and in fact actual enemies animated by the will to unveil truth to her limits as drawn and terminated inside their souls.

As each of the authorship lives explored in this book enters into mutual afterlife contact with another, those of Leonardo Padura Fuentes (inventor of Cuba's 1989 as it never was) and J. D. Salinger (the soldier who might have actually met Esmé with love and squalor back in 1945) join hands in signing-off the Romantic act of writing while holding God's hand as if it were the Devil's. If it should be true that God put his mark on Cain to brand with its trauma the need to seek copyright by copying him, even as the Devil might in confusing himself with God, the Romantic illness lies at hand: Reader, be Cain!

part one

The Star Husband

Pheidas made the Aphrodite of the Eleans stepping on a
tortoise, as a symbol of housekeeping for women and of
silence. For she must speak only to her husband or through
him, not disliking to be heard through the voice of another
as the flute player through his instrument makes a more
commanding sound.

Aesop 108

chapter one

The Sybil's Voice
(Overture)

In discussing the seclusion of girls at puberty in *The Golden Bough*, Sir James George Frazer attributes the widespread custom to the wish to protect oneself against dangers believed to emanate from menstrual uncleanliness. What is found occasionally fearsome in nubile women is not so much the filth perceived in menstrual blood as the powerful energy released by its shedding. Such energy is neither good nor bad. The dread it generates derives from the skills of those individuals capable of bending its power to their own purposes. What is dreaded, then, is a spark of divine or uncanny force essential to life, encumbered by pollution, and capable of being ruled by magic at the hands of divine kings, priests, sorcerers.

And so it happens that inside Frazer's wondrous cabinet of marvels, all sorts of girls at puberty share with a host of divine persons the ritually enforced taboo against seeing the sun or touching the ground beneath them. They are to remain hidden and suspended between earth and sky for a measure of time deemed critical until the danger of their improperly discharging blood energy goes away. Protecting girls and divine persons in particular against improper conduct or lethal contact protects others in general from two related dangers: squandering energy without benefit to life and discharging it in a manner harmful to the living.[1]

The broad perspective followed here in approaching Guillermo Cabrera Infante's tale "La voz de la tortuga" issues from the prime example given by Frazer of persons held hanging between heaven and earth on account of their possessing "the coveted yet burdensome gift of immortality" (GB 704). Such is the exemplary case of the Sibyl's plight and her unending woe in Petronius's *Satyricon* as quoted in *The Golden Bough*: "The wizened remains of the deathless Sibyl are said to have been preserved in a jar or urn which hung in a temple of Apollo at Cumae; and when a group of merry children, tired, perhaps, of playing in the sunny streets, sought the shade of the temple and amused themselves by gathering underneath the familiar jar and calling out, 'Sibyl, what do you wish?' a hollow voice, like an echo, used to answer from the urn, 'I wish to die'" (GB 704). Frazer is well aware that Trimalchio's drunken boast (in *Satyricon* 48) echoes the Sibyl's wish to die (in words further echoed in T. S. Eliot's epigraph to "The Burial of the Dead" section opening *The Waste Land*). The Sibyl's cry for release from perpetual old age is mentioned by Trimalchio, who remains oblivious that the banquet he hosts takes place in Hades. John Bodel argues that the *Cena's* readers in Petronius's age would have picked up clues of the banquet's home-of-the-dead location—sepulchral tokens in Trimalchio's house signal death's share in the ornaments of wealth—just as readers of F. Scott Fitzgerald's novel would, if told of a "Gatsby-like figure with a hearse parked in the drive and the initials R.I.P. emblazoned on the doormat."[2]

Further textual parallels would relate the actions of one of Trimalchio's banquet guests to Aeneas's descent into the underworld in *Aeneid* 6. The link is made as Encolpius scans the story of Trimalchio's rags-to-riches climb from slave to wealthy freedman painted on the house's walls, just as Aeneas halts by the gate of Apollo's temple at Cumae on his way to the underworld, as he retraces the story of the labyrinth wrought on the doors by none other than Daedalus. After he broke loose from King Minos and left the island of Crete and flew "towards the chill north by tracks unknown," Daedalus wrought on the doors at Cumae "the Bull's brutal passion, and Pasiphae's union with him."[3] The interwoven reading of "La voz de la tortuga" pursued here emulates Daedalus (the escape-artist) as it recreates and expands a tale of fatal love between man, woman, and beast.

The reading reinvents the tale as if reborn from a kernel of Romantic folklore invention. So imagined and rehearsed, the tale encircles and zigzags a path through Cabrera Infante's major writings. It burrows into them and hatches itself within the erotic labyrinth woven in *Tres Tristes Tigres* (1967) and *La Habana Para un Infante Difunto* (1979), bound together in their combined fortunes as performance novel and autobiographical myth. This labyrinth of scribbled selfhood dwells in *Satyricon* from the moment Infante's boyhood reading of Petronius's little book is enshrined at the threshold of the *defunct infant's* storytelling. Telling stories is seen in retrospect as a lonesome activity born of closet or toilet reading and energized in the aging writer's *La Habana Para un Infante Difunto* by the double jeopardy and treasured hazards of remembered sex.[4]

ROMANTIC FAME TIME ZONES

The allusion to Maurice Ravel's *Pavane pour une enfante défunte* distracts from the title's deeper implications concerning the complex temporality of authorship, authorship embroiled in a personal myth of self-making, character-building, and the Romantic earning of fame which may be rendered as follows: current adult author (the remembered or bygone *Infant* of long ago) remains as if *defunct* in the short-term cocoon time of updated obituary and funereal duties. But, unlike the Sibyl (preserved in decay inside a jar), *defunct Infant* inhabits two time zones in the authorship management of fame. Both zones are managed by that most common breed of hybrid collusion: the one involving reader and writer.

In the first, across-generations zone, occupying a background in limbo, two halves of a soul as common as the common cold are kept separate, neatly bound but distinct, except when the always-more-notorious *Writer* decides to swallow its own aboriginal soul mate in the *Reader*. In the last forty-some years of world literature, the trick in question often spelled itself as *Borges*, a signature whose fame rests on the reader's will (and fortune) in keeping his or her long-term memory of *His* (the author's) writings *infant-fresh*. Either inside *Borges* or *His* reader, such collaborative fame must cut across generations, keeping alive the illusion that no zone of the past is as truly dead as to forbid its transport on reader's shoulders into present renewal (as Aeneas carries his father Anchises on his shoulders out of burning Troy).

The renewed or reborn *infant* across-generations zone just described has its counterpart in the short-notice business of writing within deadlines. This other realm defines the perimeter work zone of the *Writer* as a technician nowadays glued to the horn-of-plenty laptop and tied (with all his/her applied know-how and fancy) to desk labor, search engine, and blogger mania. Thus, on the one hand, the Sibyl may be seen holding her Mummy-Muse office in the *Reader-Writer* collaborative affairs inside the renewal zone of elongated generations Time. On the other, a leading negotiator, akin to Melville's Confidence Man, presides (with all the powers of invisible markets and marketing ploys) over a zone of foreshortened time cycles, made up of minute-to-minute twenty-four-hour hyphenations in labor, risk, gain, loss.

Genealogical *Infant-bonding* across generations puts the label *Literature* on its own, older and ever-renewable zone, where, in the vanished echoes of the moaning Sibyl, Aeneas the *Reader* son carries on his shoulders Anchises the *Writer* father into exile. Conflagration and catastrophe, such as when Troy burns, represent the Phoenix burning-point of higher sublimity in the emotive affairs of self-renewal akin to Thomas De Quincey's literature *of power*, power fueled by emotions, which the reader *owes* in perpetual *awe* (and emotional deficit) "to the impassioned books which he has read." (The *Reader*—claims De Quincey—owes such books "many a thousand more of emotions than he can consciously trace back to them," emotions which, as dim as they may be by "their origination," yet "arise in him and mold him through life like forgotten incidents of his childhood").[5] For the moment, either all by herself at her Cumaean gatepost or scattered tenfold at every corner of the world, the Sibylline fortune-telling figure will guard, on literature's behalf, a power-nexus embedded infant-fresh within the *Reader*; the same nexus found between the *Writer* and his childhood *Infant* shade. Such nexus (most often either overvalued or devalued under the *literature* label) transforms, as if by alchemy, memories held into promises kept; but kept only as if on lease to faculties invested in foretelling and prophecy.

The actualized *Infant* subject character in the Guillermo Cabrera Infante title *La Habana Para un Infante Difunto* occupies (in absolute unbridgeable nearness) a time zone other than the one to which his *defunct* predicate character belongs. *Infant* subject and *defunct* predicate are time-zone split. Yet, their mutual separateness-in-utter-nearness means the opposite of not communicating at all. It is not for any lack of communication contact that subject *Infante* remains split from its *difunto* predicate. It is rather that, as their mutual communication grows in sheer literary *effects*, so grows in corresponding volume their mutually unconsummated *affect*. On grounds of affect, *Infant* subjectivity values time's past depth in generational terms, as it narrates from the past forward and recapitulates past lives as if they were generations lived (and exiled) within a single subject. Loss and exile make up the milk of *Infant* nursing in gross time. A great sense of loss in bodies vanished informs the abundance of laughter in *Infant* plot-making and milk-gurgling wordplay. At the edges of memory-making, *galactophagous* (or *milk-swallowing*) affect is experienced in *Infant* time as if those long-gone honey-golden, unalloyed, pleasure-pain affections were like time nuggets immune from market dissolutions. As if Marcel Proust could turn into Midas, *Infant* time treasures the gold of affect in resistance to degradation and memory fading. (The *Infant* temporal body of past and current yearnings wishes to emerge unscathed from being dipped in knowledge's pool of obsolescence.)

As such, *defunct infancy* embodies De Quincey's split between *power* and *knowledge*. Kept defunct-fresh, infancy renews its literary lease on life from the vantage point of the writer's creeping old age. *Infant* dwells in the shape of old memories embodying needs. These needs, insistently sexual in tenor, begin and end in corporeal yearnings whose best literary effect would have them exceed the figures of their own narrative enactment. These are pleasures and pains which the *Infant* writer owes to (and earns from) no other reader besides himself. And, being at heart displaced forms of rapture, no matter how much such pleasures and pains take effect in words and figures bearing knowledge, their power lies channeled in voices ineffable. Thus, listening to opera in strange Italian voices, under the familiar spell of opium, puts De Quincey (the largest infant ever born to literature) at the zero ground of power. He remains unchecked by signifying familiar English constraints as he listens (through Odysseus's ears) to the sirens' mind-beclouding Italian call. De Quincey's opium ears at the opera translate for him voice melodies in Italian into puns on those silent English words of his they might otherwise translate.[6]

Such would be the extreme transport point of unbound connectivity reached by *Infant* in the memory-making zone of genealogy, generations, elongated time. Treasured as well as encysted memories bubble up into felt images in which past affections achieve present character rapture. The rush and fear portrayed in sexual excitement may replace (as it happens in the head and crotch of the renewed *Infant* character) the gothic horrors and terror-thrills felt in the aural and visual upper registers of De Quincey's paranoid sublime. In strict Romantic Idol terms, *Infant* gets in the written and remembered adult sexual body a rush vastly minor in kind than opium's opera seance. *Infant*'s idolatry comes up short of the sublime's significant Other, found in nothing less than De Quincey's animating Christian God, behind and above whom even more powerful pagan goddesses rule.

Next to all this, and forever exempt from its moans, sighs, and wordless power-play, *Infant*'s *defunct* predicate-character celebrates time while at war with it. All at once time's celebrity and recluse inmate, *defunct* spends each day's lifetime cycle writing and rewriting his own obituary. *Defunct* occupies (on rent up- or downstairs) a stopover garret on the route that lies between funeral parlor and the grave. Just as *Infant* is a born citizen of posterity on travel between generations, his *defunct* nexus mate awaits being naturalized and dispatched into immortality, once death puts her seal on his new passport. As discussed in part 2, the nexus in question follows a small orbit adaptable to Stuart Gilbert's grand schema for Joyce's *Ulysses* in which, updated and properly *anachronized*, literary modernist and post-modern Dublin and Havana lie scrambled like a utopian bus route into nowhere.

DAILY-ROUNDS FETISH PILGRIMAGE

The *Infant-defunct* temporal dialectics begin in midmorning at the *Lotus-Eaters* point of *Bath* (the tenement toilet or outhouse enclosure) and *Genitals* (masturbation or communion with umbilical and phallic reveries). It next dwells in *Hades* (in the animation of back-and-forth traffic between the living and the dead at movie houses unframed from the diurnal/nocturnal cycle). At noontide, in *Aeolus*, the adjoining spaces of *Floating Island* and *Newspaper Press Room* would represent the workplace zone of knowledge-production at its core and zenith. The skipped lunch hour occupied in *Ulysses* by *Lestrygonians* is filled here by the *Scylla and Charybdis* of *Literature* talk at the *Library*. At the site of this *other* José Martí National Library, forensic gossip shreds to bits the higher canon of philosophic and literary wisdom. A *tabloid* zone centered on wordplay establishes itself between clashing twin rocks in whose inky whirlpool anyone's personified figure (Socrates', Jesus', Shakespeare's, Hamlet's, Che Guevara's, Fidel's, and all the chatter-serialized *literati*) replaces in caricature the living work that stood or may yet stand in his defunct memory. Then, at three, as if crossing noon anew, the small orbit skirts the *Wandering Rocks* street labyrinth in *Ulysses* and skips back to the four-o'clock-at-noon *Isle* musical womb of *Sirens* and *Daiquirí Barmaids* at the timeless *Floridita*.

Embedded in *defunct*'s small-orbit daily Odyssey lies the question of commodity fetishism. Just as Odysseus, master carpenter of his own conjugal bed, *Infant* would be glad to trade a good measure of his freedom in exchange for the embodied and concrete and tactile grasp of himself as maker of familiar objects, always inalienable from their sources in nature and family. In parallel terms, *defunct* connects with commodities by means of consuming them and renders himself a mirror of their alienated condition as finished products, severed from the material means employed by human beings in making them.[7] In terms of De Quincey's bipolar understanding of literature, *Infant* makes himself in everything he makes. His making of literature for others is as yet *of-a-piece* with making *himself-for-himself*, inalienable from others: in family, communal, pre-contractual terms. His (*Infant*'s) is the literature of power. On the other side, where literature reduces itself to knowledge, *defunct* makes himself over, for himself and for others, as if he were unknowingly buying his soul back from the Devil in order to achieve celebrity status. (Just as certain as Faust was Faustian, *defunct* is Capitalist.)

Updated, De Quincey's sense of a literature of power could help explain the *Devil-made-me-do-it* aesthetics and manic velocities at work in *defunct*'s self-advertisement and the cult of celebrity. Melville's Confidence Man represents perhaps the closest avatar to the Romantic forging in Hell of this devilishly cool, hot-commodity, authorship terminal character. He (already defunct in the instant infancy of his multiple adult role personifications) brings down, Samson-like, the twin power-knowledge pillars which so unevenly support De Quincey's temple of literature. Advertising above all the rule of affect for commodity-consumption, over any other kind of inner or public emotion in modern societies, Confidence Man plays harbinger to a familiar crisis in literary values. Prime among such values stands the valued agency of *character*. In its widest and most likable aspect, literature still identifies, in the minds and souls of its readers, with objects and practices under satyrical abuse in the serialized characters authored and personified by the Confidence Man. In the words of Jackson Lears: "a devastating assault on nearly all the cultural idioms that mid-nineteenth-century Americans hoped might stabilize the sorcery of market relations: sentimentality, rationality, mimesis—above all, the belief in a transparently communicative language and plainspoken autonomous self who utters it" (1994, 100). Yet, the chance still exists (as wagered here) to retrieve voices of genuine character from the realm of literary artifice at its *multi-vocal* best. For character may in fact prosper besides, beyond (and even at the expense of) such "plainspoken autonomous self" in command of personality. But, for any such retrieval of character to take effect, literary interpretation must examine *with affection* the work of commodity-fetishist affect so utterly layered in effects.

Affective reading (taken here as the engine of literary interpretation) should not function without spotting, digesting, and expelling the fetish through and within which that which is known from any piece of literature achieves power (power thus released from its fetish shell to become an endurable though perishable mood). This trick is attempted next in reinventing the tale "La voz de la tortuga" as an object of learned folklore making its beggar's grand entrance into the literary workshop.

chapter two

Weariness of Work Inextricable
(Folktale)

I prithee let me bring thee where crabs grow,
And I with long nails will dig thee pig-nuts,
Show thee a jay's nest, and instruct thee how
To snare the nimble marmoset. I'll bring thee
Young scamels from the rock. Wilt thou go with me?
WILLIAM SHAKESPEARE,
The Tempest, 2.2.161–66

Besides Satyricon and a soon discarded Vita Nuova in Spanish, the boy Infante found among the uncle's books a "mythology" he soon took for a bible.[1] He read about all kinds of "impossible animals" and chimeric ensembles of man and beast and discovered "exalted zoophilia [zoofilia exaltada]" (HID 42) — a fitting phrase for the tale "La voz de la tortuga" (henceforth called the "tale") whose plot outline goes as follows:

A young man from a poverty-stricken village near the seashore falls in love with a local beauty and decides to go out in search of good fortune in the company of his best friend. Together, the two friends roam the nearby beach without finding anything to earn money from. Just as they are about to quit and return home, a large sea tortoise is spotted lumbering its way back to the water. After some struggle, the two friends manage to turn the animal on its back and one of them returns to fetch a sled on which to drag the tortoise home. Left alone, the young man who plans to marry dreams about all the ornaments, hairpins, and jewelry boxes that could be made from the tortoise's shell and decides that he — not his friend — is the one with enough savvy to sell everything and get rich. It is at this point that he notices the tortoise's vulva. Aroused, the young man decides to mount the animal and mate with it. But the act proves fatal to him when the tortoise, faithful to its habits of mating in the high seas, runs him through at the genitals and from the rear with a species of horny hook or cock's spur used by the female tortoise to hold the mating male in copulating position. Upon returning with the sled, the other young man finds his friend dying atop the tortoise and decides to take him back to the village *in that same position, which is how the grieving girlfriend receives her would-be groom, as he dies hearing the tortoise's voice and dreaming that it is from his bride's mouth on their wedding night that the voice comes.[2]*

This tale of catastrophe and misplaced lust is prefaced by a sort of miracle story. When she was a girl of four, the storyteller's mother-in-law spent three days lost in the wild and was found safe on the other side of a river full of crocodiles. Ever since, she swears that it was "a tall and long-haired skinny man walking on water" (Vt 50) who carried her across on his shoulders. The family believed from the start that the girl was saved by Jesus in person ("Jesús en persona"), so she was renamed "Carmela" by her mother, in praise of the Virgen del Carmen.

Elements from the opening miracle story (1a) are set next in counterpoint with elements from the main plot (1b) and labeled as incidents and motifs of the type identified in myth stories and folktales. The three-step counterpoint progression may be phrased as follows:

(1.1a) The apparently unmotivated and perilous incursion by a girl too young to marry into an area outside her village inhabited by wild animals. (1b) The keenly motivated excursion beyond his village by a young man and a friend in search of enough wealth for him to marry a woman whom he loves and who loves him.

(2.1a) The life-saving miracle in which a female child is ferried across dangerous waters by a male perceived as sacred. (1b) The life-ending trick suffered by a young man who is carried nowhere except to his own death by an animal with uncanny attributes perceived as female.

(3.1a) The promise-keeping change of a daughter's name by her mother involving a *matronym* (a mother's Christian first name), linked by miracle to female virgin-status and its proper metaphoric relation to life. (1b) The failure by a young male to carry out a marriage promise and its attendant bestowal of a *patronym* (father's last name), improperly linked by carnal transgression to virgin-status in the symbolic relations between two species and genders and their respective life cycles.

The phrasing of the three steps in counterpoint grows in complexity. The last step may be rephrased as follows:

(3.1a) The mother gives a virgin's name to a virgin daughter whose life (and virginity) are preserved by miracle. (1b) A young man (still a "virgin") who intends to marry a woman (whom he would implicitly consider a "virgin" in her deserving his own father's last name) loses his life while committing a bestial act with a female who could (as explained below) be a "virgin" (who belongs to a species in which the notion of "virginity" would seem odd, except as imposed upon it by humans).

In looking further into the tale, one should recall Rodney Needham's plain emphasis on how frequently myth narratives deal with situations and events "physically or humanly impossible" (1978, 58), as is the case here, where the surest imprint left by myth in the tale leaves the reader face-to-face with a physical and behavioral event that appears, not only humanly, but animally impossible. For, in fact, female sea tortoises do not mate in the lethal (to humans) fashion in which the caguama in the tale does. One is left facing a tortoise-impossible, though tortoise-conceivable, event of intense mythic interest.

TURTLE LOVE

In this instance, myth works by indexing an impossible trait in the known behavior of a given animal species, turned by metamorphosis into a conceivable act born from fanciful and intrusive human curiosity about the animal. Folklore enters the picture as zoologist Archie Carr mentions "the many bizarre amatory feats that popular legend ascribes to sea turtles" (1952, 8). But science comes fast to the rescue, as Carl H. Ernst and Roger W. Barbour describe the mating habits of Chelonia in general and green turtles in particular: "Copulating pairs float at the surface, with the male atop the female. The enlarged claws on the front flippers and the strong nail at the tip of the prehensile tail provide a firm threepoint attachment; moreover, the male's claws cut into the female carapace at the third inter-marginal seam and leave deep, bleeding wounds" (1989, 121 [emphasis added]). With respect to Caretta caretta or "loggerhead" caguama sea turtles: "Mating occurs at the surface of the water off the nesting beaches. Although the female is completely submerged, the highest part of the male carapace usually is out of the water[. . . .] He sometimes bites the nape of her neck. His tail is bent down and under hers, so that the cloacal openings touch. Female mating behavior ranges from passive acceptance to violent resistance" (125 [emphasis added]).[3] Beyond myth, folklore, and science, but not literature, one is left facing a Mock Turtle of the uttermost harmful kind.

This comes as a sort of awful twist of fortune to what happens in Lewis

Carroll's "The Lobster Quadrille," when Alice is caught between two dancing chimeras, as the Mock Turtle sings:

> "Will you walk a little faster?" said the whiting
> to a snail,
> "There's a porpoise close behind us, and he's
> treading on my tail." (AA 124)

Alice is asked by the Gryphon to repeat lines from a doggerel poem (by Isaac Watts), "'Tis the Voice of the Sluggard,'" but "something very queer" comes from her echoing voice:

> "'Tis the voice of the Lobster": I heard him
> declare
> "You have baked me too brown, I must sugar
> my hair." (AA 139)

Alice blurts out a spontaneous parody in which the shift from sluggard to Lobster echoes a previous one from the biblical phrase "the voice of the turtle" in the Song of Solomon:

> the time of singing has come,
> and the voice of the turtledove
> is heard in our land. (AA 134)[4]

Echo and parody conspire in Alice's giddy breath upon dancing the difficult quadrille. Readers of Martin Gardner's *The Annotated Alice* learn that the calf-headed, calf-tailed, hind-hoofed turtle drawn by Tenniel illustrates mock turtle soup, "an imitation of green turtle soup, usually made from veal" (AA 124). One also learns that *turtle* was turned into tortoise when pupils called their "old Turtle" master by the name of "'taught us'" (AA 127). Unknowingly guilty of the capital sin of punning, the Mock Turtle betrays with his words his own status as food sentimentally spiced with cannibal humor. For parody consumes and instantly digests its own kind (just as "taught us" does when coming from a turtle pupil's mouth to yield "tortoise"). Alice's mock poem brims with fears of being turned into food, like the Lobster's:

> When the sands are all dry, he is gay as a lark,
> And will talk in contemptuous tones of the
> Shark:

But when the tide rises and sharks are around,
His voice has a timid and tremulous sound. (AA 139)

Or like the Owl, who once shared a pie with the Panther and ("as a boon")
was "kindly permitted to pocket the spoon,"

While the Panther received knife and fork
   with a growl,
And concluded the banquet by— (AA 140)

("eating the owl")—as the echoing punch line *growl/owl* is supplied by
Gardner in his notes. Indeed, when the Mock Turtle (its "voice with sobs")
sings yet another parody (turning "*Beautiful star in heav'n so bright | Softly
falls thy silv'ry light*" into "Beau—ootiful Soo—oop, so rich and so green, |
Waiting in a hot tureen!"), the mournful voice fades out and drops from
the story for good. Alice and the Gryphon hurry off from the beach sands
("without waiting for the end of the song") as the unfinished "*Turtle Soup*"
turns into a dirge to the melancholy loneliness of food, eternally in need
(and fear) of the human appetite that invents it.

Thus far, the tortoise scene of involuntary manslaughter in the tale has
yielded at least two results: first, a boldface warning in the form of humorous lying—*sex with female sea turtles may prove lethal to human male hunters*;
second, peculiar proof of the warning's groundless falsehood, obtained
through the successful hunt for the literary source behind it. Peculiar in
that something other than proof of falsehood has actually been obtained.
For, instead of replacing falsehood with the unremarkable truth it ignores
(that female tortoises lack such mating tools or weapons), a particular
tortoise-act has been cited, from a source found neither in science nor in
male folklore, on turtle-turning humor. Thus, a two-tiered reference to
scriptural text (the Song of Solomon) and poetic parody (*Alice in Wonderland*)
has left falsehood standing and has transformed the voice of the turtle into
a chunk of animated poetry authored by the vanished chimera embodied
in a singular Victorian adult writer (Lewis Carroll) and his brood of child-
mates (figuratively including in afterlife Guillermo Cabrera Infante).

In addition, turtle-voice evoked *mock soup* (*veal-for-turtle*), turned into a
verse recipe spiced with puns. Wordplay of the sort may relate to hunger,
at least for the sake of attention. Though frequent in the tale, such wordplay seems unremarkable, as when it is said that "only the shell's hardness
. . . prevents the *caguamo* from being killed, like the male praying mantis

[la mantis macho], during coitus" (Vt 16). Here the species name *caguama* is being spinned oddly on the axis of sexual difference. As it might do in Alice's own echo, *caguamo* sounds *mock-turtle* (*mock-caguama*), marking with the a/o gender switch the meridian of falsehood that divides life from death and male from female in the tale's ghastly outcome. For as sure as *a rose is a rose is a rose*, the species name *caguama* remains commonly unmodified in Spanish: it tolerates gender (as the rose needs not) by means of article and noun modifiers. When *caguama* mate, they mate as *caguama*. It is only when *caguama* species mating does not take place (as the result of human intrusion) that *someone* turns up *caguamo*. This is how *caguamo* (an *o* is all it takes) may hint at male personification inside the species common name *caguama*. (The *o* made by wordplay proves chimeric: as chimeric as female *caguama* animals would if they truly carried with them such mating lethal weapons beyond fiction.)

Fictions and myths are not invested in lying, as lying invariably is in fabricating fictions and myths. This claim requires explanation before returning to further matters in wordplay. No one *lies* in the tale except the girl, if the story of how she was saved by a stranger could be proven false, instead of being accepted as enshrined in local lore and sacred legend in the fiction-reading of a piece of fiction. In such a reading no room is given in which to boorishly unmask falsehood in what already relishes lying for pleasure at no one's expense—lying, that is, only in the sense of lending fictional vividness to what may be false (it being possible that a particular reader's uninformed or blind belief in the story's lethal *caguama* outcome could match the imaginable author who may well believe in it as true-to-life). Indeed, one discursive condition which would lend the character of *myth* to the literary tale under scrutiny lies in accepting the handiwork of such a truth-bound credulous author: an unnamed and unnameable author other than the known writer of the tale. Besides the countless instances of myth-making as willful falsehood, reading literary fictions in the mirror of myth implies the discursive presence of such an *unnamed-unnameable* and *credulous-for-sports* author (rendered impersonal and plural by Lévi-Strauss as the narrative agency he calls *myth*).

Claude Lévi-Strauss calls *zoemes* "animals given semantic functions." Zoemes "allow mythic thought to keep operations within the same framework" (1988, 97). Accordingly, features and properties in anthropomorphic appearance and behavior are attributed to various animals by groups of people in whose material culture and spiritual lives the species in question play a significant role. Brief *zoematic* acquaintance with Alice's Mock Turtle includes the punning shift of "tortoise" Master into "taught us" in his pupils' choral voice, thus lending human features to animal life. But such small operation in wit would be of genuine *zoematic* interest to Lévi-Strauss only if it played in semantic terms with the established speech norms by which a given community eats *turtle* rather than *tortoise* soup. In the same *zoematic* frame, a talking turtle or tortoise may marry a hunter or fisherman by adopting a woman's shape while remaining more turtle than ever. It is on such grounds that the youth who intrudes upon *caguama* mating habits with such dreadful results may have stepped on a *zoeme*. He becomes part of a virtual *zoematic* ensemble still to be aimed at a particular purpose (perchance, *porpoise*).

SPERM HUNT

One such purpose reflected in the tale's wordplay makes sex the main social catalyst of semantic connectedness. Moving from *caguama/ caguamo* pair-coupling, the next passage plays on differences between two men otherwise virtually alike, in order to insist that one is brighter and handsomer than the other: "They saw it [the tortoise] at the same time and together they thought the same thing. The two boys truly looked alike, except that one of them was good-looking and the other was not. Both were equally strong and often arm-wrestled with identical strength[. . . .] They were in fact the strongest boys in town, except that one was smart and the other was not. Now, the smarter of the two boys had an idea which he didn't have to relate to his friend (very often they thought about the same thing at the same time)."[5] Not unlike myth figures such as Lynx and Coyote and the unequal twins named *bright and bold* (Prometheus) and *dumb* (Epimetheus), *unequalness* between the two young men keeps in play their baseline equality, but for the purpose of best shattering it.

The two young men in the tortoise story do resemble twins of the Prometheus-Epimetheus type, who in Greek myth are opposed but complementary and are said to be *alike* in order to best highlight their unequal talents in obtaining gifts and properly conducting sacrifice. The young men spot the tortoise at the same time, but one *follows* the other ("he seconded him in seconds [*lo secundó en segundos*]"). As explained by J.-P. Vernant, in Prometheus's case, *prónoia* or *foresight* makes him *proactive* and *leading* as he deals with a situation set up by his own cunning or *metis* ("a compound of anticipation, guile and deceit"), ill-matched by Epimetheus's want of cunning, who *follows up* and always "understands after the event" (1981, 44). But the gift of cunning proves harmful to Prometheus, whose foresight "always recoils against him in the end; he is caught in the trap that he himself sets" (Detienne and Vernant 1991, 18). Likewise, the tale's leading young man is driven by his own curious lust away from potential wealth and into fatal experimentation.

Parallels with archaic Greek myth are heightened by the presence of nuptials in both the tale and Prometheus's story. Pandora (*gift-of-all-the-gods*) is taken as bride by the *dumb* twin Epimetheus, who accepts her against his brother's advice. This happens as a prototype Pandora figure is presented by the gods to humankind in the form of a *parthenos*: "a virgin nubile woman decked for her wedding ceremony" (Vernant 1981, 49). Pandora exemplifies the lure of *brideswealth*, including the bountiful seed supply (*sperma*) for the marrying man, and the gift's loss upon opening the belly-like box: "Henceforth men must toil for the female belly, which has to be fed like fire and ploughed like the land, so that they may be able to bury their seed (*sperma*) in it" (49). In the present tale's case, the better-looking, brother-like, and brighter young man wants to marry a virgin bride. Unlike Pandora, through no fault of her own, the bride becomes linked through the groom's bold but ultimately foolish actions to a female tortoise bearing promises of untold gifts. (It is the tortoise made-lethal rather than the bride who resembles gift-laden Pandora.) The groom's failure in turning tortoise into wealth in the form of gifts-for-sale contrasts with the earlier success of the villagers in extracting from the rotten carcass of a beached whale a good amount of sperm, which they sold afterward at a good price (Vt 10). Obtaining fire-producing sperm from rotten animal flesh relates to human sperm waste and bloodshed in what in such terms becomes the bright and beautiful young man's polluted immolation.

But the tale's key Pandora-Prometheus nexus concerns hunger and squalor. It is said that "a young man from the village had fallen in love with a local beauty who also fell in love with him. They wanted to marry, but he was very poor. She, too, was very poor. Everyone in town was very poor."[6] Fire theft by Prometheus in association with Pandora's box has been called by Vernant "a Story of Stomachs"; the bride's lifting of the box's lid assigns insatiable sex and hunger to women; "*gaster* represents the ardent, bestial, and wild element in man" (Detienne and Vernant 1989, 57,

59). The triangular nuptial affair between two brothers bright and dumb and a ravenous virgin bride in Promethean myth leads back to a tale of empty stomachs and a wedding's wailing widow. (The young pair of rookie hunters-scavengers split by death might have become *tortugeros* [turtle hunters] had they had the means to buy or rent themselves a turtle boat, like the *Canario* fisherman in Ernest Hemingway's *Islands in the Stream*, the final part of which occurs along the beaches and barrier keys on and off the northern coast of Camagüey Province, not too far from Gibara, the area on the coast further east where the tale has its home beyond fiction.)[7]

Thus far, a string of wordplay couplets from our tale (*caguama/caguamo*), from Lewis Carroll's *Alice* (*tortoise/taught us*), and Greek myth (*Prometheus/Epimetheus*) has yielded some insights of thematic value. The conjoined actions of *coupling* and *uncoupling* lie at the figurative heart of wordplay's sound effects. A vanishing point may now be reached in the story's focus on man-animal coupling. It comes in the Cuban vernacular *cacumen* (instead of *acumen*) for insight: "but selling the *caguama* required acumen [*pero vender la caguama demandaba* cacumen]" (Vt 14, emphasis added). Echoing *cagua/cacu* harks back to *cacuama*, more often used than *caguama*, as in: "amid the gently swaying mangroves, shells and reptiles glitter next to *cacuamas* from the sea."[8] (Here wordplay exploits the folk wish to accent the polished and seldom used *acumen* with the stronger *cacumen*, which in turns yields *insight* by echoing the older folk name *cacuama* from *caguama*.) Such wordplay syllabic trivia finally lands on a piece of precious rubbish. It happens as the young men are about to give up their search for wealth: "They searched all over the beach and found nothing but strombs [sic] and rubbish [*recorrieron toda la playa y no encontraron más que estrombos (sic) y escombros*]" (Vt 10). While the OED does list "Stromb" as the anglicized form of *Strombus* (for both the *strombidae* gastropod family and the spiral shell akin to it), "*estrombos*" remains odd and unrecorded in Spanish (and a bit absurd if conceived as a folk construct for seashell shards).

TEMPEST IN A SHELL

In his comparative study on Cuba and hurricane tempest mythology, Fernando Ortiz discusses the large spiral conches known as *guamos* or *cobos* (*Strombus gigas*).[9] A *zoematic* picture emerges out of Ortiz's writings to illustrate the tale's beach scavenging. The young men walk amid broken shards of ancient *guamos* left behind by crumbled sea walls (*male-*

cones) built by the earliest Indians ("los indios más arcaicos") on the island's beaches to trap in salt pools (saladeros) and preserve from quick putrefaction masses of sea food: "las masas alimenticias de los mariscos" (Hu 538). The seawall use of guamos for food-gathering purposes followed the eating of the conches' gastropod tenants. Guamos supplied their own flesh as well as other kinds of seafood to the Indians and were also used as horns (fotutos), turned into tools, utensils, and ornaments, and placed over the entrance of bohíos (huts) for magical, scare-away, or apotropaic purposes (Hu 544). As he had already done in Contrapunteo cubano del tabaco y el azúcar, Ortiz speculates that powder obtained from cobos was mixed with tobacco and inhaled by wizards in their shamanistic ceremonies (cohobas or cojobas) for ecstatic and visionary effects.[10] The hallucinogenic strength of tobacco inhaled in powdered form would have changed according to which alkaloids were used in combination with it. Ortiz suggests that cohobas (or cohibas, as one would say nowadays) were at times inhalations of tobacco powder mixed with dust from cobos: "The stimulating and imitative virtues of tobacco, borne symbolically up to the gods in spirals of rainmaking smoke clouds [were] mixed with mysterious substances evoking supernatural beings. . . . To inhale tobacco smoke and cobo dust combined amounted to a communion with the god Hurricane [Huracán] and his transubstantiation into dust from the ocean depths and into rain-cloud-like smoke; one of many 'communions' or theophagy [god-eating] rituals so common among indigenous peoples in the Caribbean and on the mainland."[11] Giant spiral seashells are linked to the hurricane through symbols related to sound, loud noise, and whirling motion, as when a water spout plunges its roaring, twisting tail into the sea. In indigenous lore, the shells' spiral cones would have dropped from the skies into sea waters in the form of thunderous winds and taken solid shape at the sandy bottom (Hu 550). Guamo shells kept buried in their twisting insides the storm's voice and released it back into the air (once the conch's tip had been pierced in order to eat the mollusc sheltered inside).

Ortiz's account of Strombus gigas in El huracán visualizes two types of indigenous consumption, one in which shell dust is inhaled in shamanistic drug ceremonies and another in which the shell's spiral cavity is robbed of its indwelling gastropod or belly-on-foot food. The zoematic picture thus obtained on the sacred and material uses of stromb shells transforms an odd bit of wordplay into a portmanteau word, an item or word-couple found when, according to Humpty Dumpty, two meanings get packed into a single word, as when *estrombos* swallows up *escombros*. (Rubbish shells absorb random rubbish and in thus coupling rubbish with rubbish a past full of material and spiritual richness shows forth.) But word-nurture of the sort found in such final coupling can bring no true nourishment to a tale of empty bellies.

chapter three

A Fallen-from-Use Path
Taken on the Outskirts of Town
(Cartesian Miracle)

*I should be glad . . . in this discourse, to describe for the benefit
of others the paths I have followed, to paint a picture, as it were,
of my life, of which each one may judge as he pleases; and I should
be happy, too, to learn what public opinion has to say of me, and
so discover a fresh mode of instruction for myself, which I shall
add to those I am already accustomed to employ.*

RENÉ DESCARTES, *Discourse on Method*

Thus far, the main voices retrieved from the tale "The Voice of
the Turtle" have issued from word couplets in which wordplay punctuates
in sound the character equivalent of caricature.[1] If an inchoate economy
of character is felt at work behind such a mouth-to-text process, it would
seem to hint at pervasive hunger in a small coastal village, doing so indi-
rectly, with quick heavy-handed stabs of syllabic echoes. The loaded means
at work in the type of drawing known as *caricare* and *portrait chargé* find
their equivalent here in redundant sounds, in nouns made to rub against
each other and to clash in search of some graphic resolution. In this sense,
wordplay in "La voz de la tortuga" aims at the flash enhancement of pic-
torial values in words and syllables.[2] Hunger is replaced in graphic terms
by its closest mate, sex; and sex, in turn, by its occasional shadow, violent
death, the picture of which seals off the tale's field of vision. Yet, though
upstaged in the end by a lurid carnal disaster, the sign of squalor and
hunger persists in the fetish of a made-up word for rubbish (*estrombos* for
escombros) with two meanings screwed into each other in search of mutual
satiation, as when non-food would not only feed the belly but animate the
inanimate. (The *food/hunger/life/lifeless* clues lie in the *strombus* shards and
upon the beach's present economic worthlessness, in contrast with the
shells' past value in Arawak ritual and the Indians' epicurean snail-flesh
eating.)

As examined in what follows, the absence of race and color in the story's implicitly all-white coastal community of Gibara turns into the presence of racial tones elsewhere, in a 1984 speech given by the author in Santa Cruz de Tenerife on the Canary Islands. In the talk, delivered before an audience of Canarian ancestors of his paternal family, Guillermo Cabrera Infante begins by delivering a mock eulogy to *gofio*, a gruel meal eaten by the indigenous Guanche islanders and shared on this occasion by the speaker in siblinghood with his wife: "Miriam Gómez, sitting next to me, loves *gofio*, so much so that her eyes have the color of tender *gofio*, as if they were galvanized. She grew up eating *gofio*, I myself came to naught because of *gofio*. Both of us suffer the curse of *gofio* eating, we are *gofio* addicts, *gofio* makes our mutual blood thicker than plasma; we are *gofio-maniacs*" (Gg 137). An old Canarian source describes the tribe's ambrosia in simple terms: "Toasted barley reduced to flour in a little stone grinder, set in motion with the hand by means of a small sheep bone, was the whole-some and flavorful nourishment they called *gofio* or *ahorén* and used as their daily bread."[3] (The Tenerife audience is told by Infante that the "nefari-ous vice" of *gofio* died only after his family moved from Gibara to Havana, a city said to be "less given" to the habit [Gg 136].)

The jubilant speaker tells his audience, in postprandial spirit, how, as a schoolboy of four at Gibara, he once gorged himself on the stuff and had to be carried home like a corpse to face his mother's amorous scolding: "loaded full of *gofio*, which I kept releasing on the way to the house, like ballast, coming out of my throat, nose and ears, marking a trail with *gofio*, like Hansel—or maybe Gretel: my sexuality was still not well defined. I was received at home with consternation, my mother shouting with compas-sion, 'damned you, you wretched fool,' 'it ought to teach you a lesson!'" (Gg 136). It was as if the child had eaten gold dust ("había comido oro") and had threaded a golden navel cord by spewing it back home to face his mother's anger. The mother is neither the wicked woman type who abandons her hungry children in the forest, nor the cannibal female ogre who would roast them alive. Yet, the Hansel-and-Gretel allusion seems to uncannily foreshadow the startling passage ("paréntesis violento") in the Tenerife speech about the death by murder-suicide of the speaker's pater-nal grandparents.

Told with the stark simplicity of a folktale suddenly bereft of magic, the anecdote refers to the "formidable grandfather" Francisco Cabrera as a "master of the forge" blacksmith in love with the art of making iron grills and railings. One day (rather late in what became her last pregnancy) Francisco's wife was taken by him away from Gibara and Cuba, so their child could be born, as he had, on the island of Tenerife. The man took his family on a journey back to the Canaries aboard a sloop called La Pinta (going like "Columbus-in-reverse," from where the admiral had first landed in Cuba back to where he had last sailed from the Old World). After a short stay in Tenerife and the birth of a son (the speaker's father), the grandparents returned to Gibara, where Cabrera felt the sudden urge to take a "longer" journey:

> He took his wife (who was a pious Cuban lady, a Desdemona without disdain) out on a fallen-from-use path taken on the outskirts of town, near the river. He was heard arguing with her in a loud voice, saying terrible things. Then he was seen coming back carrying her in his arms, wounded and near death: she was shot in the forehead and kept bleeding all the way back. My grandfather called the doctor when he got home, but did not wait for his arrival and instead locked himself in the bedroom. When the family's screams confirmed to him that he had killed his wife, he shot himself in the temple. They were buried together. It was never known what had caused the tragedy or what its origin was. (Gg 137)[4]

A "violent parenthesis" indeed; a violent thesis about parents, perhaps; a story offered to peel off the speaker's alien/native camouflage before the audience of his Canarian ancestors, as he declares himself a "camouflaged Canarian," brought under the spell of the islands' "atavism" and set up in conflict with (and resemblance to) the grandfather: "I am a reasonable person, but hidden inside me runs a current of irrationality, which threatens to break out as it did with my grandfather, a murderer and suicide. I am a camouflaged Canarian" (Gg 140). As such, the telling of the dark incident leaves untrodden a path it seems it might elsewhere wish to take in a retour au pays natal. In other words, what is said marks off, and turns away from, a path, as if the speaker were returning for the first time to the Canaries, after never having been there before, except in stories heard and read. The path is taken as if such a return, to where he never has actually ever been, would take him back to where he grew up, but only to the un-trodden spot on Cuba's soil where the grandfather met an alien disaster too-much at home and too-far-away from it. (Such are the territorial *soil-and-soul* matters of lethal import surveyed in the speech.)

At a stroke, with the golden halo of *gofio* still in the air, the speech turns fugitively brooding and heavy. The grandson confesses to the audience that he has "ended up being" his "father's father" (Gg 140). But, what sort of father is this other father, one generation closer in bloodline to the (grand)son? He (Infante's actual father) is claimed to be a staunch womanizer, drawn mainly to black women, and quite deaf or *sordo*, except to the sound of Communist Party watchwords: "My father survived [. . .] several illnesses, one of which left him deaf, although he could still hear watchwords[. . . .] Deafness prevented his hearing any kind of music, un-less it was *The International*[. . . .] His only passion [. . .] was for women of all races, colors and creeds, but above all black ones. Nowadays he is mar-ried to an imposing black woman" (137, 139). The father so fathered by his own son as "el padre de mi padre" is "barely an infant of two" at the time of his parents' joint death by murder-suicide, and, just within the next two sentences, he reaches eighty, after surviving the upbringing tyranny of his mother's mother, who would constantly remind him that his father had killed her daughter (137). The "violent parenthesis" in an otherwise funny speech regressively elevates the (grand)son to the father's father role. It enacts, in a speech peppered with wordplaying words, before the grand-father's ancestral Canarian audience, the grandson's assumption of the couple's murder-suicide as the catastrophic sign of transgenerational sym-bolic parenting.

Although it occurs near the same ancestral spot of family tragedy, "The Voice of the Turtle" tale is punctuated by irony and mild mockery. Set next to it, the Tenerife speech discloses the biographic murder-spot to the tale's reader, as it goes on to settle accounts with the speaker's *fathered* father. This transgenerational male is brought before the aboriginal audience of Canarians, just where the speaker's father's father (whom he now posthu-mously personifies) had brought his (his future grandson's) grandmother so she would give birth, not to a Cuban, but to a Canarian. The speaker carries out what in the glory days of psychoanalysis was known as *Entman-nung*: the unmanning of the selectively deaf and self-blinded father, whose closet philandering makes him look like "a homosexual under wraps" (139). Cases of uncovered paternal homosexuality known to the speaker are then unpacked in crude humor, such as the friend who is said to have killed himself with his father's service weapon after learning that he was "not only a police but also a pederast," and the other, an "old friend" and "Marxist millionaire" who, "upon discovering that his aging father had revealed himself homosexual," made fun of it: "with the kind of face my mother has," he confessed, "I would have done the same thing a long time ago, let us hope that the boys he hires have less of a moustache than my mother has" (139). But, in the speaker's own case, the father "was not a man chaser [*hombreriego*] but a woman-chaser [so gendered: *una (sic) mujeriego*], who, like Descartes, went forth masked [*avanzaba enmascarado*] toward each Christina, his visage [*larva*] hidden behind the mask of political prudishness: a communist can neither be libertarian nor libertine" (140).[5] (It is not reported—in final written form—whether such involved filmic allusions were actually read or ad-libbed during the speech or were embroidered later on by the writer.)

In any event, joined together, like the visual equivalent of a *portmanteau* word, the queer *woman* womanizer in Cartesian drag ("una mujeriego") and the mustachioed mother of the cynic son of an old queer cop add up to the pseudo-cinema pastiche gift of Greta Garbo's Queen Christina of Sweden and, further in the background, the Queen's mistaken boy-birth inside a caul: "The midwives heard the lusty roar of a child, [and] buoyed up by the predictions of astrologers and their own wishful thinking, they believed her to be a boy; and so the King was told. They could be forgiven for their mistake, since Christina was born with a caul which enveloped her from her head to her knees, leaving only her face, arms and lower part of her legs free; moreover she was covered with hair."[6] (In pseudo-cinematic pastiche, as the one about to unfold here, a given film is pulled back to its sources and first surroundings. What is thus witnessed and rehearsed are mainly ghost-scenes, myth-memorials played in the mind's sight.)

Enter René Descartes, who actually met the queen a few times, but never with Greta Garbo playing her as she does in Rouben Mamoulian's 1933 *Queen Christina*, in whose afterimage the speaker's Cartesian allusion/illusion takes shelter. Early in the film, the French ambassador, Chanut (played by Charles Renavent), answers the queen's news about the philosopher's upcoming visit to her court by saying: "What a happier destiny for a Frenchman than to come to you, Madame." The phrase carries unscripted irony, since Descartes' absence from the movie is both complex and trivial. His early-morning, five-hour-long lessons to the queen in the harsh Stockholm winter were hardly worth an actor's Hollywood studio salary, in a role which would have included Descartes' dying of pneumonia amid rumors of having been poisoned (Glaukroger 1991, 415). By MGM standards, old Descartes was no match for the lead role of don Antonio Pimentel de Prado as Spanish ambassador and queen-lover, played by John Gilbert. More than absent, the philosopher best known for "I think, therefore I am" occupies in film space a defunct role, just a step above and beyond the cutting floor's afterlife, in which he might be heard whispering: "*I am not, therefore I am.*" But, how does Descartes' piddling absence from *Queen Christina* matter to Cabrera Infante's cinephiliac conscience? First of all, it lends its ghostly presence to the allusion to his father, in which the son seems to be speaking (perhaps to a puzzled or oblivious audience) as if to and from the Garbo film: speaking (or writing afterwards) as he *womanizes* a womanizer who, he claims, has already womanized himself.

In the Tenerife speech Descartes approaches "each Christina" playing the speaker's father, who moves forth "masked" behind his own face as if beneath a *larva* or *larve*, a spectral visage worn by ancestors from beyond the grave.[7] The father's hatred for movies, except those from Communist Russia (Gg 139), rules out his ever seeing Garbo on screen, seeing what the speaker's early movie critic's pseudonym (Caín) calls (in a belated 1956 review of *Camille*) Garbo's "hard beauty" and "man-in-skirts" looks (OXX 112). Yet, had Descartes ever met Christina, in serial fashion from behind a double mask, as contemplated in the speech but never shown on film, his *coming to her each time* would have displayed to him the Mask. (The father, way-back-then, would have seen the *Garbo* Face while still close in time to the retro-icon aura splendor achieved by certain film faces from the silent era, when seen and studied in the wake of screen sound.)

The impossible 1930s *father-cinema-event* fits into the following time frames. First, in the foreground, Descartes' *larva* or embodied ghost is brought into the imagined film by the Tenerife speaker who, in the mid-1980s, as he speaks, is either near the age of fifty or older. Second, in the farthest background, the speaker's father never does (never would) behold Garbo's face on screen, while still relatively near the receding silent era and the film's release in 1933, when father Guillermo Cabrera López was in his thirties and his son a child of four, and both lived out-in-the-boondocks. Third, in the middle distance, and also in his thirties, the reviewer Caín, in the 1950s, sends to press his first published retro Garbo piece. Later on, in the 1980s, in the essay "For Whom the Movies [*doblan*]

Toll" (*doblan* puns *toll* with *dub*), Caín would deplore the use of dubbing as he claims the quality of sublimity for Garbo's voice as a sign of her ineffable signature, adding that the erasure of the voice by dubbing recalls her former silent-age muteness being shattered by talk.[8] In Caín's imagination, Garbo's voice survived the death of silent movies; her roles in *Anna Christie* and *Queen Christina* "allowed sound cinema not to mortally wound her" (*OXX* 113). Such a voice-spell as Garbo's lifts spoken sound up to a *blind* and *defunct* (*death-fresh*) status in which the ordinary deafness of silent movies achieves sublimity, as when, his sight all but lost, Borges "listened to movies" and denounced the spread of dubbing in films adapted for Spanish American audiences (*Cs* 73). Dubbed words delete and counterfeit voice: "No one can claim to have seen Garbo without having heard her: that hard ice-like accent, that throaty voice, that delivery in-between lassitude and disdain (which lends full sense to the famous phrase I *want to be alone*), at once erotic and asexual" (*Cs* 73). This same *cinephiliac* (*defunct*) presence (toward which the speaker's father would have remained as willfully blind as he was deaf and implicitly dumb to anything but Red propaganda) becomes, in the Tenerife speech, the scripted but unfilmed human presence in which the father is seen approaching as Descartes' own Cartesian ghost. Thus, at the same time that the ghost mirrors—in his own garb—Queen Christina's boyish cross-dressing from behind a mask, what is mirrored in return is the spectral film Face masked by Voice. Garbo's sound was her afterlife *defunct persona*, and her *voice-mask* the unburied *larva* from her dead days as silence's cinematic icon.

With its making and unmaking of parasite film memories, pseudo-cinema or *cinephilia* underscores an obvious but occluded aspect of the movies' stake in sublimity. In historical perspective, the style and mood of antiquarian affect for the remote yet recent cinema past has seen its better days. Cinephilia is all but finished as a cultivated activity now enshrined in DVD special or bonus features wisdom. In this regard, *love-of-cinema* resembles what continues to be called *philosophy* in reference to a mostly European style of bold speculation that the short-lived pleasures and remorseless toils of deconstruction helped certify as exhausted. This is why (as a sort of *paraphilia* or *cinesophia*) the desire to master everything there is to know about films with encyclopedic zest extends itself into the uncertain paths that lie beyond the outskirts of the product's stillborn or all-too-brief commercial life. Marc Vernet has placed the transcendent French version of cinephilia in the context of scarcity. The chivalrous quest after the flickering illusion of a film which he says "one might never be able to see again" transformed the one-night-stand affair into a Platonic event in the awakening of *anamnesis* as the mysterious memory of some remote embodiment of truth. Always with tongue in cheek, the marginal cinema culture Vernet recalls turned film into "a series of phantoms the cinephile was trying to capture at out-of-the-way venues" (it made the love of movies "fugitive" and "evanescent" in character),[9] just as fugitive and evanescent as the Christina tangled allusion appears to be when played before an audience of Canarians not likely to belong to the happy few among such cosmopolitan circles as Vernet's Paris and Infante's Havana.

The vanished but present past of cinephilia needs to be reviewed here in prelude to the speaker's shift to matters of color and race. In what follows, Queen Christina's historical mythic film aura should make clear that her well-earned immortality in Garbo's role is quite preposterous, not in the least due to the film's tabooed and feeble grasp of the queen's brilliant management of grotesque eroticism masked in boudoir dynastic politics. In reviewing these aspects briefly, one is surmising black-and-white memories which in the speaker's cinephiliac knowledge are set against a background of Voice and Mask emerging from Sublime Film Silence.

Beyond such specific matters of film consciousness and memories lie questions of color and race, conjured up and camouflaged in the Tenerife speaker's equivalent to a *retour au pays natal*. At the myth-making heart of the speech, he offers his Canarian ancestor-hosts the gift gimmicks of aboriginal kinship, in which the colors of black African–Cuban ancestry vanish in counterpoint with a legend about Arawak and Canarian exogamy involved in the origins of Cuban tobacco culture and its presumed passage from Indians to settlers. (It is as if Odysseus were to tell tall tales to the Phaeacians trying to persuade them that he belongs to their homeland, just as his own ancestors did, as nothing less than their earliest colonists, and all of it in prelude to his asking for Nausicaa's hand.)

Queen Christine of Sweden appears, very much unlike Garbo, in a memorable impression drawn by Ambassador Chanut to his *Secrétaire d'Etat*: "le visage de cette jeune Reine changeoit si subitement selon les mouvements de son esprit, que souvent d'un moment à l'autre elle n'étoit pas connoissable."[10] Arguing against what she calls the "Mythos of her life," Susanna Åkerman shows how Christina is represented as "a bizarre neurotic" who fled from responsibility under assault by "distorted and ill understood passion" and was cast as "the Baroque Queen who mysteriously lived a life 'mouvementée et scabreuse [shifty and risky]'" (QC 66). But it is doubtful that Christina's abdication resulted (as portrayed in the film) from her seeing, in Barry Paris's words, "the conflict between her duty as queen and her private sexuality as irrevocable" (G 293). If anything, Queen Christina seems bound by cinema formulas to widen the gap between the political and sexual realms, prevented by the censorship code and studio taste from exploring in depth the conduits between bedchamber and throne traced by the gossip and propaganda apparatus that fashioned Christina's wondrous legacy.

The film could not have portrayed Ambassador Pimentel as a married man and political instrument deceitfully involved in bringing his wife and children to Stockholm; nor could it, as part of the love story, show the queen and Pimentel bonded in lust of the sort that might have bespoken "un amour tout charnel," or made Christina write in a voice ready to serve "un amour le plus violent" (QC 40 n. 83). Instead, while not ignoring Christina's most gossiped about and slandered passion for "la Belle Comtesse" Ebba Sparre de la Gardie, the film only shows the queen's jealousy at her loss of control over the younger woman, at the same time that it makes both women surrender to a male lover of their own choice. Christina/Garbo arouses a woman's desire, not when acting as queen to Countess Ebba Sparre, but only while in male disguise before the sexy wench Elsa (played by Barbara Barondess), who in the celebrated scene inside the inn's master bedroom comes on to Garbo and touches her (young man's) leg (the same young man—one presumes—whose Christina's Garbo person the Tenerife speaker's father approaches à la Descartes). But the queen's disguise is not the film's invention. Intelligence surveillance during the trip to Rome following her abdication reported Christina's entering an inn at one point with "boots on and a carbine about her neck," and she is believed to have recognized Queen Maria Amalia at another inn, where the young Danish monarch waited for her/him disguised as a chamber maid.

Even the most sublime part of the inn sequence ("the touching scene" in which Garbo circles the room and strokes and hugs and "memorizes" objects and says: "In the future, in my memory, I shall live a great deal in this room") was deemed "pornographic" by moralists (G 300–301). A ménage à trois effect in lovemaking is noticeable in the scene, just as the trio effect is strongly felt in historical records of which the filmmakers had not the slightest clue. In triangular fashion, Barondess establishes boyish Garbo as object of her desire in prelude to Pimentel's mounting humorous uneasiness at his own attraction toward the young man after the two are left alone in the bedroom. Christina's obvious lack of interest in the stout wench Elsa contrasts with her passionate approach to Ebba Sparre during an earlier stormy scene in which the queen's desire for a woman ephemerally flares up. But at the inn, any such desire ceases and is replaced by the effects of Christina's virgin appeal to Pimentel, for whom the afterglow of her obvious male attraction (as seen in Gilbert's acting) lingers on as Garbo shows herself to him in a woman's silhouette. (It seems likely that this is the scene that best corresponds to the Tenerife speaker's Christina-Cartesian allusion to his own ghostly father.)

While Elsa the wench is entirely the film's invention, Ebba Sparre's historic role as the queen's "bedfellow" and mistress became a prominent target of rumor in Swedish court circles and beyond. Besides lewd letters supposedly addressed to the queen, but now believed apocryphal, the most famous incident starring "la Belle Ebba" has her and Christina catching the Calvinist philosopher and historian Claude de Saumaise in bed, reading (and then trying to hide from them) a copy of *Le Moyen de parvenir*, described by Åkerman as "a dialogue famed for mimicking an ancient bacchanal interspersed with pornographic allusions" (QC 39). Christina reacts by grabbing the *corpus delicti* and asking Ebba to read it aloud, but la Belle Comtesse throws the book on the floor and flees the room. (In Masson's biography, Saumaise is replaced by a ghost, as Ebba, instead of reading to Saumaise, "reads to Descartes" [153], who had died eight months earlier, also as a royal guest.) Åkerman mentions another incident in which Christina had once again positioned Ebba in a threesome situation by inviting Bulstrode Whitelocke to find out in conversation " 'whether or not her inside was as beautiful as her outside.' " In Whitelocke's account, Christina "took one of Ebba's gloves, demonstratively divided it in three and gave a piece to him, to Chanut, and to Pimentel" (QC 39 n. 83).

The threesome situation in which Christina places Ebba and herself in contact with third actors opens up a fourth dimension controlled by images of one's self linked to others, such as the libertine doctrines aided by lewd stories in Saumaise's reading hands, the inside/outside scrutiny of body and soul under Whitelocke's diplomatic gaze, and Christina's distributing Ebba's split symbolic parts in allotment to the three men. The presence of a split third actor/voyeur plays the role of insistent other to Christina's subjection of Countess Ebba to her royal designs and her further godmother-like claim over her nickname as "la Belle Comtesse" (QC

39 n. 83). Christina's desire instigates otherness in typically altered fashion. In her game, Christina splits into lots her (the queen's) complex need for Ebba by positioning the younger woman in attachment to men while making her own royal mastery subordinate to the further need of investing power in the countess's masquerade nickname.

Having unpacked the Christina/Descartes allusion in circling fashion from mask to masquerade, it is time to look at the register of color and race in which the speech remains heavily invested.

A CIGAR IS ALWAYS COLORED

Tout comme l'oppression insensée du surmoi reste à la racine des impératifs motivés de la conscience morale, la furieuse passion, qui spécifie l'homme, d'imprimer dans la réalité son image est le fondement obscur des médiations rationnelles de la volonté. [In the same manner in which the superego's senseless oppression remains at the root of the motivated imperatives of moral conscience, the furious passion, which renders man specific, and drives him to impress his image upon reality, is the obscure foundation of the rational mediations of the will.]

Jacques Lacan, "L'agressivité en psychanalyse," *Écrits*

The Tenerife speaker attempts by rhetorical and verbal means something very much akin to Lacan's conception of that "furious passion" which, with the force of the superego, renders man "specific to himself," as he "impress[es] his image upon reality," as if risen from the obscure grounds ("fondement obscur") where the rational mediations of the will rest. Such strong territorial *soil-soul* idioms seem appropriate to the tracing of racial and tribal designs in the speech.

Beginning with *gofio*'s ambrosia of golden blonde edible identities (Gibara-poor and thus as unbending as being Canarian-white in origin), the tale of race articulates a bipolar color set in which the ethnic white immigrant stock enhances its core non-colored distinction in contrast with, and proximity to, female black diaspora elements. Even when not being argued as such, the bipolar white/black set brings colors to the speech, as when the itch to diddle in puns (for example, Desdemona with 'disdain' or *desdén* for the murdered grandmother) makes Othello a Canarian ("I have no doubt but that Othello was born in the Canaries") and turns the arch-Canarian grandfather's white rage into a measure of colored madness one may label *Othello-Black*. By the same token, when the bipolar color set is being put forth outright, it creates bonding with recognized aspects of the father's person and sexual preferences otherwise repulsed: "I always carried my father inside me without knowing it: in my social behavior, my physical looks, even in casting an eye on women, the Fata Morgana of my own mythology. (It's a pity she is not black!) I must confess that I have ended up being my father's father" (Gg 140). The father remains behind in his *país natal* of Cuba, married to an "imposing black woman" in contextual surrogacy to Othello. He remains in the land of the "blonde and blue-eyed" farmers, those craftsmen of the soil who are met in amazement down to this day by startled visitors to Cuba. So the speaker asks: "Where is the citrine [*cetrino*] ancestral Cuban [*guajiro*] farmer?" The Canarian audience is told that the aboriginal non-indigenous Cuban tiller of the earth was Canarian-white: "He is [or was] a Cuban Canarian" (140). Then, the speaker further wonders: "Where are [or were] the blacks then?" His answer implies that blacks have since emancipation left their country's soil and moved in droves to cities and towns. This black diaspora would have taken place out of both dread and respect for the untilled forest wilderness. For: "African superstitions, which are their religion, declare the forest [*el monte*] a sacred place; blessed, damned, tabooed," so that there are hardly any blacks living in Cuba's countryside. Above all, "blacks are found in towns, but never in fishing villages [*aldeas marineras*]," like the speaker's Gibara hometown. Cuban blacks "do not live near the sea or beaches or ports," an egregious claim which opens the way for: "In Cuba's countryside, on its shores and in the sea that surrounds her it was the Canarian who ruled [*dominó*] the elements" (140). Thus, the *retour au pays natal* brings a considerable territorial and racial *soil-soul* gift back to the Canarian hosts wrapped in the natural elements of that other island country where their ancestors buried their labor. It also seeds the grounds of telluric nationhood with Canarian stock, in the same myth-making claim in which it uproots blacks from such grounds as if in fulfillment of their own animist beliefs. (In such tobacco magic fashion, diaspora comes home to roost.)

CARMEN'S EAR

On his way to the podium, as he recalls, the speaker was whispered something "sordid" in the ear which left him dumbfounded: " 'Why is it that you always speak of England and never of Cuba?' " He now wonders whether the sordid whisperer was deaf, punning as usual: "¿Sería sordo el sórdido?" (Gg 142). Deafness, already identified with his Communist father, makes a sordid reentry. The gift to the Canarian audience has at its core a paternal Canarian villain in the "small-town intellectual who made [the speaker's mother] a Communist"; she, who was "all impetus" to his being "all inertia" (138). The speaker's father knew that life never ends well. He knew that "each life begins in the struggle to survive and ends in death," except that, in the "father's own case, life began in death" (139). It was the mother who broke the inertia and took the family away "with gusts of willpower out of the dead small town," the same place where she had taken the speaker, at the infant age of twenty-nine days, to the movies, "exposing him to contagiousness with an incurable virus" (138–39). As it swings from convivial myth-making and funny pleasantries to morbid soliloquizing spells, the speech turns parental character differences into absolute strangeness. With the exception of the mother's spirited acquiescence to the father's Stalinist ideology as the founder of Communist cells in the Gibara region, Zoila and Guillermo Sr. appear as alien breeds of Cuban character to each other. In ancestral terms, the Cuban man who was either born on Canarian soil or was meant to be born there married a Cuban woman who could claim as hers "a bloodline that extends back to the island's original native inhabitants" (GCI 3). Facing such transmitted genealogical claims from author to quick-study biographer, one may ask whether the speaker's gift as a Cuban *soil-soul* tribute to his aboriginal Canarian hosts might not represent his own/Odysseus's way of planting his mother on pure Arawak soil, nurtured in blood pureness, untainted by the color black, as the spotless Phaeacians are in Homer, and whites are anywhere it matters dearly not to be anything other or less than *blanco puro*—pure white on the soil of Cuba's soul.

The present reading has suggested a parallel resemblance between the speaker's charter of Cuban-Canarian white ancestry and Aimé Césaire's *Cahier d'un retour au pays natal*. Resemblance by contrast. Césaire's output starts with *Cahier*, in which he records in Surrealist ways his and his family's return to Martinique on the eve of the Second World War. (*Cahier* was first published in book form in 1942 in Havana with illustrations by Wifredo Lam [David 1997, xiv].) Césaire joins the French Communist Party and becomes a leading politician in his own country as well as a very influential figure in the French Antilles and elsewhere. What distinguishes Césaire's career here or in any other context is the apparent antithesis that lies between his having coined the term *négritude* and put forth its tenets and his

subsequent success in incorporating islands like Guadeloupe and Martinique bureaucratically and politically as part of France. As both a Communist and ex-Communist, Aimé Césaire led an active and by consensus quite
accomplished political career in the affairs of what he helped to fashion as
Départments d'Outre-Mer. His elite training in Paris should be seen as a
catalyst medium for the origination of *négritude* and its exaltation of trans-
atlantic African heritages.

This last point brings into matriarchal focus the contrast between Césaire's diaspora *soil-soul* French Caribbean pride-of-place and Cabrera Infante's combined Canarian/Arawak genealogical claims on Cuba's aboriginal lineages. For in Césaire's case, his paternal grandmother attains what
has been described as a "quasi-mythic status," due to the great moral authority she exerted on her grandchildren, not the least of it on Aimé, who
stressed her being "'a woman who was visibly African in origin[. . . .] She
had the phenotype that was African in a very distinct and precise way'"
(David 1997, xiv). Baptismal names may seem appropriate here in order to
best inscribe the adult force of intense childhood filiation touched-off by
that *furieuse passion* of superego origins in Lacan's thesis. Thus, in counterpoint: African features, unmodulated by *métissage* in Aimé's matriarch's
case, match Guillermo's claim of maternal family origins in Taíno-Arawak
first-people on Cuban soil, and their *mestizaje* with yet another aboriginal
folk of Canarian origins as they settled in places like Gibara. (And from
such primal grounds these double aborigines roamed at large throughout
Cuba's ecological imaginary and cosmic ethnic diaspora—as advertised to
the Tenerife audience—they roamed in complete exemption from colors
brought from Africa.)

At the end of the speech, the whispering deaf's sordid question is an-
swered in the strongest terms of authorship: "The only house I inhabit
is the house of words in the country of writing in the kingdom of language. I do not recognize any other homeland, she is my sole teacher" (Gg
143). Even if he might have spoken into deaf ears only about England, the
speaker insists that *Cuba* is all that would always be *overheard*. (It is to such
homeland that he travels in the time machine of his memory each time Big
Ben strikes.)

Besides admitting to having acquired the vice of black melancholia in
Robert Burton's island homeland, the exile from Communism has managed to entertain his Canarian hosts (among whom one is tempted to
guess some local cigar merchants were present). In a speech where the

mother's colors and fibers have been caressed and cured as if gold-dusted like blonde *gofio* by King Midas himself, cigar-making extends the speaker's peace-pipe tale solution to his audience. Storytelling brings peace in the wake of the family fury and madness so indelibly evoked and perhaps partly blown off in bluish smoke, while gone sublimely, nicotine-half-unheard, by his listeners. In the speaker's tale, Arawaks reveal the secrets of tobacco to Canarians and Canarians the delights of golden gruel *gofio* to Arawaks. Carmen rolls and rubs pre-Freud and pre-Castro cigars or "impure puros" (*puros impuros*) on her tawny thighs, as if she wished to be herself Canarian (a Canarian Gypsy, though, being "as impossible a dream as an *habanera* blonde" [142]). It all ends in a vision of three inter-racial breeds and brand seeds among which the darkest human color of black represents the excluded third. Once upon a time, an "Indian" and a "Canarian" conceived Carmen's genesis as they traded folk secrets on the soot weed in Paradise Cuba, so that Merrimée could find his Gypsy Carmen skin-wrapped in the colors of the leaf she rolled: for "smoking is a dangerous pleasure, Cuban and Canarian." (The speech thus ends in high and bountiful pastoral praise of the Canarian cigar and its factories).

Besides the Cartesian miracle already inspected, it would seem impolite to inquire who sponsored this homecoming banquet. And just in case it might not have been a banquet after all, it is worth observing that, to the mother so strongly represented and the wife seated next to him, the speaker has added quite an occasion or excuse to hold a wedding feast for the fierce Gypsy woman who never marries but murders in *Carmen*.

chapter four

Talking about Beauty
and the Beast, She's Both
(Crime Scene)

In his quest of the origins of table manners in *Mythologiques 3*, Claude Lévi-Strauss faces a moral issue of his own making as he ponders the large implications behind the story of Monmanéki, the Amazonian Tukuna hunter, and his fifth wife, the awful *clinging woman*.[1] A possible distant relative of the Star Husband figure in indigenous North America, Monmanéki marries four animal wives in a row and then a fifth one, a woman from his own village, human in looks, but who behaves in the worst imaginable frog manner. Each marriage is ruined by his mother's distaste for the animal wife, including the fifth one, whose stubborn human way of clinging frog-like to Monmanéki gets the serial monogamist in a Tukuna divorce mess. The woman's fishing proves awesome and scary. She catches fish by breaking herself in half at the waist and entering the river only with the upper body, belly and legs left ashore. But one day, the mother-in-law removes the spinal cord from her lower body and the woman must climb up a tree split from the rest of herself. She then becomes a "clinging woman" by falling on Monmanéki's back, covering him with her own filth and preventing him from eating until, helped by piranhas, he scares her off and she turns into a parrot (OTM 25–29).

GLUED TO A WIFE TOO MANY

Just as much as the hideous (*frog-at-its-worst*) fifth wife remains torn up and wounded in the human split shape loathed by her husband, the issue of bestiality appears sutured in his treasured union with the (*frog-plain-and-simple*) first wife, such as when, out hunting, Monmanéki spots a frog near a hole and proceeds to urinate into it. A while later, he sees a "good-looking girl" on the same spot who says that she is pregnant by him, whereupon he takes her home as his first wife (OTM 26). He marries a frog who makes a pretty wife but loses her when his mother's alert fastidiousness senses some definite out-of-place frog behavior in the wife whose monogamous company she shares with her son. Besides whatever else it might imply about plausibly or implausibly mating with animals, the story seems concerned with proper and improper spouse behavior as an important aspect of being human, in this case *Tukuna* human. Yet, the implicit or explicit sexual conduct inherent in Monmanéki's marital liaison with a batrachian remains out of sight in the recorded myth.[2] Frog morals and manners show up in the good-looking frog wife's improper eating, domestic habits, and her stealing her own child, but without any graphic sexual contact with her non-frog husband.

Amazonian stories of sex with animals can be blunt, vivid, and grotesquely graphic while as a rule focused on cautionary lessons about disruptions caused by uncommon sex. In a story by a Mehinaku man named Ketepe recorded by anthropologist Thomas Gregor in *Anxious Pleasures*, the girl Kataihu encounters Tepu the worm while walking in the forest and she keeps it, feeds it, and enjoys lots of worm sex: " 'Oh, Tepu, Tepu,' she moaned, 'how delicious your penis, Tepu. Oh Tepu, Tepu . . . *ateke, ateke, aah!*' " (AP 54). Gregor explains that "*ateke*" (used here in blissful *jouissance*) can also express pain, such as from a burn. He comments that "in the [Mehinaku] myths, the animal world is dangerously tempting. Let a villager try animal sex once . . . and he may never return to human partners at all. The stories warn of sexual atavism and suggest that the line between animal and human may be all too easily crossed" (AP 55). In this regard, it seems unlikely that Tukuna views on sex with animals and strangers should differ greatly from those of other Amazonian people as they entertain in their stories the disruptive potential of sex habits. Gregor comments that among the Mehinaku, "legitimate sexual relations distinguish men from animals and tribes of men from each other. 'Humans,' say the villagers, 'have sex with other humans who are their cross-cousins. Animals don't care who they have sex with'" (AP 52). Obviously, perils and punishments in sex with animals leave deep *zoematic* scars in the affairs of improper marriage—with added incest implications. Indeed, the three incest stories showcased by Gregor concern sex with animals: "Tuluma, the Woodpecker" (father-daughter), "Tapir Woman" (mother-son), and "Bat (alua)" (mother–son-in-law).[3]

On his part, after a few analytic rounds dealing with clusters of related myths at several levels of semantic cross-reference, Lévi-Strauss draws a moral lesson of wide scope from Monmanéki's string of marriages. The myths "proclaim" or consider it "wicked" and "dangerous" to confuse "physical differences between women" with the "specific differences" that separate "animals from humans, or animals from each other" (OTM 76). To confuse different "looks" in potential wives with the ways certain animals "look" (in relation to other animals and to other women) amounts, he claims, to an "anticipatory form of racialism" and a threat to social life, which requires that women be worthy of marrying men regardless of their own looks. Hence, he concludes, in being "contrasted in the mass with animal wives, human wives are all equally valid," but, "as the armature of myth is reversed," something of a mystery (which "society tries to ignore") crops up: "All human females are not equal, for nothing can prevent them being different from each other in their animal essence" (OTM 76)—an essence worn on the face, one could add, insofar as Monmanéki behaves *frog-blind* toward a beauty type indelibly set up in figurative reference to what is already established as bedrock appealing or unappealing looks in Tukuna women.

That some good-looks norms should exist about these women seems implicit in having them involved in marriage stories concerned with frog-looks and manners as mirrored in human social rules. In Monmanéki's marriage affairs, frog beauty mirrors how the hunter husband may act as if *eyes wide shot* (dazzled or blinded—gaze shot yet gazing—regarding the species he actually marries). It is the *mirror* itself in the frog mirror of beauty and bad habits that matters most and renders singularly absurd the notion that there could be such a thing as "the literal embodiment of a frog" in Monmanéki's first wife, as claimed by Lévi-Strauss (OTM 199)—absurd, unless the *literal frog* embodies a facsimile of Tukuna standards about good or bad looks and conduct among their own females. It seems as implausible, at least in this instance, for frog looks not to mirror human looks as for human looks not to mirror frog looks, and for both not to speak loudly about improper behavior in the spouse roles of Tukuna as well as non-Tukuna women.[4]

The nexus between Monmanéki and his fifth wife transcends all of his previous marriages in cosmogonic significance. The clinging woman's terrestrial character achieves chthonian or underground depth as the bottommost point of reference in the hunter's journey from earthly paths to celestial maps. Thus, in some stories about a figure known as the *susceptible ferryman*, the woman in question is turned into a diving tortoise who drags and drowns its clinging victims. The issue of distant kinship resemblance between characters from North and South America analyzed in

Mythologiques 3 deserves a quick glance before turning to Arawak cosmogonic stories of sex involving twin brothers and female turtles.[5]

Monmanéki's Star Husband serial monogamy fails five times under pressure from his zealous mother, a strict household enforcer of proper Tukuna conduct. The formidable Tukuna resident mommy plays familial facsimile to the granny in a cluster of stories from the Plains Indians of North America known as "the grandmother and the grandson in which the Star-Husband saga widens" (OTM 201–2). A solitary old woman adopts an orphan boy who has been stealing from her garden and rears him in equivocal ways. (He is either seduced by her in adolescence or she alerts him against dangers lurking in the bush. He becomes a killer of monsters who either trades granny away to his enemies or himself kills her.) Once a hero, the young man ascends to the sky and becomes a star, sun, or moon. Following the already familiar pattern of differential resemblances between twins or matched pairs, Monmanéki's Amazonian great-hunter kinship with the Plains Indians Star Husband type involves his own leading role in a celestial canoe trip accompanied by a dumb brother-in-law whom he outshines with his brightness (OTM 199–200). Something of a lost map and a crime scene of virtual but never actualized structural affinities between distant actors transforms their diverse habitats and characters into a vast realm of familial symbols in which featured relatives from other groups may reside (as rent-free tenants of the oldest global mind ever conceived).

TORTOISE PIGGYBACK

CALIBAN *No more dams I'll make for fish,*
  Nor fetch in firing
  At requiring . . .
William Shakespeare, *The Tempest*, 2.2.175–77

A cluster of adventures whose female star is a turtle bearing traces of the clinging woman appears among the earliest stories from New World cultures recorded for European reading eyes, Fray Ramón Pané's *Relación acerca de las antigüedades de los indios*. In fragments of stories haunted by the theft of women and their subsequent disappearance, four Arawak twin brothers, believed to represent the cardinal points, take flight from the Great Yaya (Mighty Spirit). The brothers are ripped from the bloodied carcass of Itiba Cahubaba, the Arawak womb mother counterpart of Coatlicue and Mother Earth Pachamama in Mesoamerican and Andean religions.[6] The twins are led by first-born Diminán Caracaracol, a "mangy" fellow in Pané's text (*AAI* 14/R 30) but marked by syphilis in the view of Fernando Ortiz and others (*CC* 112). Flight from Mighty Yaya comes after failure to retrieve the bones of his son Yayael, which are kept in a gourd hanging from the ceiling (old Yaya killed young Yayael, afraid that his son wanted to kill him). When the leader thief Diminán Caracaracol reaches for the bones, they fall to the ground and turn into fishes. The twin brothers are next in flight from Bayamanaco, the ill-tempered grandfather, who refuses to share any of his *cazabe* bread with them. Instead, the old grump blows a *cohoba*-rich slug of mucus from his nose right at the mangy grandson's shoulder blades. After swelling and labor pains and a little stone-ax surgery with his brothers' help, a "live, female turtle" emerges from the man's quadruple twin flesh. (The notion of one common brotherly flesh shared in illness and in health seems plausible in the Adam-like twins quartet.) In Pané's account: "His brothers looked at his back and saw it was very swollen; and then the swelling grew so much that he was about to die. Then they tried to cut it and they could not; and taking a stone ax they opened it up, and a live, female turtle emerged; and so they built their house and raised the turtle" (*AAI* 16/R 31). In the ninth chapter of his first *Decade*, Peter Martyr d'Anghiera copies Pané's text but renders the *guanguayo cohoba* slug offspring as a woman, instead of a turtle, a metamorphosis that in his eyes obviously facilitates her being used mutually by the four brothers to engender sons and daughters. (In his copious notes to Pané's *Account*, J. J. Arrom argues that Anghiera creates a distortion or "deformation" of the original turtle, whose photograph Arrom believes himself quite lucky to have taken at the Museum of the American Indian in New York [*AAI* 16 n. 73/R 69 n. 73]).[7]

But the turtle woman's role in Arawak stories (as the coerced maternal means to restore her own banished gender to mankind) seems at odds with the stubborn challenge to male heroics posed by the clinging wife in Monmanéki's celestial quest. Yet, by the combined anachronic lure of myth and fetish, it should be she herself (without doubt: turtle and woman and snapped museum photo) who is forever born by caesarean means from Caracaracol's fraternal back and given food and shelter and carnal employment by the four twins.

The issue of indigenous idolatrous practices in the inquisitive judgment of European colonists lies at the heart of properly reading Pané's *Account* and its insertion in Peter Martyr's work. Serge Gruzinski praises Pané's avoidance of such vernacular labels as the Portuguese *feitiço* or "fetish" in favor of the "autochthonous" Arawak *cemí* and *cemíes* as objects of worship with multiple functions not fitting the European notion of *idol*. Pané's writings on Hispaniola are further praised for their "linguistic receptivity," "ethnographic sensitivity," and non-fetishistic focus on "themes as crucial as the body, death, visions, states of possession, and myths of origins, without ever letting his observations warp under the weight of stereotype or prejudice" (Gruzinski 2001, 11). On his part, Fernando Ortiz sees in the turtle woman "a variation of the myth of Eve, who came out of her husband's side (*CC* 112/*Cc* 292). Accordingly, the 1963 revised edition of *Contrapunteo* outlines an agrarian epic scenario in comparison with Noah and the Flood. The four twins migrate with a group after a hurricane flood. They and their people want to plant the yucca root to make *cazabe* but are refused by the grandfather. The sequence of magical *cohoba* powder spitting and female turtle birth from a male's back by means of stone-ax surgery would refer to rain and lightning, planting and harvesting. The turtle, Ortiz adds, is a symbol of the fertile rain-soaked earth. The house built for her by the brothers gives proof that settled life devoted to agriculture has been achieved, "after the transmigratory odyssey of the four sons of Itaba Yahubaba" (*Cc* 294–95).

CHIMERICAL ECONOMIES

A glance back at "The Voice of the Turtle" is now in order, after finding a mythic facsimile to match (in reverse) a piece of storytelling falsehood involving the harmful consequences to humans of mating with female tortoises. To start with, instead of resting on the "just-so" acceptance of the perils-of-bestiality tale, a specific literary source for it was found in the voice of the ("*taught us!*") tortoise encountered by Alice on the beach in "The Mock Turtle Story." Arawak myth reverses the deadly affair of mounting and dying atop a turned-over loggerhead tortoise by having its smaller earthy counterpart cling to a man's back at the moment of her apparent birth and in prelude to her serving as the first woman and mother of a group of people who had lost their women and who suffered periods of famine and often lived at the edge of squalor. The truthfulness of the Arawak myth fiction lies in the value—in pleasure and wisdom—it might have brought to its now vanished speakers and listeners, to those people who bothered to keep such stories in play as live elements in Arawak material and spiritual existence. On its part, the cock-and-bull literary truthfulness of "The Voice of the Turtle" exceeds its blatant falsehood, but without betraying it. Its truth value relates to parody as each one of the Chimera's three animal embodiments relates to the other two: as a sort of grotesque facsimile of their questionable union.

A quick chimerical reading of the literary story may proceed from two reversals: (a) the male copulatory apparatus in sea turtles switches over to the female body; (b) just as the switch in brides from human to beast takes lethal hold of the promised bridegroom. The affair turns into Chimera (a fabulous three-part fire-breathing beast: lion-head, she-goat-head and trunk, dragon-head and tail) in the shapes of (a) the dual split bride and her lost bridegroom; (b) the *corpus delicti* of two turtles-in-one (female with male mating features) and the dead bridegroom. Fuzzy or not, such chimerical math is less important than the larger picture of (a) *twosome dualism* (two young men, two sexes, two brides); (b) *threesome-marked* (two young men and a bride, two hunters and a turtle); and (c) *foursome-shadowed* (insofar as the bride's preserved virginity may find counterpoint in the bestial act that substitutes for her mating while the specter of incest clings on to the tortoise).

Incest avoidance seems implicit in the dismal affair. The chimerical beauty and beast cling together clasped by the threesome of (a) female virginity, (b) male sex with animals, and (c) the incest implications carried by the first two elements combined: female virginity turned lethal when male-aroused in male bestial copulation. At the exogamous extreme of mating with an animal of one's own (male) sex, the bridegroom meets something terribly endogamous. Bestiality in proximity to nuptials breaks up the imminent wedding as if it represented the odd copy of the incest violation tabooed in the nuptials' own success, and yet by its own success upheld as the sovereign mark of constraint in human kinship practices.

KEY GUILLERMO

In a 1948 letter, written at the exuberant horny edge of his manic mood, Ernest Hemingway spoke of his sexual prowess to screenwriter Peter Viertel, the younger biographer he seductively sought, among others, and whom he seeded with "truths, half-truths, and outright fantasies." According to Michael Reynolds, Hemingway knew that Viertel's beautiful wife, Jigee, would read his humorous praise for the virtues of turtle eggs over testosterone injections. So he describes himself in Bimini, eating the eggs and walking about "with such an erection that natives, passing in the street, would salute it," and he "would tell them if they knew someplace better to keep it than in his pants, they should tell him" (Reynolds 1999, 173).

Older by far than Hemingway's forty-eight at that point, and soon to become his most celebrated version of undying heroism in extreme age, Santiago (the Cojímar fisherman in *The Old Man and the Sea*) loves to watch turtles eat the Portuguese men-of-war at sea, eyes shut and shielded, just as much as he likes to step on the iridescent bubbles on the beach after a storm "with the horny soles of his feet" (OMS 36). Santiago loves green turtles and hawkbills but has "friendly contempt for the huge, stupid loggerheads, yellow in their armour-plating, strange in their love-making, and happily eating the Portuguese men-of-war" (36–37). The old man is no mystic about the animals; having gone on turtle boats for years, he deplores their killing and thinks that most "people are heartless" about them because "a turtle's heart will beat for hours after he has been cut up and butchered" (37). Santiago shares the same heart connection, but in sympathy, for he has "such a heart too" and his "feet and hands are like theirs" (37). It is said that the old man always "ate the white eggs to give himself strength," that he "ate them all through May to be strong in September and October for the truly big fish" (37). So nurtured but stoically famished, the old man turns his last big fish hunt into a war on time in the shape of big mako jaws and the approaching tempest.

Santiago's Gulf Stream fishing off Cojímar lies rather far to the west of the barrier keys and cay islets along the northern coast of Camagüey province and eastern Santa Clara, where the nine crew members on board the dark yacht *Pilar* pursue their hunt for German U-boats in "At Sea" (the last part of *Islands in the Stream*) and where they land on a key whose turtle hunters have been massacred by a shipwrecked crew of German U-boaters on the run. In his comparison between the "Friendless" operation (so named by Hemingway) and the fiction grown out of it in *Islands*, Norberto Fuentes observes in *Hemingway in Cuba* the reiteration of the number nine (nine murdered turtle fishermen, nine Germans, nine men in Thomas Hudson's crew) as "exorcism and magic" on the writer's part to "balance the strength of his forces against the enemy force" (HC 207–8). Once, on a visit to the barrier archipelago where Thomas Hudson finds his death in action (the same kind of death in fiction that eluded Hemingway's own pursuit in life), Fuentes followed the lead of another older and mythic Fuentes named Gregorio, forty years after the coast-patrolling days in 1943 narrated in the novel, where he is the cook and pilot named Antonio.

On Key Romano, Gregorio and Norberto visit the home of the old Canarian patriarch Alcides Fals Roque and his wife Zoila, who remembers that her mother did the laundry for "'a dark boat with Americans on board'" at the time when she was just a "little girl" (IS 213). Fuentes the writer (who at the time had read and was writing about Islands in the Stream) and Fuentes the character (who had not heard of any such book and knew not how to read and thus learns of his own role in the story by hearsay) visited two more keys (Confites and Paredón Grande). They came near the fateful spot where, in fact and fiction, the dark boat ran aground: "'I remember [says Gregorio] that we went aground between Media Luna and Guillermo" (IS 215). But the spot constitutes a fateful spot only in fiction, as the plot dictates the coordinates in time and space when and where, freed from the sand and at full blast in the narrowed channel, before it widens just ahead, the occasion of when meets the grounds of where, and where turns into nowhere, and death befalls right where stories may plot it must come. Time and place meet at last and fall into mutual place and pass into the past, as when: "Thomas Hudson felt as though someone had clubbed him three times with a baseball bat and his left leg was wet" (IS 436).

Now, heading back to the port of Nuevitas, further east (but not quite on the imagined home grounds where turtle love turns nasty and the Canarian grandfather kills the grandmother and then himself), Fuentes tells Fuentes how, back then, the Pilar found a turtle boat adrift with a wounded man, leg gored by a stingray. Following a romantic hunch, the Gregorio/ Norberto Fuentes pair looks for the wounded fisherman of yore and soon runs into "a short, solidly built man" who is lame and "walks dragging his feet" (HC 217). His name is José Roque, known as Felo. At sixty-three, he no longer fishes, and nothing seems the same to him since the "'quelonios'" or tortoise shell turtles became rare. He bemoans that nowadays "they even catch the turtle eggs" and remembers when, during World War II, he and his mates sold the tortoise shells cheap at forty cents a pound. His turtle boat was named Canario. It cast its nets for nine days. Old Felo recalls: "A dark, strong boat. A wide boat with two long sticks on its sides that looked like two lobster feelers. A boat full of Americans, with a skipper from the Canary Islands. A strong guy who was a millionaire. And another one, with a beard, whom they called the Americano" (HC 219). The elder Fuentes tells Felo that it was his boat (it was no doubt the right boat, though not yet inherited from Papa Hemingway). That he was that (other) Canarian. Thus, from one old Canarian to another, it is learned that the man gored by the stingray survived but is now twenty years gone. (It is surmised that he never limped and never dreamed of carrying his wife glued to his back.)

part two

No Wedding without Funeral

The prototype of all opposition or contrariety is the

contrariety of sex.

F. M. CORNFORD, "The Origin of Moira"

No Caliban no Prospero! No Prospero no Miranda!

No Miranda no Marriage! And no Marriage no Tempest!

GEORGE LAMMING, "A Monster, a Child, a Slave"

chapter five

Antonio's Island
(The Long Goodbye)

ANTONIO His word is more than the miraculous harp.
SEBASTIAN He hath raised the wall, and houses too.
ANTONIO What impossible matter will he make easy next?
SEBASTIAN I think he will carry this island home in his pocket,
    and give it his son for an apple.
ANTONIO And sowing the kernels of it in the sea, bring forth
    more islands.
   WILLIAM SHAKESPEARE, The Tempest, 2.1.87–90

Within the sociocultural fluidity that the Caribbean archipelago
presents, within its historiographic turbulence and its ethnological
and linguistic clamor, within its generalized instability of
vertigo and hurricane, one can sense the features of an island that
"repeats" itself, unfolding and bifurcating until it reaches all the
seas and lands of the earth, while at the same time it inspires
multidisciplinary maps of unexpected designs.
   ANTONIO BENÍTEZ-ROJO, The Repeating Island

Young people, when transferring familiar stories to their own
neighborhood, as almost all young people do, never stick at the
inconsistencies. They are like eminent Homeric scholars, and when
they mean to have things in any given way they will not let the
native hue of resolution be balked by thought; and will find it
equally easy to have Ithaca in one place and also in another, and
to see the voyages of Columbus to the tropics in their own sliding
over a frozen pool.
   SAMUEL BUTLER, The Authoress of the Odyssey

The cruelest twist of fate suffered by Odysseus on his way home
comes within sight of Ithaca and its "people tending fires" when he and his
crew are swept away from the shores of their country by the tempest, in the
crew's case forever, in Odysseus's for only nine long years. Seven of them,

the longest ones, are spent stranded on the island of Ogygia in the company of the immortal nymph and girl-looking goddess Calypso—longest if one is to judge by the tears Odysseus is shedding when approached by Hermes out on the headland beach where he sits homesick, gazing at the waves. His captivity on Calypso's island paradise is first mentioned by the "ever truthful Old Man of the Sea" to Menelaos, who informs Telemachus that old Proteus saw his father "weeping big tears," as the nymph "detains him by constraint, and he cannot make his way back to his country, / for he has not any ships by him, nor any companions / who can convey him back across the sea's wide ridges" (Ody 3.556–60). Much later in the poem, as he brings to a close the account of his wanderings, Odysseus will tell the Phaeacians that the tempest brought him alone to Calypso's home when his ship sank and his crew washed away "bobbing like sea crows" and drowned, punished by Zeus after hunger drove them to kill and to feast on Helios the Sun God's best cattle despite warnings from Circe and Tiresias (Ody 12.375–419).

The disaster that kills the crew and brings Odysseus in the tempest's wake to Calypso's nest at the end of book 12 repeats the pattern of human folly and blunder countered by divine punishment in the account of his wanderings, which begins in book 9. First, he tells King Alcinous and his court at Phaeacia of escaping the lure of the Lotus Eaters and their food of forgetfulness and of the blinding of the drunken Polyphemus and the curse uttered by the cannibal giant against him and the surviving crew. Next, at the start of book 10, he tells of the land of Aeolus, Warden of the Winds, who lives

> on a floating island, the whole enclosed by a rampart
> of bronze, not to be broken, and the sheer of the cliff runs upward
> to it; and twelve children were born to him in his palace,
> six of them daughters, and six sons in the pride of their youth, so
> he bestowed his daughters on his sons, to be their consorts. (Ody
> 10.1–8)

A settler of islands and a colonist but not himself a god, King Aeolus, perched on his floating cliff palace and nestled in convivial incest, has earned from Poseidon the gift of holding and releasing all the blowing winds kept in a cave, which he now and then breaks open to set them loose. Aeolus lends a bag full of winds to Odysseus to quicken his passage home. But the winds are unleashed within reach of Ithaca when the crew opens the bag looking for loot taken from Troy as they felt tricked by Odysseus's silence about its contents. The disaster blows them back to the Aeolian island and to the eternal banquet hall of the closest of closely-knit ruling families. On news of the debacle, Aeolus expels Odysseus and his men from his kingdom, appalled by how hateful they obviously are to the immortals. Their subsequent wanderings take them from island to island and peril to peril: to the huge and ravenous Laestrygones, to Circe's sacred forest citadel and human pigpen, to the land of the dead, and to the catastrophe brought upon them by their sacrilege in eating the Sun's cattle as they find them grazing on Hyperion's High Noon island. (The divine cattle are chased and consumed in a mad hecatomb as if they were wild animals; their improper slaughter and cooking make their skins crawl; and the meat hooked on the spits bellow like the "lowing of cattle," as if roasting did not matter and could not alter the meat's sacred grain.)[1]

THE REPEATED ISLAND

Like King Alcinous of Scheria, whose Phaeacian folk are seafarers and builders of extraordinary ships swifter than falcons in flight, Aeolus, Commander of Winds, belongs to those "People of the Sea" whose culture, according to Antonio Benítez Rojo, "is a flux interrupted by rhythms which attempt to silence the noises with which their own social formation interrupts the discourse of Nature." In less "abstruse" terms, he adds, each island culture attempts, by means of "real or symbolic sacrifice, to neutralize violence and to refer society to the transhistorical codes of nature" (RI 17). It seems that Phaeacians and Aeolians in the *Odyssey* are like those people whose cultures merge into one contiguous though fractured space, best grasped, in the Caribbean setting envisioned in *The Repeating Island*, "through the poetic, since it always puts forth an area of chaos" (RI 17). If Benítez Rojo is right in his visionary surmise of one core Caribbean island repeating itself in a fugue across latitudes, and thus undergoing untold variations, Homer's Aeolia and Phaeacia could well *repeat* Caribbean Tempest noises and stresses in sound structures returned in chaos to their echoing insular sources in what then becomes a Caribbean World *Elsewhere*. Yet, even if by such leaps and bounds and loops spanning centuries, repeating islands (borne on the sailing shoulders of pirates, fugitives, conquerors, harlots, cooks) must land somewhere, in counterpoint with *somewhere else*, which in turn may allude to yet a third landfall tied up to a potential number of past and future departures.

Nevertheless, the concept or construct *Peoples of the Sea* is meant to resist strict geographic and historical placement. The role it occupies in *The Repeating Island* sets in motion a "fable of legitimation" claimed by Benítez Rojo to be different from the great narratives associated with the "West" and its rise to world dominance, it being one of three "great paradigms of knowledge": "Peoples of the Sea, of modernity, of postmodernity" (*RI* 315). Yet, as such, the concept would lose much of its appeal if it were just a mere fable or heuristic construct. If, for instance, it could not be said that "it was the Egyptians who invented the Peoples of the Sea," or that, though blamed for "'the fall of Troy,'" the "trouble-makers" known as "Sea People" "were not 'a people,' and only to a limited extent were they 'of the sea.'"[2] Or, likewise, as when inspired by the earliest stirring in the historical narrative of such a turbulent diaspora, Victor Bérard saw in the "'Peuple de la Mer'" the ancestors of the Phoenicians, who he thought were "les principaux agents politiques et courtiers commerciaux" in the eastern Mediterranean during the sixteenth century BCE. Bérard called the People of the Sea "Normans" ("ces Normands") in reference to their incursion into the Nile Delta, where they were defeated, before settling along the coast of Gaza and Palestine as vassals of Egyptian imperial rule. As *Normans*, the People of the Sea, fashioned in Bérard's Mediterranean imagination, are further related to the adventurers and merchants who traveled downriver from Russia into the Black Sea and also to the migrant "argonauts" of the South Pacific islands (Bérard 1927, 28–29).

In Alejo Carpentier's novels *Los pasos perdidos* (1953) and *El siglo de las luces* (1962), these same People set in motion a memory apparatus of diaspora in which the transported *Traits* of lost identities in process of transformation are scattered like airborne seedlings in the winds of myth-making across insular histories of conquest, settlement, and predation. It is not unlikely that Carpentier had read Bérard's work during his years of exile in Paris in the 1930s, and it seems certain that his view of the Phoenicians as commercial diaspora agents of change derives from the same sources that inspired *Les Phéniciens et l'Odyssée* (1902–3), the first visionary source by Bérard that informs the Homeric design of Joyce's *Ulysses*.

As such, the most clear-cut Caribbean literary antecedent of the People of the Sea's role in Benítez Rojo's *The Repeating Island* is found in Carpentier's *El siglo de las luces*, as the young Romantic Esteban, in his role as "scribe" (in the company of corsairs plundering the southern Caribbean under Jacobin rule), gets in the scribbling mood while drinking wine, as if from the "nipples" of French grapes, the same wine, he muses, "that nurtured the turbulent and haughty Mediterranean civilization, now stretching into this Mediterranean Caribbean, where the Confusion of Traits [*Rasgos*] that began thousands of years before amid the People of the Sea continued" (Sl 255). The "Traits" in question (such as "accents," "hairtypes," "profiles") represent the scattered racial phenotypes from the Lost Tribes ("Tribus Extraviadas") brought in the flux of diaspora to the Caribbean along with the wine first "transported on Phoenician ships to Gades," in the Roman colony of Tartessus, near the Pillars of Hercules, from where, more than two thousand years later, a descendant of that ancient wine crossed the Atlantic with Columbus to take part in the "transcendent encounter between the Olive and Maize" (Sl 256). Thus, in the role of spores, the People of the Sea transport into infinity the still active chemistry of prehistoric myth in the visionary trans-historicist perspective framed by Bérard, Carpentier, and Benítez Rojo. However, what at first glance seems like a saga in which odyssey-quest and diaspora-scattering are combined becomes at close range a homebound voyage. Ulysses returns to a home he must reinvent, an island he must *repeat*, in the name and for the sake of another island he has forever lost.

The importance of the Ulysses paradigm in Carpentier's *Los pasos perdidos* and the recurrence of aesthetic inebriation in the daydreams of its musician and composer protagonist are repeated in Esteban's Romantic soul (inside the head behind his scribbling hand and wine-drinking mouth). In the Ulysses mold, Carpentier's and Benítez-Rojo's different conceptions of the People of the Sea can be set side-by-side at the beginning point of a heroic and erotic conflict in which epic territorial deeds of a literary sort combine with (and are in the end overcome by) repeated sexual imbroglios. Perhaps the concluding saga of this kind of heroic-erotic itinerancy —in the Romantic mold of *itinérance*—achieved by a writing hand identified with lives in Cuba and beyond Cuba is Benítez-Rojo's *Mujer en traje de batalla* (2000), in whose plot the man and the woman find abode inside the uniform of a Cuban-French cross-dressing soul on parade.

A similar pattern of epic-quest romance and comedy is caricatured in the confessional urban odyssey of sexual piracy narrated in Cabrera Infante's *La Habana Para un Infante Difunto* (in which the mock-heroic Ulysses pattern conceals the struggle between male and female authorship that lies at the core of the hero's ordeal). As illustrated below, the epic drama of territorial conquest and the rebirth of aesthetic consciousness in the story-telling man finds inner support in (his) woman-invested romantic love. But this seamless web of territorial and romantic conquest is woven only in order to be rent. The writer's Odysseus share in the authorship of his own saga becomes mortgaged to the controlling interests of a powerful Circe-Penelope Woman figure. Her long-term—and in the end renewed and permanent—abandonment (Penelope's) by the husband, and her out-right defeat (Circe's) by the same man as her enslaved lover, are two sides of the same coin. A sartorial and a numismatic version of the Romantic author's divided soul is thus envisioned. *Tailor*: the inner garments of the man's soul are woman-torn and thus worn. *Minter*: the outer visage, the soil, as it were, where his soul is shown to the conquered territory before him, wears his and her visage, by some unseen hand flipped as his sole face.

In the epic phase untouched by irony, the egotistic drama of Roman-tic conquest professes, loudly or through some ventriloquistic trick, the woman's uncanny empowering of male literary authorship. Then, when scored by Romantic irony, as it often is, the drama *repeats* itself. A second phase rendered in confessional tones and tactical evasiveness circles back to the start. It is then, curving back home, that the confessional drama of Romantic authorship declares Man's Fall on Woman's account. Such is the inherent femininity at work in the turning of outlived male heroic quest transformed into posthumous testimony of *his* literary deeds of conquest, but a conquest in the end bequeathed back to Woman.

For a long time, now perhaps exhausted, the most influential modern poetic achievement of the saga of contractual irony in the nomadic pur-suit of male pleasure and the attempt to escape the consequences of its own serial and localized seductions was Byron's *Don Juan* (among modern Romantic poems the most joyously Homeric in burlesque sublimity). As examined later in chapters 7 and 8, the *novella* form assumed by The Amazon story in Infante's confessions corresponds to the Romantic genre of ironic extravagance in the chronicle of serial adulterous love just sketched. It is a genre of excess, episodic migratory lust, and triumphant self-deprecation brought to perfection in Byron's epic poem (except that in Infante's confes-sions, erotic triumph-in-defeat seeks the masochistic transfer of author-ship power from male narrator to female love object).

THE REPEATED WOMAN

In her first passion woman loves her lover,
In all the others all she loves is love.

Lord Byron, Don Juan, 3.2

John Winkler discusses (and in witty fashion repeats) Samuel Butler's "practice of sex-detection" in search of an "authoress" for the *Odyssey* as he picks another woman besides Butler's choice of Princess Nausicaa from Phaeacia, presumed to have existed in what became modern northwest Sicily (Winkler 1990, 143–44). Taking his cue from an ancient parodist named Ptolemy of Chennos, Winkler discards Sicilian Nausicaa and considers instead none other than Egyptian Phantasia, to whom Chennos awards the authorship of both the *Iliad* and the *Odyssey*, pirated by Homer himself after Phantasia left the books at a temple in Memphis. Besides the issue of Homeric authorship-by-theft from lady Phantasy, the man from Chennos engages in wordplay parody at Odysseus's expense by pointing at large ears (*ôta*) as the reason behind the hero's *Outis* real name. Winkler shows how a wordplay echo chamber combines "ears" (*ôta* or Homer's *ôata*) with the required grammatical negative shift for "no one" or "none" (*ou* to *mê*) to ring together as *outis* ("none") and *mêtis* ("craft or cunning"), causing the Cyclopes' response to Polyphemus's cry " 'If alone as you are, none [*outis*] uses violence on you' " to ring like " 'If craftiness [*mêtis*] uses violence on you' " (*Ody* 2.410; Winkler 1990, 144). (The cunning hero's craft strikes back by making the hugeness in the Other lose its head as if felled by verbal wit.)

The Other's mythic head full of archaic memory buzz is felled as it falls to instant wit. It is at a similar switch point, but replacing epic bloodiness with comic pungency, that the play between the genealogical burden of memories embedded in *Infant* (or Infante's infancy) undergoes a dyadic transformation. As already discussed in chapter 1, memory's treasured *affect* (in which De Quincey spotted the literature of power's sublime emotional impact) transforms itself into *effects* of sheer technique. Feeling changes into craftiness. *Defunct* virtuoso authorship brings home on parade *Difunto* self-mourning. In terms of such transformation, the product of technical aura in *Defunct* operates as the posthumous modified alter ego of *Infant*.

That which relates both modalities of authorship—the glossolalia and memory-laden tonalities of *Infant* and the loquacious wit and parody of *De-*

funct—resembles the Greek-to-Latin shift from *Odysseus* to *Ulysses* in Joyce's chosen title. Why, it has been asked, should Joyce's novel not be called *Odysseus*? One appealing answer points at the gap between Homer and the gesture of serious and comic parody that transforms his Odyssey-work creating an epitaph effect, as if in the title *Ulysses* Joyce had "incorporated Homer into his fiction as the paradoxical presence of a defunct absence."[3] Likewise, in parallax fashion with Joyce's Homeric connection, the person and future writer nicknamed *Infant* can be said to reflect speech before the achievement of verbal language. In turn, that same person's predicate *Defunct* represents the falling-due deadline of indebtedness, which seems to imply that defunctness should always follow *Infant*'s infancy in the order of time and ontogenesis. Follow it, unless the onset of articulate speech toward which *Infant* progresses should imply a deadline, one dictated by *Infant*'s prior symbolic indebtedness to the established consensual domain of language. Should imply, that is, the preexisting *mort-gage* of infant speech to the aim (or teleology) of desired and compulsory linguistic competence. Already compromised from the start, and tied up to symbolic regimes in social interaction, the child-subject in question moves, as if in reverse, from *infant defunctness* to the life-talk competence of early childhood. It is such already *mort-gaged* (such in-*deadened*-ness-as-in-*debt*-ness) progression toward symbolic dialogue that adult wordplay revels in abusively caressing and arresting and transforming into punning word-sounds and glittering verbal trash.

In this particular sense, wordplay-punning performs enviously and *avant-la-lettre* its unknowing or *infant* preverbal labors. Wordplay mimics and parodies and repeats itself in envy and flash regression. It points with indexical joy toward unbound pre-verbal fragments of word-sounds and noises. (*Infant* wordplay repeats everything and nothing.) Such an instant and reiterative quest in search of *infant* eloquence aims at the fetish of polymorphous mother-tongue and throat-play unbound from actual meaning and bound to perish in articulate language beyond mouthing speech. Much of what splits authorship under man's management from women and the Woman at hand—as he writes—issues from such polymorphic conception of the nascent social self as wordplay. What in such conception answers to mother is often replaced in authorship struggles by her ability to steal or to implant evidence of creative preemption and parody of what might not yet exist of man's work.[4]

Under the sign of such parody, the Ulysses-Odysseus figure writes and composes while in erotic thralldom to a woman and to a landscape grasped in territorial bondage to her gynecology, to his own projected idioms and images of Her enveloping Earth-rule, akin to what Leopold Bloom finds in repose next to Molly's telluric rump.[5] (Transposed or repeated, the Odysseus-Ulysses hyphen suggests a prime point of heroic defeat and a comic reversal of erotic fortunes in the People-of-the-Sea Caribbean literary saga.) The romance quest genealogy sketched here (starting from the two Carpentier novels and Benítez-Rojo's euphoric treatise on islands-in-flight) ends in the bittersweet fall from bliss of the philandering Ulysses figure in Cabrera Infante's *La Habana Para un Infante Difunto*. A common case of rogue behavior by a husband in command of his one-sided authorship of each serial affair turns inward in the mirror of Ulysses and his compromised negotiations with insular women, stranded island creatures with whom his otherwise sealed-off heroic armature becomes porous, pirated, parodied.

ISLANDS BORN IN TEMPEST

Such porousness is at work on Phaeacia and the town of Scheria, the place where Odysseus regains his storytelling voice after enduring seven years of redundant bliss next to immortal Calypso. Built right on the sea, Homer's Scheria is peopled by sailors, carpenters, and ship makers who settled there after being so harassed by the Cyclopes that their leader, godlike Nausithous, took them on migration to another island and raised a "wall about the city, and built the houses, / and made the temples to the gods, and allotted the holdings" (*Ody* 6.9–10). The crafty islanders of Phaeacia listen to Odysseus's woeful tale of repeated shipwrecks and captivities and, when he is done, decide to transport him to Ithaca sound asleep in one of their self-powered ships. These ferrying People of the Sea must next atone for having so abused the ability to convey mortals from shore to shore, granted to them by earth-shaking Poseidon, Odysseus's sworn Enemy, whom they must now appease with the sacrifice of twelve bulls, or else a great mountain will come crashing on their city (*Ody* 13.170–83). Leading up to his final sleep passage to Ithaca, a core repeating-island Odyssey unfolds in the narrative loop which in book 9 begins the story of Odysseus's wanderings in his own voice and in book 12 ends with the story of the tempest that washes him on Calypso's shores seven years before the one that blows him off to the land of the Phaeacians.

The first and most crushing of these two tempests comes as punishment for the crew's letting the winds escape from Aeolus's bag. Odysseus blames himself for keeping from the crew the secret embedded in the gift of passage and ponders in his "blameless spirit" whether to kill himself by leaping into the heaving waters (*Ody* 10.50–55). The repeating-island pattern may be construed in counterpoint: on one hand, the tricky wind-bag gift from Aeolus which backfires into nine more years of exile for Odysseus and eternal banishment from Ithaca for his crew; on the other, those exchanges which occur on Phaeacia, consisting of the stories of frustrated homecoming tendered by Odysseus to his hosts, who in return offer him their ship-building and home-passage gift.

Phaeacians and their home in Scheria are often said to mark the boundary between the world of stories and the actual world to which Odysseus strives to make landfall back in Ithaca. The land of Scheria appears double in character, a model colonial settlement with arable land allotted by its ancestral founder, fields tilled by men (*Ody* 6.259), a citadel bound-off from the wild bush and untilled earth, and other ancestral rewards long sought-after by the pilgrim on his hazardous way home. But the same model island on which Odysseus crawls naked and covered in brine repeats itself in Golden Age qualities, such as a magic garden and orchard with ripened and unripened grapes grown all-at-once, olive trees, figs and fruits within perennial grasp of the Ruler and his fellow vassals, and blessed by the unchanging weather. An ideal and unattainable island society, Scheria resembles the first utopia in ancient Greek literature.[6]

For homebound Odysseus, Scheria's garden utopia and Aeolus's floating island are tied together in counterpoint repetition and joint insular reference to Ithaca. In both ruling palaces, unbroken feasting reigns. Homeric Aeolian rule accommodates royal sibling incest without hint of punishment, while the games won by Odysseus during the celebrations held in Phaeacia might bare traces of an earlier wedding narrative and song. (In both instances the exquisite corpse of matriarchy regains life attached to its Siamese sister, matrilineal descent.) In its simplest form, Odysseus's role as bridegroom to Princess Nausicaa would break up the rule of Phaeacian sibling incest, as he, a perfect stranger, would marry Nausithous's granddaughter, whose royal parents, Alcinous and Arete, are both children of the same royal pair: "Arete is the name she is called, and she comes of the same / forebears as in fact produces the king Alcinous" (*Ody* 6.54–55). Though soon corrected by declaring Arete her husband's niece, the glitch, due perhaps to interpolation, can serve as clue to the full-blown matrilineal wedding scenario embroiled in Phaeacian divine claims in sacred kingship. Thus, as the divine would-be king intruder, the alien bridegroom Odysseus takes part in Alcinous's funereal games as he marries the king's daughter, who represents her mother Arete's matrilineal clone goddess.[7]

The counterpoint between two different brands of island happiness just sketched is meant to imply that when insular repetition becomes reciprocal or mutual, it obviously engenders difference. The magical utopian realm of Alcinous, and the no less magical floating brazen fortress of Aeolus, repeat themselves as if aimed at each other. In such fashion, confronting islands in parallax flight from each other repeat a different Ithaca from the singular island kingdom imagined and imaginable at the start of the *Odyssey*. The three-prong difference between these islands (Aeolia-Phaeacia-Ithaca) confronts two other islands also caught face-to-face: Calypso's Ogygia and Circe's Aeaea. These two mutual goddess-realms or *Queendoms* stand, in what lies ahead in this and the next three chapters, as proximate contraries within the reiterative extremes posed by Woman as her figure splits itself and flip-flops in the role of erotic accomplice and sexual antagonist. Behind this specular Romantic conflict lies the larger and more intimate threat of authorship embroilment between the contending male and female parts of the chimerical Don Juan.

DON JUAN IN ITHACA

What men call gallantry, and gods adultery,
Is much more common where the climate's sultry.

    Lord Byron, Don Juan, 1:63

Memorably grasped in W. B. Stanford's "luminous daemonic creature," Circe will be remembered here in association with "a darkly malevolent" male figure represented in Greek myth by her brother Aeëtes, king of Colchis and father of Medea, as well as by the enchantress's father, the life-giving Sun (Stanford 1992, 47). Circe the enchantress acts in ensemble with her niece and sister-witch Medea and with two paired and contrasting males, Aeëtes and Helios, who are united in their sovereign power here and hereafter. Circe is the host standing at the gates between life and death. She stands for the woman who, even when all by herself in one-on-one action with her lover, is never alone. By virtue of such menacing plural relations with the living and the dead, Circe guards over the crossroads where love and poison celebrate their toxic blind date: "Fishing with *phar-*

maka is a quick and easy way to catch fish, but it renders them inedible and paltry. In the same way, women who use love potions (*philtra*) and sorcery (*goeteia*) against their husbands, and who gain mastery over them through pleasure, end up living with stunned, senseless, crippled men. The men bewitched (*katapharmakeuthentes*) by Circe were of no service to her, nor did she have any 'use' at all for them after they had become swine and asses. But Odysseus, who kept his senses and behaved prudently, she loved in excess."[8] Incorporated into the wife's role and love tactics in dire warning, Circe's *dominatrix* conduct appears here and elsewhere as overwhelmingly conjugal and uxorial. She stands not as mistress but as the sort of wife who breaks the mold and threatens to turn her husband into a sustainable ruin.

On her part, although Calypso offers Odysseus immortal youthful companionship, the offer itself sets her apart from the wife and mother in Circe and casts her as the eternal teen lover. Calypso is the nymph and girl-looking goddess, the sort of picture-perfect girl star who husband Monmanéki thinks he has found in the Tukuna woman who looks like a frog. But, where in Tukuna myth the girl serves as the first among five serial wives, in Homer, the Calypso nymph type is convinced that she should never marry. (This may have to do with her dad, who is a huge athlete named Atlas.) Calypso lives on her hideaway island at the "navel of the sea," a spot of such composite beauty that it could find itself repeated on hundreds if not thousands of island brochures.

Composite, indeed, are not only the girl and her island but the whole occasion of their Romantic encounter with Don Juan in the combined role of returning Ulysses and of all-the-suitors-in-one. After becoming the lone shipwreck survivor in flight from Spain, Byron's hero is washed ashore a Mediterranean island ruled by Lambro, a pirate slave trader and the father of the virgin nymph Haidée. Old Lambro is often compared to Shakespeare's Prospero as his daughter is to Miranda. But Lambro best resembles the sort of adventurer and freebooter that the Romantic Caliban might have become in the afterlife of Prospero's departure from the Isle and the creature's recovery of the land that his mother Sycorax had given him and his master had stolen. Lambro's sudden return to his domain ("Old Lambro passed unseen a private gate / And stood within his hall at eventide" [DJ 3.61]) kills the affair that Don Juan and his daughter had, on that same date, consummated in marriage. Lambro crashes the wedding party and destroys the sovereign bliss shared in orgiastic joy between the teenaged newlyweds and the band of servants and domestics that they have inherited after persuading themselves that her father had perished during his latest pirate raid. For a timeless instant in Haidée's eyes (which transforms itself into her madness and death), Ulysses blends into the youthful suitor and usurper Don Juan and the father and tyrant Lambro. The girl-bride looks at her boy-lover-husband:

> And gazing on the dead, she thought his face
> Faded, or altered into something new,
> Like to her father's features, till each trace
> More like and like to Lambro's aspect grew
> With all his keen worn look a Grecian grace.
> And starting, she awoke, and what to view?
> Oh powers of heaven! What dark eye meets she there?
> 'Tis—'tis her father's—fixed upon the pair! (4.35)[9]

Haidée's honeymoon coma and quick death and Don Juan's survival as a slave sold by her father's retainers in Constantinople find Caribbean counterpoint repetition in the Caliban fortunes narrated in Lino Novás Calvo's historical and biographic novel *Pedro Blanco, el negrero* (1933).

Old Lambro's piracy across the eastern Mediterranean and the wealth he has earned from the sale of humans to humans occur in the same time frame as Byron's Napoleon-post-Napoleonic composition of *Don Juan* and during the early years of Pedro Blanco's life at sea. When Pedro learns of Napoleon's death from a sailor just off Saint Helena, he reflects on the "old kabbalah of dates which had linked together his travels with the Emperor's" (PBn 421). At issue here is the Romantic sense of "portentous intensification of [one's] own history" in which Hans Blumenberg identifies the "pure anachronism" at work when "heroes still have attendant meteorological phenomena," such as "the thunderstorm that is vouched for as having occurred at the hour of Napoleon's death on Saint Helena, or the one—uncommon for the end of March, but similarly attested—at Beethoven's death" (Blumenberg 1985, 106). Pedro's pirate errancy and incest with his sister Rosa, since they were children, are only two among multiple Romantic traits stamped upon his saga in wretched tragic tones. On the one hand, Pedro Blanco embodies the darkest core figure in Cuba's economic history: the *negrero* or smuggler of African slaves into the island; while on the other, in literary values, his character would seem sufficient to represent all by itself Benítez Rojo's late-Romantic world picture of the People of the Sea.

With Pedro's career the motif cartography of repeated islands extends up to Terranova (where he was once held by pirates and worked with whalers) and down to the coast of West Africa, near the mouth of the Gallinas River, on whose cluster of tiny islands Spanish colonial rule (by then reduced to Cuba, the Philippines, Puerto Rico, and some North African outposts) had established barracoons or slave factories. On one of these barren sites Pedro established residence inside a haunt to which only he and his sister Rosa had access. From this lair he ruled and became an alien king among local chiefs dedicated to the hunt for humans who were sold and exported across the Atlantic. Pedro kept a harem as required by his merchant boss reputation as *big man*. He also gained prestige and wealth as the *Mirror-Sun-Magus* with his use of German glasses and telescopes employed in sending signals to the ships waiting off shore to pick up their human cargoes beyond the reach of the British Royal Navy. When sister Rosa died, Pedro had her embalmed by a Canarian Guanche native expert in the "Egyptian style" of mummification (PBn 480). (He also had a casket made by a craftsman as if in one piece and in the form of a ship in which, instead of his fortune, he deposited Rosa's shrunken mummy.)

Pedro Blanco Fernández de Trava died a madman exiled in Barcelona. He was held in a straitjacket inside a tower where he kept shouting orders to a sailing crew. His death of a stroke was never reported by the custodians, who broke open the casket and found a mummy dressed in silks with her doll eyes wide open. They left Rosa facing Pedro: "The two mummies seemed to stare at each other" (PBn 483). The *negrero*'s death in Novás Calvo's book stands as a monument to the character of exile from Cuba in insular flight. Pedro's character is rendered as virtually devoid of psychic attributes of the sort found in most literary narratives of the realist kind. His character wears the gift of nakedness possessed by certain statues even when clothed. Pedro is vile and saintly—if by the latter is meant a challenge to God's purpose for having created such an awful place as Earth and peopled it with all sorts of Calibans driven to the task of making it prosper. Pedro's lesson to the burdened task of being from Cuba lies in his being Cuban from afar and in flight. Pedro Blanco resembles Ulysses Unbound in his Prometheus saga and his labors as a Romantic Machiavel mired in the Torrid Zone.

PUNNING CHE'S SHADOW

It was really a great lesson for a Romantic like Pedro.
Lino Novás Calvo, *Pedro Blanco, el negrero*

At the beginning of *La Habana Para un Infante Difunto*, the Cabrera Infante family arrives in Havana penurious and homeless. They find shelter (on July 25, 1941) in a tenement building on Zulueta 408 described as a "depraved beehive" or "transformed phalanstery" (12/1).[10] The arrival bisects in meridian fashion the figure of authorship in Infante's professed biography as surmised and designed in the text you are now reading.

At the other end of the circling meridian of Romantic significance just mentioned (marked by the July 25, 1941, date of arrival in Havana) lies the moment in June 1965 when Cabrera Infante (at the time Cuba's chargé d'affaires in Brussels) rushed back to Havana to attend his mother's funeral. His intended quick exit from Cuba on July 13 was aborted when—fifteen minutes before flight time—he was asked to return from the airport to the Foreign Ministry and was told to stay put. He spent nearly four months stranded in Havana before leaving it "forever" or "para siempre" on October 3, 1965. Ithaca was then regained and abandoned by the author, who took off carrying with him his two daughters from his first marriage. (The irrevocable flight mimics Lot's escape from Sodom and his eventual entrapment in double-daughter incest—a recurrent primal myth in Infante's fiction.) Left behind was the "maddened" Penelope, held hostage by what her Communist suitors had done to her Island. She is left weaving a different tapestry each day, "certified by all of them [her Communist captors] as the true original" (*Cro* 15). In the background of the author's shuttle Odyssey between Brussels and Havana lies what has already been outlined here as Odysseus's *repeating-island* voyage toward home-(un-homely)-home.[11]

It may prove relevant to *Infante's* confessional *defunct* life (in its transcendent claim to endure as memorable fiction) that Guillermo Cabrera Infante should have left Cuba on the evening when Fidel Castro broke the promise made to Ernesto Guevara and read to the First Congress of Cuba's Communist Party Che's farewell letter to him—and to the conscience of all revolutionary Cubans—written in April 1965, as he left for Africa under the businessman camouflage of someone named Ramón Benítez. For the solemn occasion, Penelope (Che's wife, not yet called his widow, Aleida Guevara March) appeared onstage dressed in black next to Castro as he read the hero's posthumous farewell and bridges-burning-letter. Exposed and already a beaten warrior in the Congo, Che would learn of Fidel's public reading and deplore the certificate of separation that its knowledge sealed between him and his guerrilla troop: "This caused my comrades to view me, as they did many years ago, when I began in the Sierra, as a foreigner [merely] in contact with Cubans[. . . .] There were certain things in common that were no longer shared, certain common longings that I had tacitly or explicitly renounced and which are the most sacred things for each man's individuality: his family, his nation, his habitat. The letter that provoked so many eulogistic comments inside and out of Cuba separated me from the combatants."[12] Although Guevara would return to Cuba for a few months in 1966 to train in secret for his guerrilla insertion into Bolivia, the premature disclosure of his posthumous farewell made any such return to the island both dreadful and sublime in what it would have of a forfeited afterlife. Afterlife in the sense not ever to return, even when returning after vowing never to return meant that one had thus forfeited the exile's return. Even if on borrowed time, to return to the same island that Che believed he had helped to liberate would not break his disavowal of any terms of exile—in life or after life—from the soil and soul of Argentina and Cuba. Such disavowal represents the negative dialectical bond that clasps together in defunctness the authorship Romantic signature *Che/Caín* under the sign of ever-returning and ever-gone-forever Ulysses.

chapter six

The Ugly Duchess
(Cartoon Odyssey)

I speak severely to my boy,
  and beat him when he sneezes:
For he can thoroughly enjoy
  The pepper when he pleases
  Duchess's lullaby, in LEWIS CARROLL,
  Alice in Wonderland

Repeated utopias overlap and imprison Ulysses' exile fate. Aeolian blowhard incest rule and Phaeacian exogamous hospitality frame his frustrated return to Ithaca and the lengthening of a journey through places like Calypso's and Circe's insular haunts. Likewise, yet differently, in Cabrera Infante's case the Romantic Odyssey of thwarted homecoming is followed by a series of *nostoi* or returns home. The tempest as helix marks the site of diaspora as the scattering winds. Written as if on Ithaca before it becomes Ithaca, *Tres Tristes Tigres*, Cabrera Infante's first major work, represents one asp of the helix across whose vortex (on October 3, 1965) the other asp gives chase as *La Habana Para un Infante Difunto*. One asp propels and repeats the other in circular flight. The hero remains barred from home by all-too-homely repeated women figures who, in their charmed and nostalgic fixations on behalf of Woman, have brought far-off islands to haunt Ithaca. The lifeline of confessional fiction mimics the stammered looping framework of punning wordplay. (One word babbles another as it pretends to pun time into arrest.) As in: once upon a time Ithaca simply was — before it became what Ithaca once was — once it became Ithaca. The author's promise to be gone forever ("para siempre") is tapestried by the authorship's Penelope-like weaving of his home-grounded exploits during the bygone Havana-time of never-to-be-gone-from-home.

PHALANSTERY, PALIMPSEST, INVOLUTE

Bygone time is relived and retold in *La Habana Para un Infante Difunto* through the imagined occupancy of structures in whose remembrance as ruins utopia finds tenancy. Going against the grain of utopian socialism, ruins are rebuilt as narrative memorials when a promiscuous tenement ("depraved beehive") is named a phalanstery, "edificio transformado en falansterio" (*HID* 12), an organization whose design in Fourierist literature, according to Walter Benjamin in his *Arcades Project*, was meant "to restore human beings to relationships in which morality becomes superfluous" (*ArP* 5). Benjamin mentions that Fourier wanted to build a phalanstery capable of housing 12,000 children segregated from adults. Otherwise, the standard utopian site comprised 1,620 persons, "a male and a female exemplar of each of the 810 characters," who in accordance with Fourier's utopian typecasting were sufficient to exhaust all variations in personality (*ArP* 622, 639). Fourier also wanted each woman to have a husband with whom she could conceive two children, a second "breeder (*géniteur*) with whom she could have only one child," and a lover (*favorit*) living with her while she engaged yet a fourth male rank in her affairs with random "possessors (*possesseurs*)" of no particular interest to the law (*ArP* 621). Next to so busy a wife, Fourier's scheme favored unmarried teen lovers, or "filles publiques" (whom he called "bacchantes"), who could join a force of sex workers led by matrons. These young females were deemed to possess, in the words of one of his detractors, "qualities superior to those of married women" and were thought to be "as necessary as vestal virgins" in the exercise of virtuous fellowship (*ArP* 621). As reviewed by Benjamin, in Fourier's social space the regime of phalanstery and the business of streetwalking stood in militant and porous coordination.

Such is virtually the case in Havana's tenement version of the *phalanstère*. One climbs up to it with the boy Infante, up to its multiple dwellings ("I climbed, we climbed, what for me seemed a sumptuous staircase") to reach a place of tainted sublimity, a celestial hell's kitchen, a "house of transformations" (*HID* 11) inhabited by a serialized row of dwellers mingling with a "sexual colony" which includes "pederasts," a "professional bugger," ex-convicts, and a girl prostitute with syphilis named Etelvina (119/52). Although both girls have the same age, she differs from Anne of Oxford (Thomas De Quincey's "partner in wretchedness" during his period of teenage truancy in London) in the combustive warmth of her hidden disease and the casual offering of her nakedness to the Havana boy's morning gawking.[1] Moreover, the name Et-*elvi-na* suggests its scrabbled kinship with sublime *Levana*, the Roman goddess of infants with whose *levare* De Quincey identifies the "tutelary power that controls the education of the nursery," acting "not by the poor machinery that moves by spelling-books and grammars" (as does the literature of knowledge) but "by passion, by strife, by temptation, by the energies of resistance" (as does the literature of power). Levana works "for ever upon children—resting not day or night, any more than the mighty wheel of day and night themselves, whose movements, like restless spokes, are glimmering forever as they revolve" (*Conf* 147). De Quincey devised his sublime teaching apparatus in resistance to existing educational machines and under the influence of Jean Paul's "Levana, or Doctrine of Education" (1807). By the same token, the Fourier utopian pedagogical debt to Jean Paul's doctrines lies implicit in Benjamin's placement of it at the origins of his own *Arcades Project* in kindred spirit with Marx's defense of Fourier's "colossal conception of man," shown in the appropriative manner through which the phalanstery project, in Benjamin's thesis, transforms the original commercial spaces of the arcades into "places of habitation" (*ArP* 5).

A corresponding gesture in the utopian takeover of commercial activity by unruly habits of intimacy occurs when the routine chaos in Infante's tenement life spills its surplus phalanstery sex into the movie houses with their split-world interaction between the autonomous screen and the audience's consuming flesh. In Benjamin's words, the machine-like "meshing of the passions" in the organization of the phalanstery and its "intricate collaboration of the *passions mécanistes* with the *passion cabaliste*" add up to a "mechanism made of men" whose ultimate product is "the land of milk and honey, the primeval wish symbol that Fourier's utopia has filled with new life" (*ArP* 5). In contrast, and driven by its own brand of utopian impulses devoid of any prior theory, the unilateral interactivity between sexual actors in the audience and what happens on the screen (soon to be explored) offers to itself its own shadowy feedback spectacle of saturated emptiness at the cinephiliac heart of old Havana. Busy in furtive animation, as if kidnapping shadows from beneath the silver screen, some patrons in the audience surrounding the young Infante are having fun in unknowing parody of De Quincey's sublime cloning of those sacred look-alike indelible marks traced upon the shared skin of human public lives for which he coined the term *involutes*—now canonized into postmodern fashion in Benjamin's primal history (*Urgeschichte*) of Paris as Capital of the Nineteenth Century.

When elements and particles of tenement phalanstery life come home to roost in sex at the movies, something happens in the realm of excess and waste. De Quincey reached for the "involute" (as to a hieroglyph or a spiritual tattoo stamped on solid shapes he observed) in order to account for those "perplexed combinations of *concrete* objects" which "pass to us" as "*involutes*" or "in compound experiences incapable of being disentangled," and thus bearing "far more of our deepest thoughts and feelings" than "ever reach us *directly*, and in their own abstract shape" (*Conf* 103–4). The exorbitance at work in the involute's consecration of human particularism (as engraved on surface matter) serves as antidote against the fetishism it seems to preach and embrace as a species of Christian paganism.

Yet a form of mesmerized fetishism marks De Quincey's concrete indebtedness to the involute surfaces of social space. A similar economy of affect prevails when the adult Infante transports elements of sordid tenement life on his day-and-night trips to the movies. A trip is taken in quest of sex at the movies while watching the unmarked and unseen involute of forbidden sex in most every movie shown under Hollywood's moral constraints. Such is the cinephiliac afterimage created by the phalanstery's displaced extra-moral utopian regime: finding at the movies not so much a *brothel* alternative as a *brotherly* orgy enacted by twosome shadows of men and women strangers to each other. Embedded in old Havana's cinematic shadows, the Infante involute mimics De Quincey's own fetishist reiteration of the device in his account of the palimpsest. Involute and palimpsest take cinematic effect as if the surface of the screen's illusory depth spread back upon those in the audience as they grooved the ghosts of their sexual hunger into the flesh of the grind-house cinema furnishings.

APING CINEMA

As in the *Odyssey*, the dominant mode in *La Habana Para un Infante Difunto* belongs to the *nostos*, the return home, while the circular tour of cinemas and vaudeville sites suggests the island-to-island *periploi* of cabotage and piracy in Homeric seafaring and Caribbean canoeing: "We were enjoying a drama or melodrama or voyage [*peripecias o periplos*], all adventures, adventures, misadventures" (206/95).[2] The tour of over thirty cinemas in Havana illustrates the particularism of random personal dramas acting out from their scattered locations a sort of collaborative opposition to the dominant alliance between myth and cinema under the spell of sex: "But the movie theaters, more than the movies, are primordial places, the mortification of the solid sexual search interrupting the enjoyment of the screen shadows" (180/80). Beneath these projected shadows others lurk and prowl in the flesh as if risen from the realm of cartoon and folktale. In the penumbra of the Lara Cinema, a roving vampire and cyclops-like Japanese "succionador compulsivo" agitate the air offering fellation (208/97). At the Rialto, a woman feels harassed and screams for the lights; the ensuing scene reveals several men in the audience with one foot bared (181/80). Then, as if a mermaid, acting in the archaic mold of soul-sucker, had boarded his tiny vessel, his canoe, a woman (a cook on furlough) pins Infante down to the seat in furious masturbation, provoking a joint release of wasted seed and a spurt of galactic film fantasies: "rinsing the row in front, becoming a shaft shooting a stream toward the clean screen, erasing the actors, bathing the actresses, blurring the stars" (127/107). Pointed at the Big Screen, luneta or lunette or "small-moon" seat-to-seat sex would seem to parody in altered disruption the strict protocols of canoeing: who sits where, who strokes, who holds the tiller, the bar, the paddle; each name absorbing into itself the actor's own name turned into a role title.[3]

In the anamorphic mirror of Amazonia, places like the Lara and the Rialto become sites of clandestine pseudo-exogamy where a woman suddenly emerges touched by a bare foot wedged into the crack of a seat known as "luneta" (lunette): a small-moon site faces the full lunar screen; a woman appears without boyfriend, like the Amerindian "clinging woman" whose remote bridegroom in the structuralist cosmos of Lévi-Strauss keeps in touch with her from afar by means of the "immensely long penis which allows him to overcome the obstacles caused by distance" (OTM 18). Figure 1 presents a retold viewing of the long-penis story classified M252 in the shortened rendition given by Lévi-Strauss of a Waiwai myth (OTM 167–68).

This species of synoptic cartoon aims at imagining the screen's forbidden response to what the audience in Infante's cinephiliac domain enacts through the actions of some of its constituents. Myth here lies in the cinema's implicit but elided recognition of filmic signs bouncing back at it from the seats and aisles. Like treasured rubbish, body images strike back, as in mimicry, reaching and vanishing beyond the frustrations and pleasures of costumers. Shades in shadows sham-promoted by their sex practices. Lifted in figures from their bodies as if such actions represented their best self-pointing mode of bonding together in caricature. The gag-like incidents in the jungle story should be imagined in the noticeably minia-

FIGURE I

Cartoon

About the time of the first sex act, at the beginning, when there were still no people, a pregnant tortoise-of-a-woman lost her way in the forest and took shelter with a big cat, who ate her except for the eggs she was carrying, from which twin boys came out. They grew up and became hairy and bearded and had no sex organs, since at the time such organs grew only in a small plant hidden in the forest. Told by a wise bird, the twins licked one of the plants, went to sleep, and as they slept, very long penises grew on both. They felt the urge for a woman and had sex with an otter, who told them to follow the river in search of wives. Once found, the women warned the twins against having sex because their vulvas were rimmed with tiny sharp fish teeth. But one of the twins could not stop himself and had sex with his wife and was almost killed, yet his mangled organ was reduced to normal size. The other twin gave his wife some magic drugs before mating with her and as a result the sharp fish teeth in her vulva fell off.

turized style of early black-and-white Popeye cartoons, with their undulating and clashing bodies rhythmically and orchestrally committed to each other's bashing.

Amid such rolling gags, Lévi-Strauss locates the structural degradation of Amazonian myths into serial chaos. Plots become episodic and characters quite weird; their behavior and circumstances "cease to have any concrete zoological reference," the clock regulating the waning of myth in such stories ticks down from the long periodicity of the stars, the sun, and the seasons into short lunar phases embodied in "a succession of animals which make their appearance within a relatively short space of time at the ideal rate of one per night" (OTM 127). Myth lies defunct in an endless cyclic series of strung-together gags: "Like laundry, being twisted and retwisted by the washer-woman to wring out the water, the mythic substance allows its internal principles of organization to seep away. Its structural content is diminished" (OTM 129). But, whether as pristine myth degraded into serialization or not, the narrative stuff in question is reminiscent of how Norman M. Klein defines the "atomic unit" of gag action in his *Seven Minutes: The Life and Death of the American Animated Cartoon*: "The gag is a hangover from pre-industrial rituals, as well as a re-enactment of social (and narrative) dislocation. The two are held in tension, as partners: nineteenth-century animal humor and twentieth-century chaos, like a barnyard mouse building a floppy airplane[. . . .] Gags are more than random snatches of comic relief. They use the narrative code of late nineteenth-century popular culture. They are fables about surviving in an industrial world when the mind is still trapped inside a rural community (translated as the cartoon village caught inside the motion-picture machine)" (SM 27). In Amazonia: rolling heads, mile-long penises, backward-walking demons, talking dung, people cut into pieces and their innards and limbs thrown up to the skies and turned into constellations. In 1930s Paris: an "eccentric and fairly high-class American Lady," whose body is found cut to pieces, as retold in Guy de Téramond's pulp novel *La Femme coupée en morceaux* and installed as epigraph to the "Scene of the Crime" chapter of *The Origins of Table Manners*.

The world of serialized Amazonian myth is equated by Lévi-Strauss with the tabloid and *roman-feuilleton* cosmos of sensationalism during the early industrial age in cities freshly supplied with rural migrants, as is the case with Infante's family's entry into Havana in July 1941. The pulp fiction incidents encountered by the immigrants from eastern Cuba in Infante's *La Habana* befit the Amazonian decadent type heralded by Lévi-Strauss in his detection of myth's episodic death-by-metamorphosis at the hands of serialized fiction: a sleepless night of Aeolian roaring and moaning in the zoo environment of a sex inn or *posada*, mistaken for a hotel by the homeless family; a tenement lodger's orgasm-by-phone masturbation into willing female ears; the organ-grinder–murderer who scatters body parts around downtown and practices "macabre basketball" (56/130) by stuffing the victim's head in the toilet bowl at a nearby theater.

The rough verbal equivalent of such cartoon capers is obtained by phrasing in wordplay between Spanish and English the scriptural overture to an episode from another tenement residence where the Infante family lived. This will lead to a double episode in grotesque hyphenation, a phenomenon whose cartoon resonance is examined next.

THE SORCERER'S APPRENTICE

Pablo Efesio is a "mulatto" taxi driver of dangerous demeanor and "ex-jailbird" by his own admission. Paul the Ephesian, though not very efficient, had three daughters who were "by no means self-Ephesians"

(II 19); which spelled differently means that Efesio's daughters "singular-
mente no eran adefesios" (HID 46); that they were not *dephesiant* but just
deficient and also "*ad Ephesios*" in extravagantly and deficiently addressing non-deliverable Ephesian letters to the unruly Ephesians. (In Spanish,
adefesio means "aimless in purpose" or "ridiculously" dressed; from "to
speak *ad Efesios*" or "for nought or without rhyme nor reason," as does St.
Paul in the ears of his raucous listeners, according to the famous epistle,
as he fruitlessly preaches to crowds which turn on him with murder in
mind.)

Ephesus: city of counterfeit bewitchments and spin doctors, where
"talking to the Ephesians" could easily turn into talking *at* them until they
land you in jail and threaten you with execution, so you can write *ad nau-
seam* "jailbird letters" *ad Ephesians*. Ephesus: where, adding insult to injury, a
long letter written by a certain Paul or Saul and addressed to a single divine
mystery is seen by some as the pirated work of a runaway slave named
Onesimus. Which brings one back to Pablo Efesio: ubiquitous "ogre" in deficient care of his three *not-self-effacing-in-their-efficient-inefficiency* daughters:
Ester (the youngest and lame) and Fela and Emilia (who, unlike the first
two, can pass for white).

Blended in racial sounds and colors as well as amalgamated with his
daughters into a string of potential graphic gags at their own expense,
Paul, the sinister chauffeur, and his sibling motley crew fall in-between
the steps of knockabout live entertainment and cartoon painted tunes.
Pablo and his family are gagged-at and punned-with in all their interracial
malleability by the author, mirrored in the young person of his incipient
authorship. He makes them hyphenate in sound textures and shapes like
typographical creatures grown from the magic lamp of the ink spot and
the silly visual echoes of *woos whoopee* and *boop-boop-a-doops*. Next to such
cartoon affinities, Pablo's mulatto family can be pictured in a vaudeville
skid loudly etched in racist and sexist cant. For, in its archaic infancy, cartoon animation typography harkened back to stage humor more than to
drama or film. In Klein's view, "animation may have started as a form of
illusionistic theater similar to magic acts and panoramas" (SM 22). During the Hollywood twenties, the animator would still be shown perform-
ing sleight-of-hand tricks absorbed in fantastical metamorphosis (the car-
toonist art being in essence devoted to Ovid's professed purpose at the
opening of his *Metamorphoses*: "to tell of bodies which have changed into

shapes of a different kind"). Klein traces the building blocks of cartoon animation to a "vaudeville vocabulary" and notes how even animated features with symphonic aspirations like *The Sorcerer's Apprentice* "still operate like vaudeville parodies"; it took, he adds, "almost thirty years before audiences accepted Disney's *Fantasia*" (SM 23). In such hybrid terms, between cartoon, burlesque skit, and jive, Pablo, the chauffeur, becomes Sorcerer to the upstart Apprentice who is out to fool him without fooling himself.

In stewardship of his daughters, Pablo is called "hombre temible, ogro didáctico" and "ese atropellado chofer errático" (HID 54, 56), which in combined hyphenation turns him into "a-fearsome-man-didactic-ogre-recklessly-run-over-driver" (*atropellado* means "reckless in manner" but also "victim of recklessness" or "trampled upon," in common reference to being hit by traffic). This sounds a lot like (and here lies the gag) *recklessly-running-oneself-over* (a fate only a really mean sorcerer survives, and a feat only an even meaner apprentice could achieve). Yet, though "dark and dangerous" (II 19), Pablo is a figure of scorn and humiliation in the apprentice's eyes, held down, as he is, by the impossible task of daughter-control (*colored* daughters). Such a task *unmans* the sorcerer in Pablo, as when he pours his big *vozarrón* "husky voice" (56/24) impotently into the ears of Infante's mother to complain about her son's playing too much with his girls and seems unmanly in the effort.

Pablo seals the fate of grotesque hyphenation in his own affairs as a social actor by virtue of his being of more than one race and mouthing more than one voice. On one hand, it would take quite a gag to have someone, human or animal, visually *wear* a voice, such as the voice stream "chorro de voz" (HID 56) *spouted* by the scorned sorcerer's mouth into the apprentice's mother's ears, as the boy spies on them in the gathering dusk. But on the other hand, what gag-sorcery might not visually achieve (*show* that voice can be indeed be *worn* like a dress or skin), racial prejudice has already accomplished. For, even as the sorcerer's daughters are used or *worn* not quite *ad Ephesian* by the proud apprentice, the *race-branded* or *dephesiant* voice of mulattoes like Pablo booms in the shadows and enters (the non-mulatto) mother's ears. Mulatto voice booms, though not just in being *heard* as such, but rather as if *seen* in the dark. The ocular or *ophthalmic* character of the racial gag reveals a species of mimicry camouflaging racist fears in the young apprentice, fears about the mother into whose ears a kind of plastic aural matter streams as a perverse (colored) annunciation.

In another tenement story with cartoon features, the occupational hazards of inhaling hair through the mouth until it becomes a ball blocking the stomach causes the death of an obese barrio barber. The barber's awful fate hyphens with his own whale shape to form a celestial *catasterism* or elevation to *a place among the stars*, a sublime spectacle not itself unhyphened from his wife's and daughter's sublunar abode. This happens as the wife and future widow ("a very ugly woman with tremendous [*enormes*] breasts") and her daughter ("a fat dwarf") rest within reach of Infante's gaze and elongated arm length (65/27). As discovered by the author many years later, the Havana mother is mirrored in Quentin Massys's *Portrait of a Grotesque Woman*, best known as *The Ugly Duchess* (figure 2).[4]

The boy's fascination with the huge breasts on Dominica's chest beneath her remarkable face brings him closer and yields a profile which finds unmarked allusion in Tenniel's picture of the Duchess in *Alice in Wonderland* (figure 3), seated in her peppery and noisy kitchen, crying baby on her lap, smiling Cheshire cat at her feet, enthralled Alice in front of her and about to catch a flying baby turned into a pig, and frowning cook at her right, in whose profiled face the Duchess is caught sideways.[5]

A composite view of Dominica obtains in simultaneous reference to Massys's grotesque woman and Tenniel's caricatured kitchen ensemble: "Even in profile it was possible to notice the narrow forehead, protruding eyebrows, ball-point nose and great distance between this and the upper lip, which together with the lower formed a muzzle more than a mouth: all this was blurred by the promise of her breasts and, more important, her sex" (69/29). On his part, the barber is perceived in the boy's mind "almost crushing" his opulently-breasted ugly wife under his bulk, like a "lubricious Leviathan" (67/29), in whose stomach lies, in mute prophecy of doom, the horrible product gestated by years of hair-inhaling work.

Barbers and dentists were once birds of a feather. Dominica tells the boy he should become one of the latter, as he excels in pulling her daughter's baby teeth ("milk teeth" or *dientes de leche*). The two occupations hyphenate in the boy under the spell of Dominica. He is her frustrated lover, the successful dentist of her daughter, and the brooding gynecologist who leaves the scene of dentistry (and instruction) with a pitch-tent erection, while thinking that his "milk" (semen) and the girl's milky teeth and bloodied mouth add up to his own arrival at puberty—in synchrony with hers at menarche—under the care of his combined art in dental gynecology.

FIGURE 2
Quentin Massys,
Portrait of a
Grotesque Woman
(*The National Gallery,
London*)

At this point Monmanéki returns. The Star-Husband-serial-monoga-mist, whose climbing-to-the-moon canoe transforms itself at the end of his Amazonian odyssey hunter's saga into a water beast. A water Tukuna lagoon beast (*dyĕvaë* or *Lord-of-fish*) not unrelated to the barber-Leviathan, Gerard, whose wife is virtually segmented by Infante's adolescent lust, as Dominica gets lodged by his gawking into her upper bust-half, like Mon-manéki's fifth wife, the "clinging woman," whose body is broken in half and whose long-distance lover ("long penis") is mimicked in the boy's thoughts: "I imagined an arm longer than mine (monstrously longer in fact) like a darling hand reaching the edge of her slip salaciously and gently caressing her breasts" (69/29); while her husband the barber, like a balloon whale, "expands through the tenement, which was like saying the universe then" (67/28). Such moments of omnipotent thinking on the boy's part,

FIGURE 3
Sir John Tenniel,
Pig and Pepper
(Alice in Wonderland)

in the midst of the tenement's dense routines of abasement and squalor, transform him into a mural painter, a besmeared maker of frescoes tainted and painted and glued by the shapes and substances of his creation; a creation in which he actively wallows.

Then, surrounded by creatures from film (but who are tabooed from cinemas, like ghosts exuded by what is not seen as desired in what is seen), Infante finds, in advance of his adult movie-house sex predations, modalities of aesthetic misrule that foreshadow the art of composition that his fictional recollections, now, in the act of late authorship, rediscover in such vanished creative moments. It is as such (and only in such enraptured visions) that Ithaca travels in flight and repeats itself upon the stranded imagination of her bygone and buried dweller.

ULYSSES IN KIMONO

As if these ruins were not in Havana, but instead
in the ideal meridian of an ideal geography.
Abilio Estévez, *Los palacios distantes*

Infante's old tenement phalanstery communicates with other corresponding sites besides cinemas, as when, from the besotted and "tenebrous tenement" of Zulueta 408, the boy could see "a structure of rusty iron" that "rose like the ruins of a bridge, supporting a glass roof—a crystal palace now completely in ruins, with vitreous blades still sticking to the metallic frame. These dangerous man-made stalactites, veritable guillotines, sometimes came off and crashed against the floor of the alley. Only Havana luck prevented them from beheading some wayfarer, ignorant of the dangers threatening those who crossed the perilous passage" (15/49). Nothing as grand as the glass roof and iron girders of the *Passage Vivienne* in Paris, Capital of the Nineteenth Century, ever stood there, in Havana, before it became Ithaca. The boy scans from his tenement watchtower rooftop "this decidedly evil construction," next to the Hotel Pasaje, whose windows overhang the ruined arcade (*HID* 49). No one in the neighborhood can tell whether the decadence of the Hotel Pasaje followed or preceded the ruining of the adjoining glass roof arcade. A space so emptied of life and marked by the chance of random death from fallen debris evokes, by coincident contrariness, more authentic ruins, certified as such by their extramural location at the outskirts of the City, of Paris, in a "virgin forest," where an old hotel stands, the center of which gives access to "catacombs" and the haunted grounds where "the Romantic gatherings of the Carbonari" were held (*ArP* 603).

What Walter Benjamin thus recalls as ferments of utopia and nationalist revolution in his own post-imperial *Das Passagen-Werk* allows for passage into repeating ruins where vestiges of Romantic soulfulness lie as if marooned in the millennial Havana of 2000: "The mansion has been divided into tiny rooms, so it should not be called 'palace' any longer, but tenement, little convent, phalanstery, corral, slum quarters. To stop in front of both buildings united into one by a blackened scaffolding and name them 'palace' and 'hotel' would seem cynical and even perverse" (Estévez 2002, 18).

The roving glance at work here: ubiquitous, omniscient, in melancholy surveillance over ruins cluttered with human squalor, dwells inside the shambles of a theater, deserted, except by the man who observes and two other squatters of recent vintage. Part Sorcerer, part Ulysses in kimono, part clown, the grotesque sensibility in him lifts itself into sublime musings, in which Havana and the theater ruins merge in sameness, so that the City might be said to derive from the Theater's remains, as if risen from its ruins and then repeated in them as they in it: as he, the novelist, lies repeated and entombed in both.

chapter seven

Amazon I
(Psycho-Analysis)

Further Indications that the Writer is a Woman—Young,
Headstrong, and Unmarried.

SAMUEL BUTLER, The Authoress of the "Odyssey"

If a woman repudiates her husband, and declares, "You will
not have marital relations with me"—her circumstances shall be
investigated by the authorities of her city quarter, and if she is
circumspect and without fault, but her husband is wayward and
disparages her greatly, that woman will not be subject to any
penalty; she shall take her dowry and she shall depart for her
father's house.

Laws of Hammurabi

Possession by love and dispossession by politics mark the extremes of sentiment, militancy, and affliction examined next under the sign of vertigo. The case of erotic possession in question is that of Psyche's captivation by Love or Cupid. This prime instance of the soul's seizure by passion in the realm of myth and religion casts its spell upon the adulterous romance between husband Infante and the unmarried woman named Margarita, whom he calls the Amazon (la amazona) in what is probably the most celebrated and autonomous episode in La Habana Para un Infante Difunto. Setting aside for the moment the political vanishing point of the lovers' polymorphous affair, the issue lies in erotic possession and its consequences: how male sexual opportunism founders in romance as the man's exclusive literary hold on authorship (on his recounting the pains and delights of sexual pleasure and clandestine love) is breached by the object of his authorial passion, by the woman turned into Woman and rival Authoress as the central creature of his literary invention.

In the fourth book of Apuleius's Golden Ass, the story of Cupid and Psyche begins when an old woman tries to console a cheerless girl with an old wives' tale. Once upon a time, a king was urged by an oracle to array one of his three lovely princesses as a Bride of Death and to set her upon a rock to await the arrival of "something cruel and fierce and serpentine" to be joined in a "funereal wedlock" or *deadly wedding* (Apuleius 1998, 74). Psyche, the chosen bride, had enraged Venus with her beauty. Cursed by the Goddess, she will be denied her Prince Charming. She will not have him unless she is first burned by the love of an *extreme man* ("amore frag- lantissimo teneatur hominis extremi"), an affair entrusted by Venus to her son Cupid.[1] But the childlike man, who in Cupid's disguised personifi- cation Psyche marries, turns out to be *supremus*, rather than *extremus*; *deus* instead of *homo*. So personified, Cupid is not the "creature cursed by for- tune" and "degraded" in the extreme, as requested by his mother, Venus; nor is he, as a boyish winged daimon, the slithering snake claimed by the jealous sisters to be the crawler who lies each night cloaked in darkness next to Psyche, the unravished maiden, during her protracted honeymoon. Peppered by wordplay concerning the inseminating virtues of the phal- lus, Psyche's bridal virgin rest beside her celestial and unseen groom puts on hold, though not forever, her being pricked by the bite of fecundity, a piercing that satisfies and transforms the hunger of the dragon who came to the wedding in the first place expecting both a consort and a meal.[2] At the turning point in the affair, Psyche disobeys her groom's orders not to lay eyes on him and enters the nuptial chamber holding a candle, armed with a blade, and ready to behold and to kill the winged snake she has ap- parently married. But what the light of the candle reveals is Cupid asleep; it shows to Psyche's gaze in human shape the immortal spark of Love now dwelling within herself as her personal *daimon*.

It is in such a strict fashion that the Soul is possessed by Love in the alle- gorical tradition that connects ancient philosophical and religious mys- teries with modern literary and psychoanalytic fictions. The *mise-en-abyme* picture of the Soul's gaze being captured by the Image of Love silhouetted in the Soul's own *camara obscura* (as the psychic erotic possession that, in fact, possesses its own possessor) looks like a flagrant allegory of Jacques Lacan's central specular mystery.[3]

In his own case, youthful Infante makes love to seasoned and volup- tuous Margarita under a double restraint. He is to perform in the dark and to leave the unseen right side of her torso untouched. So restrained, the lover thinks distractedly of defloration and of how the act would leave an indelible ownership mark on the woman, whereby her first possessor would own her as if for life: "not in the sense of possession of the body but of the soul [. . .] which seemed to reside behind the hymen and thus liberated would come to lodge in the lover like an incubus," or perhaps a "succubus," for in the act of deflowering "man becomes woman a little" (553/291). Constrained possession of Margarita's Amazon body activates the apparatus of virginity and defloration in her lover's mind as a mock version of Freud's views in "The Taboo of Virginity" concerning the whole-sale perils involved in the loss of maidenhood. In Freud's account, the woman's resentful and wounded narcissism upon being deflowered comes in reaction to her harbored feelings of sexual dependence on man. Her "sexual bondage" (*geschlechtliche Hörigkeit*) combines with hostility against him (TV 193). Bondage of the sort (though exclusively roped to the mast of a woman's passion) shows up in Haidée's virgin union with Byron's Don Juan: "In her first passion woman loves her lover, / In all the others all she loves is love" — and since then, with the unbound passion of her promis-cuous *liberté*: "One man alone at first her heart can move; / She then prefers him in the plural number, / Not finding that the additions much encum-ber" (DJ 3.3).

Such is not the case with Freud. He saw male fears concerning blood shed in defloration as part of a comprehensive "dread of woman" (TV 198) that included attitudes toward menstruation. He explained how the "mys-terious phenomenon" of the monthly flow of blood "brought about sadis-tic ideas" in "primitive" people, who interpreted menstrual blood, "espe-cially at its onset, as the bite of a spirit-animal, or possibly as the token of sexual intercourse with this spirit" (TV 197).[4] Such is the dread of woman, Freud claims, of "her eternally inexplicable, mysterious and strange na-ture, which thus seems hostile," that man "fears that his strength will be taken from him" and "dreads becoming infected with her femininity" (TV 198–99). Having married just three months before his affair with Margarita the Amazon, Infante encounters in her the occasion on which to repeat and upgrade an already faded honeymoon with a bride whose traumatized and hemorrhaging hymen-loss brought back to him childhood memories of his brother's frequent bleeding and of another boy who often bled with-out apparent cause. His bride's bloody hymen-loss becomes retroactively involved in the Amazon warring love mystery about to ensue, in which In-fante plays the complex role of male initiate, lover, and sex rival.

In Greek mythology the marriage chant is personified by Hymen or Hymenaeus, a young hermaphrodite musician who dies while singing at the wedding between Bacchus and Althea.[5] As already seen, while mating with Margarita in enforced darkness, Infante imagines a death of the hymeneal kind, but in mock allegorical terms. As pictured in his mind, during his bride's deflowering, Psyche ("the soul") hid behind the dying hymen, and now, as if in answer to her profuse bleeding and unilateral suffering on their wedding night, Infante conjures up a scene of reciprocal bondage and possessed *daemonic* eroticism between him and Amazon; a mystery scene haunted by the revelation of Margarita's childhood loss of her right breast. Just as the ancient Amazons removed one breast to fight and to resemble in odd ways the men they vanquished, Margarita's accidental breast-loss will in the end suggest the symbolic restoration of her hymeneal integrity in the role of female avenger of all brides. Indeed, Margarita's graphic erotic subordination to Infante's male sexual exploits includes her role as the avenger-in-woman, but such a romantic supporting role distracts attention from the no less romantic, as well as ironic, invasive character of her uncanny intervention in the affairs of authorship.

SPELLBOUND

In Margarita's embodiment, Woman plays the *Other-in-sex* to both men and women. Her role as *Other* to *both* sexes supports her simultaneous (phallic) embedment and detachment in the lovers' conjoint sex. She dwells like the *daimon* of male libido inside (t)he(i)r lovemaking. The Amazon lies embedded in Love's play to a degree as alienable and prone to prosthesis in *both* lovers as her missing and now cratered Amazon breast is to her injured and repaired or patched-up selfhood. Amazon proves spellbinding as a phallic mirror-fantasy of assembled body parts in flight, while the mystery of her tabooed missing part still rules the scene: "her body in flight, stretching toward a horizon while leaving behind the vigorous vulva, surrendering her pelvis to me as she stole away her torso. She broke into two as if coitus sawed her in half in a vicious vaudeville act: it was as if she fled to surrender, half and half, half escape and half embrace[. . . .] I could see nothing of that zone of eclipsed body, her umbra[. . . .] The left half of her body revealed a thigh" (573/336).[6]

As if all at once alluding to and denying the hysterical wandering of one body part into another, as when the clitoris would wander in climbing fashion into a (missing) nipple, Margarita's childhood breast-loss to a botched surgery marks the fetish-invested absence-as-presence combined at the *site* and *sight*. The present absence of "something that should have been there but wasn't. Simply because it doesn't exist [*algo que debía haber y que no existe*]" (577/294). The hymen's spectral token — in the one and shorter

Spanish epitaph sentence—lies in the tautology enunciated in the *locative* and *possessive* (*positioned* and *possessed*) meaning of "to exist" in "debía haber" (*something that should exist but does not exist, or that should obtain therein but does not*). The loss of hymeneal virginity (and its breast-lost-breast restoration elsewhere in Amazon's body) remains spectral insofar as the existence of Margarita's breast, prior to its unveiling as a cratered, scarred tissue, mirrors the visible absence of the hymen's loss. The lost breast beside the sole one that represents Amazon power offers proof of the former regulatory existence of the hymen in women believed to have been *deflowered*.

Rules, *règles*, *reglas*, of another but related sort are present in the philanderer's exogamous schedule. His bride's recent defloration, her current three-month wife-pregnancy, and the emergence of Amazon's clandestine-honeymoon sex from tabooed illumination into garish display. Infante's menstrual calendar links in coordination Margarita's pregnancy claim and threatened abortion, her sister Tania's actual abortion, and his wife's eventual birthing of a baby girl. From the start, Infante hunts down Amazon and finds her at first engaged in acting "menstrual mimes" at a family theater (679/383). When he asserts consort-kinship ties with her sister Tania's unseen lover, who has paid for her illegal abortion, a lucky pun occurs on love's oldest regulatory watch. As he puts it: "The relationship between this indistinguishable gentleman and Margarita's sister was just like ours: he was her lover, period" (II 483). In this anxious view, the *other* or monthly period hangs with redundant emphasis over the serial duplications of philandering in whose tribal affairs Infante plays the role of wandering minstrel.

The only instance in which money is mentioned in his affair with Margarita comes after she misses their first date and Infante responds by giving her in cash an entire week's salary inside an envelope. But treating her like a prostitute (for services not rendered) ignores the possibility that Margarita might have had her period. As a result, periods of employment cash-flow and gynecological blood-flow overlap in conflict (just as the cash-nexus eliminates the threat of Tania's presumed pregnancy). In either case, the agencies and remedies involved in adultery entail spouse obligations and contingencies in the unadulterated mold of polygamy.

The blood ties dissolved by Margarita's false abortion and Tania's real (or perhaps decoy) one are in synchrony with the birth of a green-eyed daughter to the married couple: "Those green eyes were, in fact, another form of adultery: they were the eyes of Margarita[. . . .] She had been inside me, not I inside her" (674/374). This is the same woman who blood-marks Infante with tattooing kisses—"like the stains of Lady Macbeth, they were indelible" (615/321)—and who tries to repeat such blood-tying antics by dropping tiny remnants of her ovulation (as a love potion *bilongo* or *amarre*) into a drink eponymous with her *Margarita* assumed name. Nauseous Margarita—"this Nausicaa, now a nausea" (II 318)—in Circe's role, fails in her attempts to enforce solidarity with men through direct maternal blood ties unspoiled by *his* (Infante's) semen. She would have his seed wiped out by her vampire or "Bulgarian bacilli brew" (II 312). Margarita appropriates *his* male seed in declaring her vengeance on *all* men as potential lovers: "I avenge myself" (she tells Infante, with the Margarita taste still on her palate); but she also means "I come" (punning on *vengarse* and *venirse*), "in order to collect the debt society owes me for making me bitter" (HID 609). Embittered, *amargada*, Margarita comes into his bitter, mixed, and invisibly bloodied Margarita drink. Whether a fake or not (or prompted by his own aphrodisiac fear), Margarita's love-philter revenge acts out a parody of male seed being absorbed and mimicked in each of her avenging orgasms. It happens as if Amazon sexual bliss resulted in the climactic emptying-for-nought of her stolen male seminal gift through lovemaking.

The absence of hymeneal defloration in Margarita wanders off in fetish fashion from her genitals into her right breast, as horribly maimed in life as it is triumphantly severed in myth, in order to make a revenant Amazon out of her. Her bonding with each male lover, of whom the current one represents a star case, appears ruled by symbolic and psychic affinities between loss of maidenhood and castration. Were she to triumph, Amazon would hold in bondage to herself a man singularly attached to her masculine sexual rule; a rule akin to the spell he has already winsomely recognized in saying that, in the act of deflowering, "man becomes woman a little" (553/291). But not, one may add, a *little woman*, if inspired by Her as Other. Unless what the Other in Amazon succeeds in inspiring is a little picture of woman lodged within her male lover's psyche as his own castrated double or erotic daimon.

While insisting that sexual resistance coupled with bondage (of the sort crystallized in defloration) is "more frequent and more intense in women than in men" (TV 194), Freud alludes to the phenomenon's increase among modern men he either treated or knew from the analytic literature. In his own practice, Freud dealt with this sort of male bondage "as resulting from an overcoming of psychical impotence through one particular woman, to whom the man in question has remained subsequently bound" (194). A similar bond, resulting from sexual impairment and taken to melodramatic extremes, holds together the duo of love-at-first-sight virgins played by Ingrid Bergman (Dr. Constance Petersen) and Gregory Peck (John Ballantine) in Hitchcock's Spellbound (1945), a film in whose "theatricality" Lesley Brill perceives psychoanalysis acting as "a sister to cinema rather than a rival" (but, why not, as well, as a daughter and a rival?).[7]

Dr. Petersen follows pair bonding interaction in her masterful analytic scrutiny of her patient John Ballantine in response to his apparent compulsion to kill. The woman analyst takes charge of the amnesiac impostor who has usurped the name of Dr. Anthony Edwardes and with whom she falls in love at first sight upon his arrival as director or "new chief" of the Green Manors psychiatric institution. John Ballantine ("J. B.") suffers from lethargic amnesia and trance episodes caused by murder-guilt. These include moments of hysterical anguish and one spellbound incident during which, razor blade in hand, he behaves like a would-be killer automaton or somnambulist. As John discovers under Constance's probing questions, he must have stolen Anthony Edwardes's name after killing him ("Anthony is dead. I killed him and took his place. I am someone else. I don't know who").

The romantic view of this therapeutic affair is given by Lesley Brill. She finds John's "real healing" not in psychoanalytic "inadequacy" but in the "miracle of love," or in how his "illness resembles the curse put on Sleeping Beauty by an evil sorcerer," release from which is obtained as the woman analyst confronts Dr. Murchison, the evil psychiatrist, and leads him into confessing that he is Anthony Edwardes's real killer. Through the magic of gender-switch, "Sleeping Beauty" (Gregory Peck) is thus released from the spell by "the heroic kiss that awakens not just him, but his rescuer [Ingrid Bergman] also." (Behind Dr. Constance Petersen's all-too feminine and feminist analytic success story stands Freud's caricature as Dr. Alex Brulov [Michael Chekhov], characterized by Brill as "Constance's professional 'father,'" who in the end, as Brill puts it, "does not lose a daughter but gains, um, something," or, as Brulov himself puts it: "I always say, any husband of Constance is a husband of mine"—marked by the quoting knowingness of that "um," father and husband lend the bride their joint citational support.)[8]

Constance's unmasking of Dr. Murchison as Edwardes's killer prevents the murderer's therapeutic manipulation of the amnesiac patient's guilt complex. Her analytic victory wins back the stolen psychiatric institution and business at Green Manors, and it restores to Anthony Edwardes's scholarly legacy the books he wrote on psychic disorders, among which *The Labyrinth of the Guilt Complex* stands in obvious allusion to Freud's *Totem and Taboo* as the unquestionable paragon. According to Lisa Appignanesi and John Forrester, Freud found sons "wanting" in his quest to pass on his own succession "and also found that he was never quite ready to be the murdered father of the 'horde'" — in the archaic role he had invented as he delved into the origins of ethical conscience in the primal father's murder by his male brood. Instead, the authors see "the line of succession passed through the youngest daughter, vestal virgin Anna, who guarded the shrine of psycho-analysis and the word of her father," but with the ambivalence proper of tragically rebellious daughters from the psychoanalytic archive, such as Antigone ("Anna-Antigone") and Lear's Cordelia.[9]

In her commentary on *Spellbound*, Marian Keane claims that "the battle that will ensue in this film is over authorship," as well as over issues of contested "proprietorship" between Director and *Author* Hitchcock and his Producer and presumed *Master*, David O. Selznick.[10] The double battle points to current issues of intellectual property and to the Romantic notion of the author's genius in troubled possession of his work (it being understood that the gender mark or imprint of genius on work and of work on genius is *masculine*, regardless of the author's sex). In Keane's interpretation, Murchison's murder of Anthony Edwardes creates in the victim the "absent author of the story, the film's deceased, surrogate author" (chap. 17). The murder renders in actual proprietorship terms the unwitting usurpation of Edwardes's name by John Ballantine in his amnesiac's authorship role of, among other works, *The Labyrinth of the Guilt Complex*. To the winner go the spoils of conscience found in guilt. For when, in their final confrontation, Dr. Murchison confesses to Constance that he acted as "the angry proprietor" of Green Manors in killing its owner, the twin-prize of Director's artistic genius and Proprietor's absolute rights at stake from the beginning ends up as a terminal ethical burden upon the winner.

While initially identified in Keane's compelling reading with Selznick's ownership as the intruding author in Hitchcock's work, now, as he is upstaged by Constance, Dr. Murchison becomes the victim of his own surrogacy. As the murderer's "impotence" is exposed and he is driven to suicide, it is Constance's higher surrogacy to Hitchcock's directorship that does the deed. But, in Keane's apt words, "in order to demonstrate the proprietor's impotence, Hitchcock had to demonstrate his own" (chap. 22). Yet, what may be added to Constance's (psychoanalytic) and Sir Alfred's (cinematic) joint success—and to the Director's and Proprietor's combined defeat—is John Ballantine's successful release from the burdens of authorship, as measured by his not being any longer the author of Anthony Edwardes's *The Labyrinth of the Guilt Complex* (or, allusively, the symbolic author of Sigmund Freud's *Totem and Taboo*).

Virgin honeymoon rewards therapy. Two virgins may wed once released from authorship guilt in Freud's legacy. Neither bride nor groom has written such awful books as *Totem and Taboo* on how the sins of primal brothers bring about the ancestral burden of their combined fraternal murder-guilt to act as midwife in the birth of civilized discontent (including Freud's view of defloration and shared male-female sexual bondage in modern marital sex). Accordingly, John and Constance are released, not so much from transgenerational psychic burdens as such, as from the arduous author-reader literary nexus reworked by modernism. This burdened nexus—to which Freud's psychoanalysis contributed from *Totem and Taboo* to *Moses and Monotheism*—would prove inseparable from notions of guilt-debt to primitive ancestors. It is as if the heavy burden of reading the high canon of modernist literature were to find release in the thematic leisure and gothic melodrama, the narrative legend that in plain and bold strokes within one chapter of relentless plotting runs from primal horde and father-murder to civilized religious compromise. As an act of reading with a peculiar share in literary invention, this readable modernist activity cannot, in its own terms, be saved (if not through therapy) from the syndrome identified, in Frank Sulloway's words, as a "disease-prone heredity, either in terms of inherited residues of noxious, ancestral experiences—the now-discredited Lamarckian position that Freud himself endorsed—or in terms of some other form of genetic anomaly" (1992, 92). Sulloway is thus bent on tying psychoanalysis to biology and proving Freud's vestigial adherence to Lamarck's theories of inherited behavioral traits. In this regard, John Edwardes's treatise on phylogenetic guilt caricatures Lamarck's presence in Freud's search for ancestral guilt. But, even if Lamarck's trace is removed from Freud's conception of the unconscious, the latter's habit of relying upon art and religion in order to illustrate psychic maladies justifies the melodrama of ancestral guilt exploited in *Spellbound*.

The film bypasses what Donald Spoto calls the "turgid grotesqueries" of Francis Beeding's *House of Dr. Edwardes* (in which psychoanalysis supports devil-worship, human sacrifice, and orgiastic sadism).[11] But a closer view of Freud's embattled science in *Spellbound* reveals two levels of analytic interest: the individual or *ontogenetic* and the extra-individual or *phylogenetic*. For instance, Dali's notorious film nightmare offers a montage transparency of ontogenesis in its representation of the "surreal" game of Twenty-One, played with two-out-of-three blank cards. In it, John Ballantine plays against the man whose identity he has usurped in becoming the insomniac who fears he actually killed him. But, as decoded by none other than the killer-analyst himself, Dr. Murchison, the dreamer in John is "denying it is a gambling house by using spurious cards," a view which turns the usurper into a bastard, as it translates the possible mark of sterility or impotence in the blank cards into the identity-anguish of being born out of wedlock. The symbolic effect of blankness on spuriousness and the erasure of legitimate paternity refers back to John Ballantine's signature in his note to Constance as *Anthony Edwardes*. Her comparison of John's signature with that of Edwardes's (in his dedication of the copy of *The Labyrinth of the Guilt Complex* that she is reading) unravels Ballantine's impostor authorship of the treatise in which his own psychic malady is constructed and resolved by the authority of the psychoanalyst whom he comes to believe he has murdered. In the history of the psychoanalytic movement, such divestment of authorship evokes Freud's tacit denial of his founding act of self-analysis to subsequent practitioners. Other analysts would not approach his *opus magnum* in the self-analysis of the therapist's own Oedipus complex, the act of introspection that led him to achieve his early (at once modernist and retrograde) masterwork, *The Interpretation of Dreams* (1900).[12]

Joining the personal incidents of ontogeny with the group designs of phylogeny, in the rooting-out of obsessions, requires the sort of introspective task best left in the hands of a few masters in the art of analytic self-intrusion. John Ballantine is spared such a role as he proves innocently impotent of doing any writing of consequence—beyond that of someone else's stolen signature—under the nursing and editorial care of the woman analyst. Instead, the phylogenetic type of obsessive anguish is felt by Germes, the patient who believes he killed his father, and by John himself, as the enthralled hallucinating patient whose belief in having caused his brother's death exceeds his apparent blame for that accident and makes him feel guilty of additional killings. Such parricide and fratricide joint fears manifest what Freud thought was the phylogenesis of obsessional neuroses and pathological repression, a subject he discussed in terms of "Man's archaic heritage" as the "nucleus of the unconscious mind," and about which he wrote "four separate books and the major part of a fifth," centered "on the intimate and antagonistic relationship that he perceived between civilization and sexual life."[13] (Censorship codes and taste blocked the brutal phylogeny of sex from *Spellbound*, leaving the exquisite corpse of archaic murder to fester in its lurid source, the novel *The House of Dr. Edwardes*.) Phylogeny intersects ontogeny in Freud's account of the taboo of virginity. The same can be said of the film when viewed as the story of a broken honeymoon of which only traces show, and during which the virgin couple shares in the impotence caused by the man's fear of Woman in the person of his analyst. Punctuated by the ethereal and creepy music of the theremin, the couple encounters tokens of fetish dread and castration in naive transparency, as when Constance's silver fork draws on the white tablecloth a swimming pool shaped like a vulva (or chastity buckle), over which she then rubs a knife back and forth, causing John's first vertigo spell and his anguished complaint about the waste of "linen" at the institution, a material found in bed sheets and in some wedding traditions required to be shown crimsoned by the shedding of the bride's hymeneal blood. Earlier, Constance overlooks through her office window John's arrival at Green Manors as she cuts open an envelope and makes a ripping sound next to Germes, the patient who later on will slit his own throat, and who is evidently seized and cued by the sound effect of blade on paper. Germes will confess to Constance that he killed his father just as John looks at him, spellbound by the nascent awareness that he, too, shares in the same guilt, a guilt eventually discovered to be *double*, since, at one point, John will blame himself for killing Dr. Edwardes (the paternal surrogate) besides causing the death of his own brother during childhood. John's sense of kinship with Germes' delusional parricide is aided by his total lack of knowledge of *The Labyrinth of the Guilt Complex*, the book on the phylogenesis of guilt which he has written, but in the person of the author whose impersonation he unknowingly performs and believes in the end he has killed.

John is the virgin male reader of a treatise on the extra-individual foundations of guilt which Constance has already mastered and absorbed before she applies its learning in saving him, its pseudo-author, from a type of obsession directly linked to suicide. Empowered by such reader's mastery, Constance, the analyst and passionate interpreter, revives the *defunct* self in John. She brings *Defunct* back into the living. Constance *name-of-the-father's* or *nom-du-pére's* John back into the living from his *defunct* limbo.

When John enters the operating room followed by Constance (both dressed in white surgical gowns) and he suffers a spell of dizziness as Germes' throat is being sewn up, he takes down his mask, gasps in desperation, and nearly grabs his throat with both hands in a gesture of identification with the injured. (The surrealist visual alchemy-wedding between the umbrella and the sewing machine on the operating table is replaced here by white surgical wedding gowns and the mimicry effect cast by a repaired throat-wound in the groom's virginal seizure of his hysteric's neck.) Cut-throat mimics are also present in John's spellbound wielding of the razor blade as he ambles by the sleeping and intact Constance and heads downstairs in search of Dr. Brulov, an expert in pacifying primal fears with cookies and milk laced with bromides.

The presence of the benign father image in Dr. Brulov (in his self-appointed double role as both giver of the bride and symbolic bride: "I always say, any husband of Constance is a husband of mine") is opposed by the sinister version of the incest-father in the murderous Dr. Murchison. The icy touch of restrained debauchery that Leo G. Carroll lends to his evil part aptly suggests what the film otherwise keeps unsealed about the role of incest in the psychoanalytic view of unconscious repression. In the virgin bride's case, repression puts a dent on the daughter's expectations of primal or perverse sex. According to Freud's account of the taboo of virginity, "the husband is almost always so to speak only a substitute, never the right man; it is another man—in typical cases the father—who has the first claim to the woman's love, the husband at most takes second place" (TV 203). In the shot that ends the operating room scene, Dr. Murchison takes down the surgeon's mask as his face is shown edged by shadows in near closeup. He has been officiating in the parricide's operation and the stitching of his throat-wound, actions which in Freud's phylogenetic scenario put Dr. Murchison in the lord's role during the enactment of actual or mimicked defloration, in accordance with the jus primae noctis ritual custom (which is the dramatic centerpiece of the essay on tabooed virginity). The lordly role is defined, in this specific context, by Alian Boureau, as he underscores Freud's reliance on Westermarck's monumental survey of wedding customs: "Freud's conclusion approaches Westermarck's because in both cases the lord in the jus primae noctis serves as an institutional interpreter of a universal mode of psychic organization, marked in one case by a horror of virginal blood and in the other by the female's desire for the father and the male's fear of the initial bond" (Boureau 1998, 27). When Murchison steps on the sealed envelope that John has slipped under Constance's bedroom door, informing her that he has fled to New York, the doctor is accidentally planting his foot on a hymeneal token, just as the proverbial medieval lord is said to have stretched his leg across the nuptial bed as the signature of his authority over the affair's investment in the bride's maidenhood.

Regardless of one's views on Freud's essay, the lasting impression it might leave in the reader centers on its analysis of Judith's decapitation of Holofernes in Friedrich Hebbel's tragedy. In what amounts to a case of sham nuptials, the accidental groom of a widow who is regarded as a virgin loses his head to the lethal powers lodged in her tabooed though absent hymen. As a widow, Judith's virginity is endowed with symbolic effects greater than those of a plain or hymen-intact virgin. The fate of Judith's surrogate and decapitated bridegroom, Holofernes, illustrates John Ballantine's throat anguish at the critical moment of his phobic identification with Germes, the wounded parricide, in whose self-inflicted ordeal and surgery John's own castration fears and nuptial impotence are deployed in specular dread.

Whether actually inflicted or just mimicked, the type of patient self-injury under surgery and therapy at the Green Manors psychiatric clinic disowns individual suicide, since in Spellbound the cause of delusional parricide is wholly determined by phylogeny, by the murder of the primal father. Parricide remains in bondage to ancestral guilt, just as those male fears embroiled in Freud's conception of the taboo of virginity are kept, in dread and fascination, bound to elements in shed female blood of analogous phylogenetic remoteness.

chapter eight

Amazon II
(Vertigo)

With which grotesque biped can one compare a pregnant woman?
GUILLERMO CABRERA INFANTE,
La Habana Para un Infante Difunto

I found no traces of the first in the charnel where I laid the second.
EDGAR ALLAN POE, "Morella"

Just think of a Madame Tristan!
DENIS DE ROUGEMONT, *Love in the Western World*

Just think of Tristan Junior. Think of him and a character named Morella. Think of both Tristan Junior and Senior in love with *More-of-Her*. The two of them in succession or at the same time in love with a woman character whose name comes prefixed perhaps by death (*Mors*), doubled up as *more*, and suffixed (*encore!*) by *elle* or *ella* or *Her*. But hold it. Thus far, the adulterous affair between the Amazon Margarita and Infante played (in *encore* and parody) the mystery scene of hymen-loss lost, botched, during his lawful honeymoon of three months before with a screaming and bleeding virgin bride. The spellbound Infante-Amazon X-rated affair (yet to play itself out in full) was also shown on two screens: on one, pre-cinematic, Psyche and Cupid enacted the mystery of the Soul's seizure by Love and the attendant sacrifice of hymeneal maidenhood; on the other, cinematic, the ancient erotic mystery found solution in the *honeyed* wedding of analysis and romance between female therapist and male patient.

REBECCA'S REACH

Foreshadowed in John Ballantine's dissociative proneness to flee from the cure taught him by the bride virgin therapist Dr. Constance Petersen in *Spellbound* lies the deeper and incurable Romantic mourning manifest in *Vertigo*. The film's review (dated November 15, 1959) is based on three successive nights of viewing by Cabrera Infante's pen-name G. *Caín*: three nights of "obsessive and fatal dating" immersed in *Vertigo*'s "absolute adherence to the magical world" (OXX 364). Those three nights of troubled Orphic ecstasy will be examined here in retrospect from the perspective of the lectures delivered by Cabrera Infante in the summer of 1962 and published much later (1978) with slight revisions as "Hitchcock's Bacillum" (Atn 83–118). Besides the difference in perspective created by Psycho (1960), the 1962 lectures add the Tristan and Isolde "myth" (Atn 109) to the story of Orpheus and Euridyce, the original focus of the first three viewings of Vertigo in November 1959.

The effect of Psycho upon Vertigo brings back Rebecca (1940) in belated fashion as the first piece of a "Hitchcock trilogy" on "the loneliness of love lost" (Atn 111). The 1962 lecturer reinterprets Scottie Ferguson's loss of "Judy-Madeleine" in Vertigo as willful ("he loses her in an act that now appears to me voluntary"); and then, without mentioning Rebecca's death, in which a cancerous growth replaces her presumed pregnancy, the lecturer reminds his audience that in Psycho, "the son loves his mother so much that he does not reconstruct her from present to past times," but instead "preserves her in the eternal present from which all future times are challenged: he [Norman Bates] lives with his mother's mummy" (Atn 111). The presence of Vertigo as the third element between Rebecca and Psycho finds support in the paradox of the "vampiric double" identified by Joan Copjec in the scene from Bram Stoker's Dracula in which Mina Harker sucks blood from the master vampire's breast. Such polluted nursing alters Mina's own breasts into a single object embodying obscene alien excess, now lodged within her uttermost sense of self. Applied to Hitchcock's film, "the object [the breast] which 'completes' the subject [Rebecca's], filling in its lack, is also always a disfiguring surplus"; the paradox functions as a plot device "when the baby with which Rebecca was supposed to have been pregnant when she died is revealed to have been a fatal cancer." Moreover, adds Copjec, the deceased/diseased Rebecca "reminds us that the breasted, vampiric double is not only a creature with 'too much' body, it is also a 'body too much'[. . . .] As a double of the subject, it always stands in the way of or crowds out the subject's own actions."[1]

Viewed askance from Psycho, the pregnancy-into-cancer growth inside the womb of Rebecca's heroine's corpse transforms Norman Bates's avenging madness against women (as potential mothers) into the haunting symptom of his own posthumous condition, akin to being the unborn issue which aborts into cancer in the dying Rebecca and into his own death-ruled life as the son forever tethered to the mother's fetish mummy in the house behind the Bates Motel. The *Rebecca* effect on *Psycho*'s Norman Bates turns his madness into the *unborn-fetal* and *post-partum-post-mortem* psychic remnant of the *body-too-much* issue that haunts Scottie's relationship in *Vertigo* with his loss of two-women-in-one: with the *two-ness* of her, with her *More-of-Her*, with the specter of a dying (murdered) woman's pregnant death.

Enter "Morella" harbored inside the *Rebecca* effect. The 1962 lecturer on *Vertigo* speaks of the "Lord of Manderley" (Laurence Olivier's Maxim de Winter) assisted by his zealous female housekeeper (Judith Anderson's Mrs. Danvers) as joint custodians of the lost wife's possessions. The Judy-Madeleine-Scottie *Vertigo* knotted love nexus is thus seen by Cabrera Infante as the altered replica of the Rebecca–Maxim de Winter and the new Mrs. de Winter nexus, in which the second and unnamed wife cannot but replace and be haunted by the first one. However, no explicit mention is made by the lecturer concerning Mrs. Danvers's maternal housekeeping of her defunct mistress's curse, nor of Rebecca's posthumous evil tyranny over the widowed de Winter; the curse on account of which the connection with the dead (Bates-son-murdered) mother gives origin to the proposed trilogy's *Psycho* effect.

The accursed replication of Edgar Allan Poe's Morella character in the figure of her posthumous daughter ("to which in dying she had given birth") as the tutor and soul mate of, first, her husband and, second, her father is subject to its own *Rebecca* effect. The effect's kernel is found in the heroine's death (or murder) as written in Daphne du Maurier's novel, but not shown in Hitchcock's film, under his own or someone else's censor rules. Near the novel's end, the second Mrs. de Winter tells her husband of a dream in which she has seen him holding his wife's "hair in his hand," and, "as he brushed it" and "wound it slowly into a thick long rope," facing the boudoir mirror, the hair "twisted like a snake," and "he took hold of it with both hands and smiled at Rebecca and put it round his neck" (du Maurier 1971, 379). The avoidance of *her* neck (and of wife strangulation) in de Winter's suicidal gesture connotes all at once the act of murder using the woman's hair braided by her husband's hands as well as *his* unborn death, strangled by the umbilical cord (or his after-birth hanging death by means of the same mother-thread).

The mother-son death duel inscribed in such dream-fears lies implicit (though barred from view) in Poe's "Morella." However, in *Rebecca*, mind contact between Mr. and Mrs. de Winter does not occur in the same spiritualist realm in which Morella's tutorial emanations of arcane wisdom penetrate her husband's knowledge of all she has taught him. If the same spiritualist emanation existed in *Rebecca*, the dream of umbilical wife strangulation and husband-son suicide would require no actual disclosure by the second wife to her widowed and haunted husband, the Lord of Manderley. Bear in mind that Morella's nameless husband and pupil pours over "forbidden pages" as he feels "a forbidden spirit enkindling" within himself, as "her cold hand" is placed upon his own, "to rake up from the ashes of a dead philosophy some low, singular words, whose strange meaning burned themselves in upon [his] memory" (Mor 230). The mute language of Morella's copious readings echoes in her husband's soul, except that his *reading* is a singular encrypted emanation issuing from her bilocal presence in the realms of both the living and the dead.

The porous spiritualist screen through which back-and-forth medium-transit is obtained from one realm to the other in "Morella" becomes a matter of communicable conjugal boudoir dreams in du Maurier's *Rebecca*. The nexus thus established between du Maurier, Hitchcock, and Poe concerns the implantation of soul-to-soul or virtually telepathic vertigo in the husband. It also underscores the issue of contested husband/wife authorship through the channels previously surfaced by spiritualist means. Thus, as the second Mrs. de Winter is writing party invitations in her dream, she looks down, not quite in vertigo ("I looked down to see what I had written"), and her "small square hand-writing" becomes "long and slanting, with curious pointed strokes" (du Maurier 1971, 379). In such fashion, the nascent office of woman novelist is foreshadowed within her as harbored in an old-fashioned dream of spouse possession. The haunted office of conjugal authorship might be said to unite in one stroking arm-reach two scribblings. The horrible and sublime alliance between the demonic and domestic brands of *Mrs. de Winter*'s handwriting script helps measure how, in her husband-pupil's haunted grasp, Morella's "powers of mind were gigantic" (Mor 229). The pupil in the husband becomes the *infant* of Morella's vast *defunctness*. The resulting spiritualist increase equals the *More-of-Her* afterlife effect.

The vastness of Morella's reincarnated soul (as embedded in her posthumous dwelling inside her eternal husband-pupil) institutes vertigo inside her pupil, who is now taught by her as she lies in possession of her daughter. It is from Morella's own eye pupils that her pupil's climb to perilous heights emanates: "I met the glance of her meaning eyes, and then my soul sickened and became giddy with the giddiness of one who gazes downward into some dreary and unfathomable abyss" (Mor 231). Across the abysm of bottomless time and unmeasurable numbers of vanished human lives lies the bridge of reincarnation: the "modified Παλιγγενεσια [Paliggedenia] of the Pythagoreans" (230). Yet, nothing gets actually written on the substance of this endoskeletal bridge, except the scribbled and printed tale of the 1831–35 Folio Club entitled "Morella." It is by word of silent mouth between soul mates in reciprocal bondage that the husband-pupil acts as medium-amanuensis of the Immortal Soul. (In the 1860s, writings of Lizzi Doten and Sarah Helen Whitman—by Poe himself, in the afterlife—became a prominent agent of spiritualist mediumship [Cottom 1991, 84, 270 n. 17].)

Just as *Rebecca*'s reach into *Psycho* brings to the Bates Motel matters of life-and-death inside the womb, "Morella"'s effect on *Vertigo* reaches beyond the two sentences in whose last two clauses the kinship between Poe's tale and Hitchcock's film would rest: "Yet, as she had foretold, her child—to which in dying she had given birth, and which breathed not until the mother breathed no more—her child, a daughter, lived. And she grew strangely in stature and intellect, and was the perfect resemblance of her who had departed, and I loved her with a love more perfect than I had believed it possible to feel for any denizen of earth" (Mor 233). The husband's and father's discipleship in soul reincarnation is abetted by the "wild Pantheism of Fichte" and, "above all, the doctrines of *identity* as urged by Schelling," in which the sense of being "*ourselves*" and having "*our personal identity*" confronts the "*principium individuationis*, the notion of that identity *which at death is or is not lost forever*," an object of "intense interest" on the pupil's part, "not more from the perplexing and exciting nature of its consequences, than from the marked and agitated manner in which Morella mentioned them" (230–31). Fichte and Schelling taught philosophy in Jena and Munich respectively, as both would later on in Berlin, to a group of young men called by Friedrich A. Kittler (in *Discourse Networks: 1800/1900*) a "male brotherhood of educational bureaucrats" (DN 170). Morella's training "in those mystical writings which are usually considered the mere dross of early German literature" (Mor 229) takes place in "Pressburg," a citadel of black magic associated in Poe's fiction with the making of android automata by the Hungarian "mechanician" and official of the Vienna court chamber, Wolfgang von Kempelen, also known as "the modern Prometheus" (the readymade Romantic nickname given to Victor Frankenstein in the subtitle of Mary Shelley's novel).[2]

The wedding of souls into a single though partitioned human frame in "Morella" has been best explained by John T. Irwin, for whom the site where the tale unfolds implies (as it does in "Berenicë" and "Ligeia") the figure of "a womb tomb in which the narrator was born and his mother died (presumably in giving birth)" (MS 232). Irwin adds that human pre-existence is sensed and scripted by the male voice "as a kind of amniotic dreamworld" in whose remembrance "psychic stagnation" shrinks "his present existence into a series of meditative reveries within the womb-like chamber" (232). Husband and wife become wedded to each other in soul implosion: "Since she serves as a kind of Psyche figure, the beloved woman's physical deterioration in the grip of a wasting illness mirrors (and thereby exacerbates) the man's psychic deterioration" (233). The terminal condition thus witnessed could be diagnosed as the *soul-surplus* of the More-*of-Her* syndrome caused by transgenerational women like Morella.

Kittler observes that at the time of Fichte and Schelling (the two German professors active in Morella's extramural education), "there were no women in philosophical discourse," which remained "in a neutered mode between friends or men" (DN 171). Women as *significant-others* were routinely given masculine names as objects of poetic worship and latent philosophic wisdom, above whose sublime enunciations their actual human selves were deleted. If, either by discursive deletion or actual suicide, as Kittler insists, in the saturated environment of German Romantic poetry "the homosexuality of philosophy and poetry" very often destroyed women (DN 172), in Morella's distant discipleship something akin happens. Except, perhaps, that a man's own destruction seems to crop up in Poe's story beneath the remains of the *body-too-much* that his own *body-too-many* has both gestated and murdered in his kindred woman soul mate.

More-of-Her may now be seen in nutshell vertigo: falling like a prodigal celestial body at Earth reentry, Morella's male mate was "thrown by accident into her society," and from their first meeting his soul "burned with fires it had never before known"; but, alas, "the fires were not from Eros" (Mor 229). One soul (his) survived the inflamed fall away from sexual passion and into the Soul's hard core by kindling the fires of philosophy dressed in the noncombustive garments of Poesy. But what survives of him after the Fall?

HARD-BOILED SURGERY

Παλιγγενεσια
Itself, by itself solely, ONE everlasting, and single.
  Edgar Allan Poe, "Morella"

Él mismo, para él mismo, con él mismo, homogéneo, eterno.
[*He himself, for himself, with himself, homogeneous, eternal.*]
  Guillermo Cabrera Infante, "Hitchcock's Bacillum,"
  in *Arcadia todas las noches*

The summer of 1962 Havana lecture on *Vertigo* performs quadruple bypass on Poe's Greek-quoted epigraph from Plato's *Symposium* (rendered in English in preface to "Morella"). The lecture in fact ends by quoting film director Eric Rohmer, whose French text on *Vertigo* the lecturer Cabrera Infante annexes ("these words which could also be mine") and renders in Spanish. Rohmer, who in his first film, *Bérénice* (1954), plays the role of Egaeus (the obsessed lover oral surgeon who saves in a box the "thirty-two small, white, and ivory-looking substances" he pulled from his deceased beloved's mouth), writes in quotation: "If I have placed at the top of these remarks a phrase from Plato, which one can read inscribed by Edgar Poe at the head of his *Morella*, whose plot reminds one of *Vertigo*, it is not because I wish to equate our *cineaste* with the author of *Parmenides*, nor with the one who wrote *Extraordinary Tales*, but simply because I wish to propose a key capable in my view of opening more doors than any other such key" (Atn 117–18).[3] Plato's epigraph (adds the lecturer) should have the last word on this "esoteric film": " 'He himself, for himself, with himself, homogeneous, eternal' " (Mor 118), in which, by grammatical accommodation to Spanish, the masculine subject "él" replaces Beauty's "it" in Plato's text. How can the words picked by Rohmer whole-cloth from "Morella" support such a definitive open-heart Platonic glance into *Vertigo*? The answer sketched in what follows incorporates the Amazon-Infante love affair into the Hitchcock trilogy under review, with some surgical help from Aristophanes and the consent of Judy Barton, the woman who at some point, in the shape of Kim Novak, would emerge, naked and unfilmed, from the wedding-cake female fabric of a love-object person called Madeleine.

The words in Plato (also rendered as "it [something beautiful] exists in itself alone by itself, single in nature forever") belong to Diotima, as spoken by Socrates, who recalls a conversation he once had with the wise-woman on love and the ascent of human knowledge to the Beautiful.[4] Diotima situates Eros in an *intermediate* region, a messenger who moves back-and-forth between *immanent* and *transcendent* realms. Her speech on Eros (*Symp* 201d–12a) follows an upward climb from lesser to greater mysteries, up to the last segments known as *The Ladder of Love* and *The Ascent to Beauty Itself* (*Symp* 209e–12a). At first glance, Poe's epigraph choice from Plato's *Symposium* may seem to allude to the unperishable union of souls into One single Soul reached between Morella and her husband and pupil. Indeed, the "ONE" in Poe's epigraph is reached by the Socratic knowledge of one who has been educated in matters of love and who sees "something marvelous, beautiful in nature," which "ever is and neither comes to be nor perishes, nor has it growth nor diminution (*Symp* 210e–11a). It (Beauty Itself) is that of which each instance of beauty partakes and which, while other beautiful things "come to be and perish" by sharing in it, "comes to be neither in greater degree nor less and is not at all affected" (211b). In matters of love, one is "led by another," beginning "from these beautiful things here, to ascend ever upward for the sake of *that*, the Beautiful, as though using the steps of a ladder, from one to two, and from two to all beautiful bodies" (211c). Thus, in close up, the Platonic "ONE" in Poe's epigraph for "Morella" grounds its immutability on the unperishable Beauty toward which one ascends in climbing up the Ladder of Love. However, in its downward thrust into the "charnel" where the second woman is brought to rest by her father, in the emptied space left by the first one, her mother, and somehow left void by *herself*, the story's last sentence shatters Diotima's mystery effusions on Eros into a kernel genealogy of human ruins.

The Platonic relevance of "Morella" to *Vertigo* perceived by Eric Rohmer brings with it a lethal measure of Romantic irony. Behind the door that the story opens into the film lies the ruinous fate of that in which beauty may appear in unfathomable excess. What is perceived as excess underlies the inalienable sameness which causes arrest in what appears so obsessively beautiful. Excess also undermines that same sameness by suggesting that it should remain immutable and unperishable, but only by remaining all at once *other* and the *same* in the replica foreshadowed by its own perfection out of its own genealogical past.[5]

Figures of excess breathe easier and in larger gulps in the high ether of Socratic Eros than they do in the cloistered incestuous air of "Morella" and "Berenicë" —or in the fainting gasps of *Vertigo*. Diotima's teaching on

Eros applies to "Morella" as one contrasts her (and Socrates') notion of "procreation and begetting of children in the beautiful" (Symp 206e) with the specter in "Morella" of what nowadays is popularly known as cloning. In Poe's case, the spectral awful chance exists that the genealogical mother-daughter reincarnation cycle at the heart of his story could translate into the chimerical genetics of generation-through-single-parenting and the exact reproduction of traits from one sole ancestor or ancestress. Beneath Morella's beauty and sameness lurks the recycled and chimerical imprint that emanates from the "modified Παλιγγενεσια [Paliggedenia]" of her applied learning in Pythagorean reincarnation, leavened with heavy doses of German Idealist Romantic philosophy. By contrast, in Diotima's view, beauty assumes the role of midwife to generation, as when "one who is pregnant and already swollen is vehemently excited over the beautiful, because it releases its possessor from great pangs" (Symp 206d). Contact with Socratic Eros, echoing from Diotima, upgrades itself in ascent through Beauty up to a summit beyond discourse: "to beget, not images of virtue, because he does not touch an image, but true virtue," which enables the initiate in the higher mysteries "to become dear to the gods, and if any other among men is immortal, he is too" (212a). (The time comes to glance back and downward from such summit to Aristophanes, who, recovered from his hiccups, delivers a speech on hard-boiled primeval surgery later on challenged by Diotima as spoken by Socrates.)

At the start, pre-humans were round creatures with eight limbs and a double male-female set of genitals, a single head with two faces, and terrible strength. These rolling stones in restless motion tried to climb up and storm Heaven to displace the gods (Symp 189e–90c). A team of surgeons made up by Zeus and Apollo cut them to size in stages. Here, the operation's most relevant stage concerns the suturing of the middle section from chest to groin, after the aboriginal humans have been sliced in two (as "eggs are cut with a hair"): "Apollo turned the face around and drew together from all sides the skin of what is now called the belly, as purses are closed by a drawstring, and, tying it off in the middle of the belly, he made a single mouth which people call the navel. [. . .] He smoothed out most of the other wrinkles and carefully shaped the chest with a tool of the sort shoemakers use to smooth out wrinkles in the leather on a last; but he left a few wrinkles around the belly and the navel, as a reminder of the ancient suffering" (190e–91a). But the suffering is far from over, since the split creatures still seek each other, to the point of embracing at random the dead halves of those who had, in the earliest of their former body shapes, made up a single whole creature, and then died in due course after surviving being halved from each other. Zeus takes further pity on them and turns their respective genitals to the front, so that, if only one could picture this correctly, they would stop "begetting each other but in the earth like locusts" and could instead beget children "in each other" (291c). Ever since, Eros "is a name for the desire and pursuit of wholeness," since "even in The Place of the Dead," as Hephaestus forewarns, people will seek and love to be rejoined into one as of old (192d–93a). As a result, erotic desire appears in resistance to ascent, to the type of climb from lesser to greater mysteries subsequently enjoined in Diotima's speech as the highest human reach in pursuit of the beautiful, the good, the virtuous life.[6]

WRINKLES IN THE ABYSS

The hero undergoes a disjunction through a fall into a subterranean world instead of one through the growth of a tree that lifts him up to the sky. This disjunction is the work of very close kin—in one case brothers, in another a father—who make the hero disappear as to appropriate his wife or wives.

Claude Lévi-Strauss, *The Story of Lynx*

The abundance of wrinkles (mentionable and unmentionable) in the account of Olympian surgery given by Aristophanes brings up the scene of lovemaking between the Amazon and Infante, in which the lovers have been at it since early in the afternoon and, as the sun is about to set, are themselves all set to reach their sixth climb to ecstasy. The plunging solar brightness brings into bold relief (and into view for the very first time) the sight of the Amazon's missing breast, lost to a bad burn and clumsy surgery during puberty, and now reduced to the nipple surrounded by wrinkled scar tissue. The man's hand is brought by the Amazon's into contact with the "flatness" ("chatura") and the rippling scar surface, "wrinkled back upon itself" or "replegada sobre sí misma" (HID 651) at the breast's past and present site. Upon finger contact, he comes in "great contractions" as she does, too, in silence.[7] Something in the order of a visual breast afterimage turned into palpable gift prompts Infante's arduously achieved sixth climax. He comes (and comes up dry) as if wanting to give Amazon a gift of flesh, a gift in place of the residue scar memorial that the lost breast erects to the blooming twin breast resting next to it. The sense that the lovers' last match in bed should end in a sort of orgy-for-two between two frustrated vampires increases as they go for yet another climb. She now finds a hidden "hood" in his "shrunken scrotum" and starts "red-riding" or rubbing his anus with his own epididymis: "She seemed like a midwife helping a masculine birth. But I felt my penis growing, the erection getting harder, its thickness gone bigger [*parecía una comadrona que auxiliaba al parto masculino. Pero sentí mi pene crecer, la erección endurecer, hacerse mayor el grosor*]" (HID 651). (The OED gives a single case of what is performed upon the *epididymis* by Margarita's Amazon massage rub. It is taken from Ben Jonson's *The Alchemist*, where, in bawdy shouts, barnyard and brothel are meshed: "shee must milke his epididimis, Where is the Doxie [whore]?")

The wrinkled remnants of the Amazon's breast and the rubbed-together wrinkles of her lover's anus and scrotum make up a chimerical pose for a sculpture in mock celebration of the Olympian excisions and sutures of archaic human flesh retold by Aristophanes in *The Symposium*. The dramatist comedian speaks of himself and everybody else as a "token of a human being, sliced like a flatfish; two from one," so that, ever since, each half "seeks his matching token," with the men who were "sectioned" from the "common sex" ("then called androgynous") becoming "woman-lovers" to the corresponding women "man-lovers" who were cut from the same prime stuff. The resulting two heterosexual matching sets include the bulk of adulterers and adulteresses (*Symp* 191d–e), wounded soul mates, no doubt, of Margarita the Amazon and Infante.

It was claimed in the previous chapter that the "absence of hymeneal defloration in Margarita wanders off in fetish fashion from her genitals into her right breast," to which it should now be added a surgical amendment from Aristophanes (with a rider from Poe's "Morella"). According to which, *More-of-Her* accrues as the "lower organs" of reproduction climb up the heaving and undulating ladder of her flesh over navel and chest and find their mansion in the ruins of a vanished breast. But, hold it. Mammalian abode, yes, but not without kinky contact with the rubbed-up wrinkles and birth-areas of a Fallen Adam's ass.

JUDY'S JUDY

In adherence to *Vertigo*'s plot strictures, the role of Judy Barton, played by Kim Novak, should earn Kim credit as supporting actress to the lead role of Madeleine in which she is also cast in more ways than one. Just as there is only one Madeleine in the one-and-only figure impersonated by Judy, there are two of the latter: one and then another Judy, neither of whom is ever Madeleine. This extra other Judy is never Madeleine except in Scottie's captive eyes, in Judy's knowing act, and in Gavin Elster's sinister Pygmalion directorship over her and his ghastly trick on both eventual lovers. A fabrication in garments and cosmetics, Madeleine cannot die; she can only cease to exist or be unplugged from Judy's or some other impersonator's performance.

In the absence of a substitute for Madeleine—besides the one once supported by Judy in Scottie's mesmerized purview as her own customized replacement—the matter of Madeleine's loss could be addressed (Orpheus-wise) as if one's back were turned to her trailing face. Turned to Madeleine, that is, while facing the impossible Sphinx riddle posed to Scottie by twice-Judy. The riddle's performance has Judy seducing Scottie on Elster's behalf and, hopelessly, seducing Scottie, under his own directorship, into accepting Madeleine back after he discovers that he lost her in the person of the Judy he now finally faces. The spectator who identifies with Scottie as he falls for Madeleine and then attempts to regain her in Judy is presumed masculine, a man of recent vintage or brand, but still a descendant from those archaic surgical "woman-lovers" and adulterers named by Aristophanes tongue-in-cheek.

Before taking a closer look at the film's masculine-centered perspective, a scene near the Espada Graveyard in *La Habana Para un Infante Difunto* must be examined, in which an encounter with two versions of Judy takes place, on the same spot and all at once. The uncanny comic *Vertigo* lesson learned from the instant serial interval between sighting a first and then a second Judy, on the same spot, amounts to this: the Madeleine decoy is neither secured nor regained through Judy's instant dissipation—her non-existence—and rebirth as a pair of facsimile women, otherwise properly acknowledged as identical twins. The loss of Madeleine-as-Madeleine-the-lost-woman obtains, alas, only if and when one runs into Judy and only Judy twice on the same spot—with no in-between museum painting replica. This is just what befalls Infante as he escorts home Margarita the Amazon, in the environs of the old and now demolished Espada Graveyard. Although *Vertigo* is in-retro out of the picture, as the recollected scene takes place in 1954, Infante learns of Margarita's ongoing liaison with a potential Gavin Elster figure, a father-like older man and former (though perhaps still current) lover who owns a radio station and who arouses in Infante, without a trace of irony, fears of father-daughter incest.[8] His phrase "incest is a serious matter" (*II* 299) is followed by her "you're funny [*eres cómico*]" (584/299), and then, as he is about to respond with some acrid jive, the look on Margarita's face makes him, his back to the street, "turn around" at the point where she says: "Ahí viene mi hermana" (*HID* 584). The sister's arrival is what brings Judy upon Judy on the same spot. Everything in her, the arriving sister, turns into something *about her*, about both sisters, the one that is and the one that is not the one in question. Everything spotted in her looks and presence seals in Infante her resemblance to Margarita, just as it underlines the slight but remarkable difference it creates in him about the sisters. Infante's visual inventory of the other sister is made up of comparative phrases in the negative prefaced by "although" and headed by "it did not," "were not," "she did not have," and other Margarita-depended clauses (584/299)

Everything mentioned about sister Tania is caught in Margarita's mirror, it is about her, or rather, about the *she-has-a-sister* factor emanating from the mirror effect felt by Infante when gazing at both. Tania bears the *she-has-a-sister* look that allows the uncanny presence of Judy *and* Judy on the same spot—even when she actually *is* at the spot.

Enter Isolde in double-take. The Isolde link takes place on the spot next to the Espada Graveyard in the interpolation of close to one page added to *Infante's Inferno*. Margarita's smile, just before Tania shows up, provokes in the English version two paragraphs' worth of extravagant high praise tainted with scorn and turning on the notion that from Ireland has come a "green-eyed Isolde with a bit of black," with teeth "like a pearly potion from a certain Celtic chalice" that could render one (Infante) "uncertain" (*II* 298). The Isolde interpolation puts the signature of *Vertigo* on the sister pair, since the Hitchcock lectures delivered in 1962 altered the Orpheus-Euridyce connection established in the 1959 review, influenced by the essay on the Tristan myth and *Vertigo* first published by Barthelmy Amengual in 1960.[9] Cabrera Infante points out that, like Tristan, who renounces Isolde in favor of a "poor facsimile," another Isolde, the one with the "white hands," Scottie loses the original woman he fell in love with (*Atn* 113). Except that Scottie's loss of Isolde seems worse than Tristan's, in that the medieval knight named *sad* (*tristis*) did not have to cope with the catastrophe of having Isolde, the one and only, become someone else's handiwork copy of someone he's never met. Also, when compared with Tristan's fate and the two Isoldes, Scottie's predicament (whether tragic or just pathetic) would end in his required Romantic death, instead of the disputed cure from psychic impairment that the loss of Madeleine and then Judy grants Hitchcock's anti-hero.

The uncanny or *unheimlich* effect has laid the ground for the sister encounter with Margarita and Tania. Before the encounter, as he approaches the chunk of graveyard wall left undemolished, Infante recalls that the spot is familiar to him because of two sisters he knew and visited nearby to listen to guitar music played by a friend of his who was seeing one of the girls. One sister is pinheaded, "her minuscule head" makes her seem "like a little girl grafted onto a fat woman," as she rocks like a metronome seated next to her beautiful redhead sibling (580–81/296). At times they resemble identical twins and trade features, the one lending beauty to the other as she takes on the other's grotesque smile.

The metronome beat that measures in standstill fashion the dissonant resemblance between the false twins evokes for Infante the instrument's invention by Maelzel, as well as the commercial exploits with von Kempelen's chess-player automaton on tour through Europe and America. Besides the elaborate right-versus-left-hand arguments engaged by Poe in his efforts to unmask the hidden man inside the chess cabinet, one bit of detective work proves of uncanny relevance to Margarita the Amazon's breast loss. Ancient Amazons were willing to trade debreasting for the more powerful use of their right arm and shoulder in shooting arrows at their men enemies. According to the Hippocratic Corpus, Amazon mothers would have employed a red-hot bronze instrument and applied it to the right breast of their infant daughters to cauterize it, so that in being so destroyed the breast would surrender " 'all its strength and fullness to the right shoulder and arm.' "[10] In what might be labeled, from the Amazon's point of view, *The Mammalian Chest Mystery*, one is invited by Poe to come inside Maelzel's cabinet and the attached Turk figure, to visualize how "[the] man within [. . .] gets up into the body of the Turk just so high as to bring his eyes above the level of the chess-board[. . . .] In this position he sees the chess-board through the bosom of the Turk which is of gauze. Bringing his right arm across his breast he actuates the little machinery necessary to guide the left arm and fingers of the figure."[11] As the reader is drawn into Poe's partly mistaken guesswork on how exactly the man and his sight are deployed inside Maelzel's chess cabinet, one would also enter the corresponding uncanny site inside the Amazon's single-breasted chest and peer through the opening covered by the gauze out into the audience. The person peering from inside the furniture chest and through the

Turk's chest would be the same subject who imagines the action while seated in the audience and feels the effects of the other's gaze from within. The Mammalian resident hostage inside Maelzel's chest would in this case peer through the Amazon's missing breast nipple-sight. He would peer at what might be termed the always reserved and forever occupied *Poe Seat* in the audience from which the bilocal or double position of looking into the chest and looking out from inside the chest originates.

The Morella *More-of-Her* factor returns at the core of *The Mammalian Chest Mystery*. It returns attached to the *she-has-a-sister* factor which, embodied in both Margarita and Tania, equates *More-of-Her* with the object of desire. The hyphenated claim *More-of-Her-equals-she-has-a-sister* constitutes on this occasion the *Vertigo* mystery to the solution of its symptom in enjoyment. In this regard, John T. Irwin's *The Mystery to a Solution* (1994) and Slavoj Žižek's *Enjoy Your Symptom!* (1992) are on the same page and in pursuit of the same analytic cache, though in different styles and for seemingly different purposes. First, Žižek's rhetorical question: "In the *noir* universe is evil not epitomized by the *femme fatale* who poses a threat not only to the hero's moral integrity, but to his very ontological identity? Is the axis of the *noir* universe not therefore to be sought in the relationship of the male detective to the woman *qua* his *symptom*?" (154). Followed here by Irwin's own question (as if on the philosophy of composition issue), apropos his quotation from Borges: " 'Mystery has something of the supernatural about it, and even of the divine; its solution, however, is always tainted by sleight of hand' ": "But [asks Irwin] if in the analytic detective story the solution is always in some sense an anticlimax that in dissipating the mystery exhausts the story's interest for us, an interest in speculative reasoning that the mystery empowers, how does one write this kind of story as a serious (i.e., rereadable) literary form? How does one both represent the analytic solution of a mystery and at the same time conserve the sense of the mysterious on which the analysis thrives?" (1994, 2). One possible answer lies in the serial reiteration of the mystery inherent in both the analytic and *noir* genres, where the story proves rereadable when repeated in another story. Irwin's own answer may lie in his writing a book on *noir* as his first major prose work after the book on the analytic detective story. A *noir* book which, by Borges's precursor rules, would represent a *pre-sequel* to its predecessor. By making the analytic story its own sequel, *noir* replaces the "supernatural" and "divine" origins mentioned by Borges and puts in their place the male hero's erotic bondage to the fatal (symptom) woman.

The cache mystery that rewards the *More-of-Her* solution involves three intractable claims on truth at the heart of the plot: (a) the aborted pregnancy-nexus claim involving *two* sisters and the unborn's putative father; (b) the father's claim that the child born to him and his wife in the meantime is also the offspring of *one* of the two sisters, most likely the one who would have aborted the unborn issue in question; (c) *the father's claim on death on behalf of life and on life on behalf of death.* Obviously, this last stressed and enigmatic and perhaps arcane claim or demand is what lends to the solution its intractable air of mystery.

JUDY'S NUDE

In his "psychoanalytical (and political)" scrutiny of alternate and separate shots in *Vertigo*'s first four sequences, Robin Wood identifies the "regression to the infantile stage" and the "unconditional demand for the 'lost breast'" in the "heterosexual male," instilled since infancy particularly in boys under the rule or "logic of patriarchy" (HFR 384). In this view, women are taught to repress the "original desire" for unchecked bliss so much encouraged in males. Men seek pleasure through the demand that best embodies masculinity; a sort of whole-hog quest for pleasure that, when found in women, under similar patriarchal strictures, is deemed to promote bisexuality and sexual "activeness" in them (384). Men are therefore on a train bound for mammalian paradise. They simply regress easier than women might into a condition called "'romantic love'" in which, as Wood sees it, the "demand for perfect union" and the "tendency to construct the loved person as an idealized fantasy figure" takes hold as a "denial of otherness and autonomy" (385). Wood concludes that this romanticized regression is what *Vertigo* "so incomparably dramatizes"; he knows of "no other film that so ruthlessly analyzes the basis of male desire and exposes its mechanisms" (385). Two of the sequences he examines require attention in reference to the *Vertigo* cosmos created in G. Caín's November 1959 review, Cabrera Infante's summer of 1962 lectures, and what has thus far transpired about *The Mammalian Chest Mystery* in Infante's Amazon affair.

Although it results from his detailed observation of shot sequences, Wood's allegory of love under patriarchy can be studied in less formal ways. For instance, Scottie's meeting with Midge Wood in her apartment —as she designs lingerie at a drafting table—should make even casual viewers aware of breast matters and brassiere engineering. Brassieres are made, Midge says, on "the principle of the cantilever bridge" in order to provide "revolutionary uplift" (a quality that in late 1959 Havana should have struck a chord in the reviewer G. Caín). The pink "doohickey" contraption about which Scottie asks Midge as he points to it with his walking cane remains in view from several shot angles. The fashionable breast contraption brings into focus Midge's mothering her former boyfriend, whom she dumped while back in college. Robin Wood recognizes comedy in the scene mainly in terms of Midge's "mother" role with "a defined ego" and her having "her own drives and demands," as she expects "a relationship of equals" and thus "demystifies sexuality" ("specifically in relation to the breast") by explaining "the mechanics" of the new uplift device. Midge resists the core requirement of female mystification in the male romantic lover. She "is finally disqualified by her accessibility" (HFR 385). Wood's analysis shows all-too-well that "the spectator constructed by the film is clearly male"; that Judy (its ultimate and residual female lead) "never becomes the film's central consciousness"; that "she is permitted only six point-of-view shots during the entire film" (386). If, as Wood argues, Midge demystifies the (breast) object of "original desire" on behalf of the primal male in Scottie, showing him that it has never existed, Judy puts the object's everlasting nonexistence right back under his nose.

This happens quite literally in the scene where she lies undressed (in the viewer's retrospective imagination) and *pretending* (also *imagined* in retrospect) that she is unconscious as Scottie attends to her. The woman he rescues from her (staged) suicide plunge in San Francisco Bay is Madeleine, the naked bait, now at rest in his bed at a moment regarded by Wood as one of "cinema's most perverse (and most 'romantic') love scenes"; a scene "so perverse it couldn't possibly be filmed" (HFR 385). The nude that in the unfilmable scene leaps, while at rest, before Scottie's eyes may be seen as prelapsarian or untouched by original sinfulness. Judy's nude appears Eve-like before the Lapse, the Slip, the Fall that enters Scottie's memory later on. Judy's nakedness comes in place of Madeleine's unthinkable nudeness. It would be the difference created between the naked and the nude by Judy's exposed body that renders her in Robin Wood's eyes untouchable to the besotted male romantic: "When she is Judy, Scottie can't bear to touch her" (385). This implies Scottie's romantic resistance to see past the nude Judy into the naked woman in whom she lies.

Yet, perspectives may vary on the issue of Scottie's sexual abstinence with Judy and the occasion of their final lovemaking. For instance, Peter

Conrad believes in the venereal magic of a Frisco steak dinner. He reminds us that Judy feels, as she says, "suddenly hungry" just as she blunders by choosing to wear the necklace that Scottie once saw worn by Carlotta Valdes in her oil portrait at the museum. Conrad is persuaded that Scottie perceives in Judy's sudden hunger that she is no "goddess" and that he will then "do more than ruffle her hair" (HM 317). But Conrad is mistaken. The steak dinner in question occurs earlier in their relationship, as they return to Ernie's restaurant and confront a Madeleine lookalike woman whose sight puts Judy at cross-purposes, as explained in the shooting script: "Judy is staring at him [Scottie] anxiously. It is her first defeat, and her first victory: defeat, in that although he is with her he is still searching [for Madeleine]; victory, in that she is sure, now, that he does not think she is Madeleine." [12] Judy's sudden hunger occurs later, on the last evening of her life. In the necklace recognition scene, Conrad has her asking Scottie to " 'muss me a little' before they go off to dinner" (HM 317), instead of her "Oh, no, you'll muss me" in coy refusal of any kissing or caressing, just before Scottie's gloomy realization before the mirror that she is wearing Carlotta's necklace. So the steak dinner is postponed forever, as they head back to the place where Judy once died and is about to die again that same evening. (If indeed they ever make love, it could be in between this scene and the previous rhapsodic moment of transport in the same room when they kiss to echoes of Wagner's Tristan und Isolde in Herrmann's score.) Charles Barr calls the following scene, where Judy puts on the necklace, "one of post-coital contentment" (V 72). Their mutual happiness does seem to suggest consummation and to cast doubt on Scottie's sexual inadequacy or impotence with the double-woman he so treasures and has such a hard time detaching from fetish worship.

Back in the scene, after her rescue from the bay, Madeleine appears in Scottie's bathrobe, and they touch hands as if by chance as he offers her more coffee, but the erotic spell is broken when the phone rings. It is Elster who calls. As Charles Barr points out, "in retrospect and on repeated viewings," one realizes that Elster is in control of events, but how, Barr asks, "does he know the exact moment at which to phone?" It seems as if Elster's "co-conspirator" (Madeleine) "has pressed a hidden button to alert him," or "as if he has been monitoring the scene via closed-circuit cameras" (V 59). A good deal of directorial magic hangs on how such exquisite timing is judged. Let judgment in this instance be found by taking a look at Pedro Almodóvar's Hable con ella (2002).

PEDRO'S ORPHEUS

At the beginning, the curtain rises to choreographer Pina Bausch's picture of extreme sadness in *Café Müller*. Two female dancers, one rather aged, the other much less so, but neither of them young, are dressed in flimsy slips. They appear absorbed in grief (informed by Henry Purcell's plaint from *The Fairy Queen*, "O Let Me Weep, Forever Weep"). They drift, glide, bump their chests and backs against the side wall, as if sleep-walking through an empty room crowded with tables and chairs. A man hurries about pushing furniture off their aimless path but suggesting no exit. In the film's first close shot, the older dancer moves her hand left-to-right across her chest as the one in the background does the same in replica. Nipples show beneath the slip's soft surface. Breasts (so prominent through most of the film) are first glimpsed, briefly, when the younger dancer leans forward. Bodies adopt in succession a stiff pose with legs slightly ajar and raised while lying sideways on the floor against the wall. Whatever *Café Müller* suggests seems far removed from sex or any sense of female erotic embodiment.

But such is not the case with *Masurca Fogo*, the choreography that ends the film. A sense of nuptials fills the air in the wake of Benigno's (Javier Camara) suicide death and the testimonial letter he leaves for Marco (Darío Grandinetti). The swaying bodies of seven young couples dressed in flowered colors shuffle across stage in syncopated pomp suggestive of folk dancing. Two of the women wear slips like the first pair does in *Café Müller*. Almodóvar has spoken of the "vitality and optimism" and "bucolic air" and about "el nacimiento de una pareja" ("the birth of a couple") in Marco and Alicia (Leonor Watling), the film's definitive romantic couple, who meet for the first time at the performance of *Masurca Fogo*. (Another couple is being born in the pair of dancers left on stage as the mazurka ends in seduction: the man throws his hat on the floor and moves it with his foot luring the young woman into joining him.)[13] The whole affair exudes warmth in the blues female lament "my baby is gone" heard against a luscious green foliage backdrop with dripping water. *Hable con ella* frames its cyclical plot between these two contrasting choreographies, from which one's focus may shift in order to consider issues of psychic and reproductive timing in the plot.

Benigno cares for Alicia, a patient who lies in a four-year coma at the private clinic El Bosque after being hit by a car. He tells her stories and speaks to her in the hope that Alicia will awake. As Benigno afterward tells Marco, Alicia's eventual lover, men in particular should always talk to women, they should *talk to her*, the woman in question. Looking back at *Vertigo*, the assumption of such *object-her* in need of talk—to whom any given man's speech ought to always aim—would seem to add tokenism to the dismal male romantic malady diagnosed by Robin Wood, among others, in Scott Ferguson's character. (Just think about how much *talking-to-her* and *listening* Scottie shares with Madeleine and Judy in *Vertigo*.) But such tokenism is far from Benigno's mind, unless it is precisely something like it that he recommends in earnest to Marco, as Almodóvar and Geraldine Chaplin do to the rest of mankind (*Pedro*: "It is a recommendation that should serve all men well; one ought to [*hay que*] treat women this way, take an interest in them." And *Geraldine*: "I have a lot of experience with that"). People everywhere (and "from all cultures") laugh at the film's title as quoted by Benigno, says Almodóvar. But he implies that the joke is on them, since Benigno speaks "naturalmente en serio." Almodóvar sees his character living "in a world apart" ("un mundo aparte"). In fact, Benigno spent fifteen years living with his bedridden mother, as he tells the psychiatrist Dr. Roncero, Alicia's father, on the occasion of their first meeting, arranged by Benigno for the sole purpose of setting foot inside her home. (During the session, Dr. Roncero listens to a story that rings in Freudian ears like the perfect script for male homosexuality as the product of maternal influence in isolation from the father's presence.)

Almodóvar makes fun of such psychoanalytic bias in his comments even as he speaks of Benigno's "abnormal" situation, "all alone with his mother," of his nursing and grooming of her, and then of Alicia, of his going "from one bed to another bed, from one woman to another woman." Later on, Almodóvar speaks of another mother, "a bit in the style of Hitchcock, that woman" ("un poco a la Hitchcock, esa mujer"), as he confides to Geraldine Chaplin. He is not talking about Benigno's case, but about another man's mother and their mutual problems. It is the shrinking or *waning* lover from the silent movie who causes such an impact on Benigno, as he tells Alicia, while rubbing her comatose body, and just as he (unbeknown to the viewer) is about to have sexual intercourse with his patient.

A brief shot in the silent black-and-white pastiche film *El amante menguante* (*The Shrinking Lover*) shows the maternal mansion to which the diminished man returns after drinking the elixir that reduces him to the size of a toy. In that first shot, his mother's house bears the softened though unmistakable Gothic look of the house behind the Bates Motel in *Psycho* (perhaps by chance Almodóvar's reference to Hitchcock's style of woman comes right after this shot). In the rest of the silent film, not shown in *Hable con ella*, the diminutive man discovers in a letter left by his father that, as he had long predicted, his wife had set out to kill him. In what is learned from Almodóvar's comment, the son is rescued from the mother's mansion and is taken back to a hotel by his girlfriend, the young woman who concocts the elixir, whose name is Amparo (shelter, *refuge*). In what corresponds to their wedding night, and upon learning that he will never regain his former size, the shrunken man bares Amparo's body in her sleep and climbs over her breasts and then comes down between her thighs and after some exploratory foreplay with his hand enters her vulva naked never to come out again. In Almodóvar's words to Chaplin: "ahí se queda" ("there he remains").

The viewer watches this other film in place of the scene that would prove far more perverse than the one imagined by Robin Wood when he contemplates Scottie's undressing of Madeleine's body. This happens as Judy, the actual woman to whom the *body-too-much* belongs, feigns that she is unconscious. There is in *Vertigo* a suppressed instance of the type of bed-trick scenario in which a bride takes the place of another, as Brangane does in King Mark's bed on behalf of Isolde, in order to substitute her own intact hymen for the one the real bride has already surrendered to Tristan, while both lovers are under the effect of a potion different from the drink that makes the shrunken lover in *Hable con ella* seek shelter and final rest in his bride's womb. Just as there are two women in only one body in *Vertigo*, and one virgin-bride in place of a non-virgin decoy-bride in *Tristan*, there are two women in two different films, one film inside the other, in *Hable con ella*.

El amante menguante intervenes so that the foul business of impregnating Alicia's comatose body and violating her unconsciousness and her soul is not shown. In the nudity scene not shown in *Vertigo*, the woman (Madeleine-Judy) cannot be meant to be menstruating. The uncanny precision timing of Gavin Elster's phone call—dissected by Charles Barr in terms of directorial coordinated control from inside the plot (Elster's) and outside (Hitchcock's)—would follow Judy's implicit decision that she could not be on her period when she fakes suicide by drowning and then unconsciousness in order to further snare her rescuer Scottie. If not, poor Scottie's stoicism in laundering her garments and Judy's in resisting wakefulness while being cleaned and swabbed by him would seem perversely admirable. On its part, Benigno's own angelic perverseness in mounting

Alicia seems relevant to such imaginable embarrassment in the unfilmed *Vertigo* scene. From the very first scene in the film, when Benigno is shown talking to and massaging Alicia in full display of her breasts, the early arrival of her menses comes into play. Benigno agrees with the other nurse that she is "early" as they prepare to clean and swab her. How *does* he know? Or, how could he *not* know, knowing Alicia's menstrual rhythms as well and as faithfully as he does?[14]

This is what makes Benigno's watching *The Shrinking Lover* the night before he violates Alicia's coma seem so timely. For there is something of the moon about the tiny lover who inspires Benigno. More than with any other usage, *menguante* in ordinary Spanish is most often heard in reference to the *waning* moon. Besides, the earth's satellite sister is present in the silent film. In his comments, Almodóvar refers to the round mirror seen on the wall just as the tiny lover is about to descend into the woman's bushy pubic zone. He says it represents either the sun or the moon. But, it being nighttime, the celestial body in question should be the moon's. In addition, the surface of mirrors in Spanish is called *luna* or moon. So the quality of "naturalness" in Benigno that so impresses Almodóvar and causes admiration in him hints at the ability to keep in tune with how the moon, too, *Talks to Her*. By the period rules of such calendar, Benigno mounts Alice quite moonstruck, just as she, deep in the lapse of her coma, remains under the spell of the oldest and oddest of sister rules.

Further Orphic matters occasioned by watching *Vertigo* on three successive nights in Havana in late November 1959 are examined next. For the time has come to witness how Odysseus and Orpheus (and Cain and Lot) may cross paths on Home soil.

chapter nine

Orpheus in Vegas
(Tabloid)

It was Ulysses and it was not.
WALLACE STEVENS, *"The World as Meditation"*

The film reviewer or *cronista* known as G. Caín, who on three successive evenings in November 1959 watched *Vertigo*, had already seen and reviewed *North by Northwest* a few weeks earlier, well aware of its immediate and more notorious predecessor's delay in reaching Havana. The reviews (dated October 25 and November 15) appear back-to-back in *Un oficio del siglo XX*. Besides relating forward to *Psycho* and backward to *Rebecca*, the first three viewings of *Vertigo*, which centered on the "myth of Orpheus in its American version" (*OXX* 367), could also relate to *Topaz* along the lines of a deepened political crisis in the sphere of Romantic love centered on Cuba's soil.

A sustained attempt to cast *Vertigo* in trilogy form (with *North by Northwest* and *Psycho*) is pursued along strict psychoanalytical lines by Ayako Saito, strict in the sense in which the injured psyches of characters find mimetic projection in the films under scrutiny as if these aesthetic products were imprinted with individual and transindividual mental disorders. In such a clinical mood, one is asked, for instance, to disengage from the comic nuptial environment of *North by Northwest* and to shift attention away from the upcoming honeymoon, already foreplayed aboard the westbound Twentieth Century train and now about to be replayed beyond the ending as it enters a tunnel eastbound. As a result, the cliffhanger on Mount Rushmore (just before the lovers' last triumph over evil) is to be seen as if their "magical reunion *was* indeed a screen memory" and they had fallen to their death.[1]

Working from the already examined trilogy, which crystallizes in *Psycho*, with *Rebecca* at its center next to *Vertigo*, another film trio suggests itself. The cinematic threesome could work a bit like a *ménage à trois* with a fourth-dimensional shadow. Two of the films involved would interact with the third one in kaleidoscopic fashion to produce a series of locked-in theme clusters made up of images, sites, and altered resemblances animated by a synoptic view of the trilogy effect in question.

First, going back before *Vertigo*, a review from April 20, 1958, yields a case of "Argentinian Necrophilia" concerning *Más allá del olvido* or *Beyond Oblivion* (1956) by Hugo del Carril, an all-but-forgotten older relative of Hitchcock's masterpiece. Though remarkable in its baroque excess, the film's lurid necrophilia provokes laughter in the reviewer with its treatment of "stubborn monogamy" and the husband's discovery in "strange lands" of the "empty facsimile" of his dead wife, which he "fills up with his absurd love" (*OXX* 277). A stolen resemblance to *Rebecca* is noted, and pardoned, since du Maurier's novel might itself be copied from a Brazilian romance.

A second glance at *Más allá del olvido* occurs much later, in connection with the Amazon, whose "weakness" for Mexican movies has taken Infante to the Florencia cinema as her escort in search of reruns. But it was only after "Margarita had already vanished" that he first watched *Beyond Oblivion* (possibly as reviewer G. Caín) with its "theme of the double and necrophilia" (*HID* 619) and the mad lover that kills its own woman facsimile creation (a deed which applied to *Vertigo* would turn Scottie into Judy Barton's necrophiliac killer). This is how the *Vertigo* and Orpheus matrix takes root at the Florencia cinema: unknown, foreshadowed, extant, amid ghostly third-world underworld reruns, and caught in the Romantic absurdities of Argentinian necrophilia, with its species of widower's wife-murder ancestor worship.

ORPHEUS AND THE PHANTOM JUDY

Orpheus cannot prevent himself from being the lover and seducer
of a woman whose lawful husband he also is.
 Marcel Detienne

The word *tabloid* was patented and trademarked by London druggists in the 1880s to distinguish the compressed goods they sold from the common pharmaceutical *tablet*. The "fancy word" (*OED*) soon took off in popularity to name the treatment of any topic in compressed doses, particularly in the press. Nowadays tabloid exudes the strong smell of Norman Mailer's *factoid*, a word coined in the early stages of his fanciful 1973 biography of Marilyn Monroe in reference to those facts that lack existence before showing up in the media. Or, being not yet on the Web: "facts which have no existence before appearing in a magazine or newspaper, creations which are not so much lies as a product to manipulate emotion in the Silent Majority. (It is possible, for example, that Richard Nixon has spoken in nothing but factoids during his public life)" (Mailer 1973, 18).

On his way to transmute base factoid elements about Marilyn into golden fact-benders of a mythical kind, Mailer ponders how, in the biography of a "great actor" (meaning her), the "abominable magnetism of facts" always attracts "polar facts" (a fit prophecy for bloggers). An actor, he claims, "lives with the lie as if it were truth," and "a false truth can offer," he finishes off, "more reality than the truth that was altered" (18). Take for instance the case of Plato's Phaedrus, a character who in the dialogue that bears his name appears best qualified by virtue of his own mediocrity to stand next to Socrates at perhaps the most sublime point ever witnessed in the utterance of philosophical truth, and who even shares in the aspirations to spiritual wealth expressed by Socrates in his final prayer to the god Pan. (There seems to be a bit of Phaedrus in Mailer's Marilyn and a touch of Marilyn in Socrates' Phaedrus.)[2]

In Phaedrus, Socrates disowns previous views of his blasphemous to love, in which he believes he treated eros as mere physical lust, just as Lysias does in the speech that Phaedrus approvingly reads to him in fresh transcription. In conveying to Socrates what is regarded as Plato's pastiche of a professional writer's morning column on love, Phaedrus fulfills his role as "a person of shallow and uncritical enthusiasms, the eager but superficial follower of a new fashion in culture, although at the end he seems to be genuinely converted to Socrates' view."[3] The fashion in question involves the ancient Greek professional litigants known as sophists, who offered their services in public as attorneys for hire. In recognition of their influence in the handling of facts, Mailer's definition of factoid may designate anything that, by virtue of being in the mouth of a sophist, performs truth.

In R. B. Bury's words, Phaedrus is responsible for "the arbitrary handling of the Orpheus myth" in "striking illustration of the sophist manner" (which happens just at the point in the Symposium where the Orphic Vertigo connection—first proposed by G. Caín in his 1959 review and expanded by Cabrera Infante in the 1962 Hitchcock lectures—grows in complexity).[4] In late 1959 it seemed clear to the reviewer that Scottie and Madeleine were meant for each other, but that, like Orpheus, the man would fail to see danger in the woman who obsesses him as he descends into hellish nightmare to rescue her. As Caín sees it, Vertigo's first part is ruled by supernatural tokens and symbols. In the second part, after Judy turns her face to the audience to reveal in flashback fashion her complicity in wife murder, these same signs turn into police clues pointing at necrophilia. Scottie takes himself, Judy, and the audience beyond the coveted solution of "who killed whom" toward the unanswerable mystery of "who is who," reaching into the realm of the dead (OXX 367–68). Later on, in the summer of 1962, the lecturer reexamines the review as he speaks of Phaedrus's account of the trick that the gods played upon Orpheus when they returned to him a phantom woman instead of the wife he had chased into Hades. But before he cites Phaedrus's allusion to Orpheus in the *Symposium*, Cabrera Infante mentions the two Isoldes in Tristan's life in their double role as *who-is-a-truer-blonde* ("one a poor facsimile of the other"). Two Irish blondes are compared with the phantom Helen of Troy fabricated in the *palinode* of the poet Stesichorus, whose sight was restored after he recanted his bad-mouthing of Helen's adultery and wrote that "another legendary blonde" (*Atn* 113) had never been abducted and taken to Troy, for she was replaced by her *eidolon*.

Earlier in the lecture it is claimed that "all myths are only one myth" (*Atn* 105), so Orpheus's ill-fated lapse in looking back, only to see his wife vanish, should stand in mutual reflection with Lot's obedience to the angels' warning (in Genesis 19.17) never to look back upon the conflagration in the cities below, an injunction broken by his wife, who in glancing back turns into a pillar of salt. But the speaker adds that "Lot's wife had ideas of her own, just like those of her predecessor Eve" (*Atn* 105). So Orpheus's wife-vanishing backward glance compares oddly with Lot's *not* looking back, as his trouble-making or suicidal or simply dumb wife fatally does. Is such a backward gesture a hint of the automaton in her (or in *More-of-Her*)?

The bond between Orpheus and Lot and their lost wives concerns two cases of wordplay in English added to *Infante's Inferno*. In one scene, Infante knows without turning around ("sin volverme") that Margarita follows him to the corner (*HID* 622). In English, the added allusion to a play by Tennessee Williams is followed by a biblical pun: "Upon turning around, Orpheus condescending," Infante "saw that she had followed [him] to the corner. She stood there looking a lot like Lot's mistress" (*II* 329). So Infante *does* turn around Orpheus-like and Margarita does not vanish, but turns instead into Lot's mistress, though not into a pillar-of-salt dead wife. The Orphic lost wife's fall into Hades duplicates the Havana mistress who turns into the biblical pillar of salt—but transformed into a dead wife.

A second Lot addition-and-subtraction in the art of wife elimination follows. Infante's plain "like what?" answer to Margarita's "I like you like this" ("me gustas mucho así") turns into the question "Like Lot's wife or like his daughters?" (646/348). Behind such wordplay lies a matter of allotment touching on the lot (and lottery) that will correspond to Lot's two foxy daughters.

In the Bible, Lot is a potential felon involved in the punishable-by-death crime of abetting in the possible rape of his two virgin daughters, whom he offers to a gang of Sodomite night prowlers in place of the two alien angels sheltered under his roof, who were the intended victims of the homosexual abuse first requested by the intruders. As one comment puts it, "It is reasonable to infer that Lot evinces a disquieting readiness here to serve as accomplice in the multiple enactment of a capital crime directed at his own daughters." [5] Grievous moral guilt is confirmed when afterward, on successive nights, Lot is made drunk inside a cave by his two virgin daughters, who seek, in being deflowered by their own father, to become the founding mothers of two separate peoples. As already mentioned, Cabrera Infante left Cuba for good in the fall of 1965, taking with him his two daughters by his first wife, Marta Calvo, in whose fictional shadow the affair with the Amazon and the birth of the first of the two daughters are set. It looks as if, in leaving Ithaca for good (as well as Penelope weaving tapestries to Fidel's suitors), Sodom and Gomorrah are left in the rearview mirror by a fugitive and forward-sailing Odysseus, who like Cain just won't stop, except in the double and contradictory Janus-like gesture of Lot (who never looks back) and Orpheus (who always will).

Emblazoned in the *ekphrastic* shield of such *mise-en-abyme* ensemble cast rests the author's signature of authorship, perhaps essayed beyond recall in his punning autobiographical caption for the year 1987: "His second grandson is born in the Jewish faith; circumcised on the third day. Begins to visit Ithaca anew. Who would his hero be this time. *Ohddyseus [Ohdiseo]* or *Judysses [Judises]*?" (Cro 360).[6]

VEGAS HONEYMOON

Tying up the *More-of-Her* motif with its variant in *the-woman-to-be-named-later*, it seems as if the cluster of women gathered in the *Vertigo* matrix includes, besides the two Isoldes, a bond between wife and mistress. On the one hand: Lot's pillar-of-salt wife, turned into both Infante's first and divorced wife (betrayed while pregnant shortly after their honeymoon) and the mistress Amazon (abandoned after the birth of the first daughter in whose conception she is implicated). On the other: Orpheus's lost wife (who is inseparable from the other two wife-mistress figures in association with the phantom woman embodied in Helen's *eidolon*). This implies — in the deadly and fuzzy math of myth — that in Orpheus's honeymoon (whether in Vegas or not), wife and mistress, while not clones, act as if conjoined. They are hitched, in more ways than one, to a diet of honeyed excess unsevered from flesh taboos applied to the woman as nymph at odds with herself as seasoned lover. From a bleeding bride honeyed in the blood and tears of her lost hymen and soon, after such ordeal, made pregnant, the Orphic Infant comes to the full banquet. Now, in the mistress's flesh, blood tastes as honeyed as when flavored in the salty juices of lovemaking and its mimic cannibalism. (That missing breast of hers — restored by her own tongue to the wrinkles of his sphincter — adds to his bliss the further *jouissance* of being the afterimage of the other breast, the one devoured by him as tabooed by the Orphic regime against consuming any kind of flesh.)

The substantive and detailed reference to the phantom Helen in the Hitchcock lecture alludes to Euripides' *Helen* and Stesichorus's *palinode*, but it does not refer to Socrates' comment about the affair in *Phaedrus* (Plato 1973, 243a). This happens even as the figure of Helen's replica leads directly to the discussion of the Orpheus-Euridyce passage in the *Symposium*.[7] In a wider context, Phaedrus speaks of men in pursuit of other younger men, of "lovers and their beloveds" (*Symp* 178e), who are tied together by mutual bonding based on martial valor. He claims that "only lovers are willing to die in behalf of others — not only men but women too" (179b). He holds Alcestis as such an exemplary lover, for she was willing to die in place of her husband, Admetus, even though his parents might have assumed the awful task, but "she so much surpassed them in friendship that she made them appear alien to their own son and related to him only in name" (179b–c). Next, Phaedrus accuses Orpheus of cowardice opposite Alcestis's courage, who received her soul back from the Place of the Dead when the gods honored her for dying on behalf of her husband, Admetus. By contrast, the gods thought that Orpheus was "soft due to being a musician, and didn't dare die for the sake of Eros as Alcestis had, but contrived to go to the Place of the Dead alive!," so the honeyed lyricist was shown only "an appearance of the wife he'd come for" instead of Euridyce herself (179d).[8]

As if such slander were not enough, shreds of fact adhere to the Alcestis-Orpheus passage, either causing further damage or enhancing, in spite of any blame, the lurid shine of the heroic and divine persons involved. Factoid accretions of the sort found in King Admetus's honeymoon often cling to convoluted mythic lives. Besides a pair of lost wives, Admetus and Orpheus experience honeymoons or short marriages finished in death. Their weddings are haunted by instituted passions to which marriage itself seems resistant, but to the point of serving as the occasion for the lethal recurrence of just such passions. It is fitting to delve briefly into these affairs if one is to appreciate in full the Orphic *Vertigo*.

King Admetus (*the untamable*) was among many suitors who competed for Princess Alcestis, daughter of Pelias, king of Iolcus. He won her hand with the help of Apollo but then failed to sacrifice to Artemis, whose tutelage Alcestis had left in order to wed him. As punishment, on the wedding night, Admetus found the marriage couch crawling with snakes. He ran to Apollo, who had his sister Artemis relent and to grant to him that Admetus should be spared from death, provided that a member of his own family took the man's place and died for the love of him. When the fatal day came much sooner than expected, Apollo managed to detain Admetus's passage into Hades by making the three Fates drunk, allowing Alcestis time to poison herself. Persephone, however, thought it heinous for a wife to die in place of her husband and sent the queen's soul back to the upper air. If, as Richard Lattimore helpfully suggests, Admetus should be seen as the principal tragic character in *Alcestis*, the theme posed by Euripides could well be, not the wife's bravery and devotion when she dies for her husband, so much as what manner of man that husband must be when he allows his wife to die for him. Thus, Admetus "lacks the courage to die as he ought to instead of letting his wife die for him," just as he "lacks the courage to admit, to himself or anyone else, that he ought to be dying but dare not do it."[9] To summarize. In the *Symposium* the uncovered case of Admetus as cowardly husband comes up when Phaedrus debunks Orpheus for being soft and holds up Alcestis as a paragon of heroic love. This happens at the point where the account he gives of Eurydice's phantom-trick played by the gods at the expense of Orpheus's reputation is picked up by Cabrera Infante as the main clue behind the Orphic *Vertigo*. (Though no mention is made of the ridicule against the poet and musician promoted by Phaedrus at the cost of his own amateur reputation in philosophical circles.)

Thus exposed, Admetus's cowardice could not stand in greater contrast with Scottie's victimized uprightness and overwhelming sense of guilt in the related triple deaths of Gavin Elster's wife, Judy, and Judy's phantom in

Madeleine. In addition, Elter's sinister role is enhanced upon further looking into the Orphic character of his honeymoon. For it so happens that in his *Eroticus* (761e) Plutarch makes Admetus the object of Heracles' pederasty as well as Apollo's. The Sun God's love for Alcestis's suitor (and for the husband Apollo helps him to become) would account for the further favor Apollo exacts from his sister Artemis in order to prevent Admetus from dying. The latter's craven resignation to his wife's suicide in order to save himself as beloved or *eromenos* of Apollo prompts eerie thoughts about Elster's own murder plot. Furthermore, Admetus is seen by some experts as none other than Hades himself, in which case he becomes the anthropomorphic husband version of the god of the underworld.[10]

A quick glance at Orpheus's story in Virgil's fourth *Georgics* discloses that beekeeper Aristaeus lost his hives in punishment for his attempt to nab and assault the nymph Euridyce, who in flight from him was bitten by a serpent at river's edge and fell into the underworld. The beekeeper's sexual savagery violates the protocols of chasteness regularly observed in caring for bees, whose mythical counterparts were the Bee-Women or *Melissai*. In myth, bees were equated with the lawful wife and were notorious for their hatred of perfumes and other signs of extra- or infra-marital voluptuousness or debauchery. Beekeepers were advised by some to go as far as to shave their heads in order to avoid carrying traces of scent or cosmetic aromas near the hives. In chasing Euridyce, Aristaeus worked against his own invention of honey, which he brought about through the technique of *bougonia*, the art of generating bees from the rotten carcass of an ox. In Marcel Detienne's words: "It was because the inventor of honey had the smell of seduction on him that he was deprived of his bees. Orpheus' bitterness and the Nymphs' anger are therefore reactions to a sexual offence" (in Gordon 1981, 99). Such odor of seduction clings to no one in *Vertigo* except Scottie: as he embraces and kisses Madeleine, undresses and dries Judy's body, and directs with utter fastidiousness her sartorial and cosmetic transformation back into Madeleine, the phantom woman who ought not to exist after shedding her garments and facsimile appearance once she is restored to the living.

At first glance, the compound woman in Madeleine-Judy does not fit the strict status of nymph in the Orphic honeymoon environment. The role of the nymph figure to whom Eurydice owes her awful bridal fate goes back to her place in Demeter's entourage and to Melissa's discovery of wild honey in the forest. The nymph mixed wild honey with water and fed it to humans, who up to that time had known no other food besides their own flesh. Under the influence of Melissa, humans ate only the honey found in forest trees and were shown how to weave and wear garments—the nymph's second prime invention. In line with such innovations in the culture of life, elaborate purification protocols were observed in the prenuptial marriage rituals, in whose environment, according to Marcel Detienne, the honeymoon of Orpheus and Eurydice begins to unfold. This is how a razor's edge separates the nymph's lawful enjoyment of bridal pleasures from lethal excesses of the kind in which " 'to sprinkle oneself with honey,' " as the saying went, could turn the young bride into a hornet or "carnivorous bee," a throwback forest brute driven "to gorge without measure on honey" (in Gordon 1981, 100, 103). And this is why, from the start, Euridyce's affair with Orpheus leans on bride debauchery, which is what Aristaeus, master of honey, tries to carry out later on at the cost of losing his hives and sending the nymph to the realm of the dead. (Aristaeus acted as if he knew that Euridyce had been swept away enraptured by the love sounds of Orpheus the enchanter, much like, in another myth corpus, Isolde is enchanted by Tristan's music, the young knight's peerless attribute.)

Aristaeus's mad lover's abducting actions are prefigured in Orpheus's own loving acts. Detienne calls him "the lover and seducer of a woman whose lawful husband he also is" (in Gordon 1981, 104). Here lies the biggest yet minimal difference between the Orphic honeymooner wife-lover and Gavin Elster. Elster plays mad hunter to the enraptured bridegroom he never is. He kills his own spouse and discards her by proxy in Scottie and his enthrallment by phantom Judy, who, it seems, came to him already the victim of wrongful lust. Anti-patriarchal readers like Robin Wood should ponder how the origins of Scottie's seduction attachment to his romantic prey (besides his own Narcissus self) might lie in what Judy tells him about her flight from home. She tells him that she could not get along with her stepfather. Was he a molester whose version of a lost honeymoon in Vegas was to try it on his stepdaughter back in Salina, Kansas? Inside the patriarchal closet, is Aristaeus, the mad honeymooner, a primer of the lyrical bridegroom lover's fatal lust?

ORPHEUS TALKS TO HER

Vertigo leaves unhealed the scission between the sexes so central to Orphism when defined as a strict doctrine in which the conduct of life splits "between woman and man, between the impure bestiality of one and the pure spirituality promised the other" (Detienne 1979, 92). In such terms, the lethal bullfight presence of beastliness in Hable con ella proves essential to the healing of sexual wounds attempted through the film's magical view of sacrifice and metamorphosis. Lydia González's body is shattered (destrozado) by a bull named Thunder (Trueno) whom she chooses to face "a puerta gallola" as she kneels right at the start a few feet directly in front of the swung-open door. Lydia's recklessness is anticipated when a member of her crew tells another that for the love and admiration of her now former boyfriend and fellow bullfighter, el niño or "Kid" from Valencia, she would "allow her entrails [entrañas] to be spilled." Lydia's desperate bonding both to a man and to the man-ruled art of corrida (the blood-sport fight known as lidia) comes from her dead father's wish for her to achieve the full status of torero which he never reached, as he remained just a bull-baiter ("se quedó en banderillero"). Lidia is played by Rosario Flores, whose face and sinuous body seem ideal for the role of a bacchic maenad. Rosario cuts the most intense and theriomorphic or animal-like figure in the film, a human soul mate of the noble beast she fights as if imbued with sacred fury.

The bull figures prominently in the worship of Zeus and his son Dionysus. In Euripides' The Bacchae, a chorus of Asian women leap and dance as celebrants of the orgiastic "bull-horned god" who was born of Zeus.[11] The women of Elis call upon him to come "leaping on a bull's clog," as Dionysus "is invited for the day of bounding and spurting [. . .] supposed to appear in his animal form as a raging bull at the gallop, leaping with a single bound into a temple described as pure." (If it were true that, as Detienne claims, "in Dionysian anthropology the heart muscle is like an internal maenad in the body of the possessed, constantly leaping within," Lydia González could embody the thumping organ in a film about two women in coma.)[12]

One half of the Orphic connection in Hable con ella lies in Lydia's purifying sacrifice and her dismal but ennobling bond with the lidia and the bull god. She fulfills the horrors of slaughter shunned by Orphism, an abstention from sacrifice and meat consumption very much mindful of the countervailing forces invested in the worship of Dionysus. (Understanding the film in resistance to such mythology results in unplugging it from its main source of passion linked to the erotic.) The other Orphic half involves a foursome—Angela, Marco, Benigno, Alicia—and a nameless Cuban woman, the woman to be named later.

Marco's frequent travels with his young lover Angela resemble periodic honeymoons, taken while he researches his guidebooks and she recovers from drug addiction. In the one travel Marco recalls for the camera, when questioned by Lydia about the source of his tears, Angela is seen by the light of a campfire running naked in the African night at water's edge. Her flight is caused by a serpent that crept into their tent, the same animal that crawls into Lydia's kitchen and puts her in need of Marco's help. The incident attests to one of the worse superstitions among bullfighters: their loathing to see or to run into a *bicho* or snake. (Lydia considers it so polluting that she decides never to return and to sell the house.)

The African flashback scene is followed by the first shot of Lydia's face lying in a coma next to Marco, and then by Marco's first look at Alicia, whose mostly nude body lies slightly reclined on its left side, accentuating Leonor Watling's shapely forms. He seems spellbound and then aghast as her eyes suddenly open. When he next speaks with Dr. Vega about the length and prognosis of Lydia's coma, Marco's words seem haunted by the sight of the nude young woman he has just seen open her eyes in what he must now accept, from the doctor's advice, as "un acto mecánico" (like yawning, crying, and other vegetative functions during a coma). Marco is shown a magazine article about the case of a woman named "Meryl Lazy Moon" who lapsed into a coma after delivering her third child and who emerged from it several years later. Clustered in this sequence, the nymph-evoking nudity of the two young women blends in contrast: Angela runs madly in alien darkness, Alicia lies oddly in erotic and clinical stillness, falsely and yet truthfully awakened by Marco's gaze. (The Lazy Moon adds a touch of allegorical candor and pastiche humor to the nocturnal mysteries so central to the film.)

Both snake episodes occur at night, and the traffic accident that puts Alicia in a coma interrupts her reading of Davis Grubb's novel, The Night of the Hunter. This prompts comments by Almodóvar about Alicia being "hunted down" ("cazada") or abducted by something or someone ("cazada por algo o alguien"). Like Euridyce's fatal flight from abduction by the beekeeper-turned-hunter, Aristaeus, Alicia has been ravished into darkness by ill fate; her careless jaywalking in Madrid is a sign of pure abandonment, so typical of nymphs in their wild Arcadian home.

Although they do not look at all as if born in Lesbos, at this point in the film, Javier Cámara's Benigno could well play Daphnis to Leonor Watling's Chloe, except that his "naturalness" (a sign of his unpolluted soul), so praised by Almodóvar, includes the bold capacity to commit a species of abduction and rape (adult crimes for which the ancient Lesbian pastoral pair of youths often serve as prey). The pair of foundlings in *Daphnis and Chloe* informs the sibling nexus between Benigno and Alicia. It is through Benigno's point of view that a copy of *The Night of the Hunter* is seen on her night table, when he intrudes into her bedroom as if to reclaim, not only a fetish souvenir, but a lost, though still extant, familiarity with—in his case —his haunted maternal origins and prolonged nursing of his bedridden mother. The ancient pastoral view of the couple could regard Benigno's love spell as a manifestation of erotic nympholepsy, of being possessed and enraptured by the nymph's powers to bring inspiration into the soul.[13]

In association with *The Night of the Hunter*, Benigno would turn the sylvan hunter and rapist Aristaeus inside-out (a figure of utter innocence who is also capable of rape). This puts Marco in the corresponding role of Orpheus as the would-be husband of the woman who is jolted back into conscious life by her ravisher. The Orphic signs and sounds are underscored in Almodóvar's DVD comments on the film. He sees Benigno entering Alicia's coma in search of her in the darkness ("entrar en el coma para buscarla, meterse en la oscuridad"). Once Benigno is doomed to commit suicide, as he is kept in the dark about Alicia's renascence from coma, Almodóvar speaks of him facing the rain, as if it were the "door" through which she "disappeared" and which Benigno must now enter in death. Benigno's punishment would have him grope in darkness in search of the lost woman whose body integrity he transgresses, as the waning lover does in the black-and-white silent Orphic night in the film in which his tiny self returns to the womb.

When Marco regains sight of Alicia—who is seated watching the dancers in the studio across the street—he is at the window in Benigno's apartment, where he now lives. He "has her" (Almodóvar's words) "in front of him, asleep, just as Benigno saw her." Besides such comments, film language speaks for itself. Marco "has her," indeed, before him, in a photo of Alicia resting in coma taken by Benigno. Marco will soon face the photo a second time, after he turns his back on Alicia's epiphanic sight, across the street, at the dance school. (Euridyce splits in two, her photogenic image and her own recovered living presence among the living. Perhaps she is also found in Benigno's retinas—in the afterlife he equates with the oblivious rest he dared violate in her, after so much talking to her.)

In the director's view, when Marco speaks to Alicia, face-to-face for the first time, at the intermission of *Masurca Fogo*, "she hears him from the coma" ("lo oye desde el coma"). Her aural magical hearing comes in response to Marco's earlier visual seizure of her nymph's nude stillness, in which Almodóvar claims that he is not seeing her as a woman in a coma ("no la ve como una mujer en coma"). The magical notion that Marco's imprint image captured itself in Alicia's retinas the first time he saw her—and saw her nude, as she opened her eyes while in coma—revives itself now in her live listening to him.

In pastoral Greek myth, at various ancient sanctuaries, particular nymphs exercised powers of divination. Along such lines, from the sheltered grotto of her coma, Alicia *divines* Marco.[14]

The insertion of *Hable con ella* in the *Vertigo* trilogy imagined here begins and ends in Havana, between late 1959 and 2000: between the review of Hitchcock's film by Caín and Benigno's last meeting with Marco who visits him in jail. Benigno has read all of Marco's travel guides and finds the one on Havana his favorite. He tells Marco that he identifies with the woman shown in a photo leaning on a balcony as she looks at the sea across Malecón Avenue. The inmate sees himself in the woman, who, like the rest of the people there, he says "have got nothing and invent themselves everything," and who go on "waiting uselessly as times goes by and nothing happens" ("I thought I was that woman"). The photo taken by Marco in Havana is seen once more when he reads Benigno's suicide letter (in which Javier Cámara is heard in voiceover saying: "I write to you moments before my escape; I hope that all I've taken is enough to put me in a coma and reunite me with her"—Alicia). As this is heard, the shot scans the photo of the woman on the balcony down to the bottom of the picture, covered with the drug pills Benigno is about to take to kill himself. It may be asked whether the woman in the picture contemplates an exit flight from life not unlike Benigno's—pictured in Benigno's own mind and in her own. How many times has she taken the plunge—if not from that balcony itself, then from another loftier spot? Has she spotted herself an afterlife like the one Benigno ensures himself in joining Alicia's coma sphere—the same inner sphere he once visited as he ravished her quietness? Almodóvar tells Geraldine Chaplin that he wants no one to draw any conclusions about the Havana photo but that it is all rather expressive ("no quiero que nadie saque conclusiones, pero también es muy expresivo"). Yet, the circumstances in whose halo Benigno's unassisted suicide in a Spanish jail goes through are worth a backward glance.

"Unassisted" heightens the irony of Marco's complicity in Benigno's "escape"—it stresses Marco's good faith as he assists the lawyer (for whose services he is paying) in denying Benigno fresh knowledge of Alicia's recovery from coma. Indebtedness to Alicia and to Benigno grows in Marco's moral conscience. What he knows and may or may not share with Alicia in any future intimacy between them makes Marco the custodian of Benigno's posthumous fate in what Alicia may or may never learn about the role that her male nurse played in talking to her and violating her coma. Marco owes Benigno in death the news he withheld from him in life: that Alicia woke up from her coma. He owes his friend the news that would have broken the suicide's will in him at that moment and perhaps for good. He also owes Alicia the equivalent of a suicide letter unwritten, disavowed, inalienable from what he might feel he owes Benigno. A letter with the disclosure that he might judge only Benigno could make to Alicia. Something said, written, or taped, at the earnest zero degree where the first person addresses the extra-grammatical person committed to suicide through a speech act.

Such saturation in the debt owed to the gift of death—so terribly and perhaps unmindfully acknowledged in the news of one's killing brought to oneself and to others—is what glues these actors together (Alicia-Benigno-Marcos) in what they most certainly have not in common with the automatism all-too-often at work in self-inflicted dying solo.

chapter ten

Home Alone

I am God in nature; I am a weed by the wall.
RALPH WALDO EMERSON

The *Vertigo* catastrophe point in the life of Guillermo Cabrera Infante comes in 1972 when the drawn-out writing of the screenplay for Malcolm Lowry's *Under the Volcano* (1947) led to his collapse into a catatonic state. Besides any current or kinder clinical name, it was paranoia that copied in the screenwriter's personal life the British Consul's trip into Mexico's realm of the dead on November 1, 1939: "'I ended up a classic vegetable. I had no visible reactions, neither ate nor relieved myself or apparently heard anything said to me" (*GCI* 118).[1] Overloaded with high-literature indicators and religious symbols, Lowry's *Día de los Muertos* Mexican Inferno appears as the tragic black-hole version of core elements in *Vertigo* and its French *D'entre les morts* source. (As if Carlotta Valdez's Mexican ancestry has dragged into Hell her villainy as the Madeleine betrayer of France to the Nazis in Boileau and Narcejac's plot.) The emotional psychic wreckage caused by the screenplay fiasco represents a late hit suffered by Cabrera Infante at the hands of the ponderous European modernism so strenuously aped in Lowry's drunken visionary novel—and parodied in Infante's best delirious moods in prose.

Betraying modernism in earnest or in parody is one thing, but betraying the country with whose homeland-allegorical-woman one is linked is quite another. For nothing tops the excesses of romantic love worse than allowing it to surpass itself in the love of Nation as the ultimate She.

JUPITER'S JULIETTE AND ROMEO'S CASTRO

Enter Helena in tow of Julieta as harbingers and coupled contraries of Juanita de Córdoba, the murdered heroic widow of a Cuban revolutionary. Her death in *Topaz* (a code name used by a rogue cell of the French intelligence in dealing with Soviet defectors during the Cold War) is seen, as choreographed for the camera, with Juanita (Karin Dor) clinched tight, as if ready to dance, by her Fidel Castro–clone killer, Rico Parra (John Vernon). The Helena figure dates back to 1950, the year in which the author

entered the National School of Journalism and held a brief job as pollster for a presidential candidate and worked as translator and watchman.
She comes into view seen in distortion through Hitchcock's *Rear Window*
(1954)—as if foreshadowed in pure fictional time—in the chapter "The
Near-Sighted Voyeur's Vision" written in the 1970s for inclusion in *La Habana Para un Infante Difunto*.[2]

In *Rear Window*, photographer L. B. Jeffries is confined to a wheelchair
and forced into sexual abstinence by one and eventually two waist-to-toe
plaster casts. The comic predicament of Jeff's hold-off celibacy on the eve
—or at the brink—of marrying Lisa Freemont turns perverse in Helena's
apparent incest bondage to her father spied through binoculars by Infante.
She is a blonde from a nearby building—a "radiant beauty" with a "yellow mane"—likened to Helen of Troy and her ghost replica: "Many nights
I awaited the apparition of Helen, my future phantom" (412/216). Infante
dismisses the neighbors' legends about Helena's father's mad love for his
daughter. But, when finally seen naked in the middle of the night, she is
caught busily adjusting the leather straps on a large chastity belt, an "archaic contraption" she wears only after turning off the bedroom lights long
enough to cause Infante to doze off. What at first resembles an "ortho-
pedic contraption" or "evil machine" does not turn into "the chastity belt
designed by Goya" until he dreams of Helena, "covered with an atro-
cious armor that went from her white chin to her hairy vulva" (415/217),
and wakes up to the recognition that she is wearing the dream belt. (A
soft pencil drawing by Goya on a subject already depicted in *Los Caprichos*
shows a grotesque man aiming two skeleton keys at a huge padlock over
an armor-like neck-to-knees leather girdle worn over the groin by a taller
and distraught woman.)[3] Sickened by voyeur sights and Goya nightmares
he dares not fully explain to himself, Infante allows his father to "inherit"
the field glasses, to which he becomes attached: "My father, on the other
hand, armed with my former spyglasses, locked away on the balcony, late
at night, secretly scrutinized the buildings across the avenue" (231/441).
(A spot from which he might have caught sight of his son Infante, cruising
at night on the avenue, reduced to sexual indigence after sublime Julieta
dumps him.)

For Infante is left hung to dry by the adult woman with whom he enjoys his "first success" in adultery. She is the former *Most Beautiful Girl in
the World* and the truest Helen figure in being always unfaithful to men
while remaining ever so faithful, in the choir of her howls, to the attendant

phantoms summoned by lovers with their coupling noises. Julieta stands in lovemaking between her male lover's captive pleasure in her heat and the bliss she performs on herself as if given to her by Zeus-Jupiter. As if she were tracing sound shapes on musty walls, Julieta enjoys making love while listening to Debussy's *La Mer* on a record player she asks Infante to truck into her marriage bedroom. She fills the airwaves of a famous sex house *posada* with her *periphonous* howls of joy and overload of echoing fantasies. (Like De Quincey, surfing waves of sound at the Italian opera on opium, Jupiter's Juliette's Julieta translates into above-sense sublime noises the stereophonic glossolalia of sacred wantonness.) When patrons complain, Julieta stops: "dejó de perifonear [interrupted her broadcast]" (387/201). She wants loudly and lewdly "to establish her presence in the *posada*" (386/201). (After all, *posar*—to "alight" or to "pause"—issues from the Greek for "I detain," "bring to a halt.")

The verb *perifonear* dates back to the days of wireless radio transmissions of music and speeches and the sound-transport of images to listeners. In the absence of a concordance of Cabrera Infante's work, it seems for now probable that the only other *perifonear* lexical instance besides Julieta's love-making *posada* broadcast belongs to Fidel Castro's verbal virtuosity as recalled by the author in *Mea Cuba*:

> I remember having seen him [Castro] one day in the waiting room of a television studio about to go on the air [*a punto de perifonear*]. Meanwhile, he killed time joking, strolling around calmly as he slowly smoked his habitual Havana, talking about cows and green pasturage and milk production, smiling satisfied: the agreeable agronomist. But no sooner had they introduced him to the well-lit studio and the camera had focused on him, than he came on the air transformed into a true Zeus thundering terrible traumas against an invisible opposition. He was not the elder Marx but the young Jupiter. (MC 430/440)[4]

Perifonía transmits—as loudly and as far as sound waves may wish to carry it—a message self-addressed by double-gendered Narcissus to the world near whose oracular navel his or her singular power dwells. For Julieta's *perifonía* lies just off from Paradise ever since the days of the *primal horde*, those terrible golden days where early youth finds itself over again in the lost sibling it used to be and was severed from before the time Oedipus turned tyrannous. (Before Oedipus first graduated to Zeus and Zeus to Jupiter, Juliette already sang the Sound of Music. This uncanny lesson in the self-delusions of power regained and power lost is owed to Juliette's Sybil knowledge of her pleasure as Julieta.)

Julieta's transcendentalist agenda in howling sex alters Emerson's borderline kitsch effusion ("I am God in nature; I am a weed by the wall") into an ornament of self-rapture: *I'm a weed in nature; I am Goddess by the wall.* Throughout the section dedicated to her, Julieta's textual presence is wall-papered with *dora* and *doro* golden sound clusters. Though not a natural blonde, her golden-girl dazzle creates a soundtrack of gold-related syllables, a litter-and-glitter dust trail. Like precipitates of nervous tics echoing in the Spanish of *La Habana Para un Infante Difunto*, these clusters come in bunches, such as in Julieta's passionate style of reading: "pasión arrebeta*dora*"/"dedos *dora*dos" (346); in the rocker where fellatio is performed on Infante: "la mece*dora*" (349); in his fly being opened: "puerta pu*doro*sa"; and in her mouth-and-head rhythm: "or*de*nado . . . mono*corde*" (350). Such particles work like symptoms of comic autism, of self-pointing and self-caressing in Julieta's automaton aura.

Her sublime kitsch and Helen-allure are related to the vulgarities of pollster politics and prison inmates population. During his job as "surveyero" or canvasser for a political candidate, Infante tells a fellow worker about Julieta's sex antics. In a passage added to *Infantes's Inferno* about a supposed honeymoon letter sent by her to him from the Isle of Pines, she tells the story of her visit to the Presidio Modelo penitentiary, modeled after Bentham's panoptic jail. Julieta went there in the middle of her honeymoon to meet with René Hidalgo, body-hacker *descuartizador* of his wife, the six newspaper-packaged parts of whose remains he scattered throughout Havana. (Apparently he is the same fellow "policeman lover" who in Hemingway's *Islands in the Stream* enters Thomas Hudson's mind as his auto crosses over the bridge near Finca Vigía beneath which the trunk of the victim was found and was first thought to belong to a North American tourist.)[5] But, spoiling whatever expectations she brought to the jail rendezvous, Julieta found in Hidalgo "an incurably mediocre man"; her thrill, as imagined by Infante, came instead while walking to and from the waiting room to face the man under the glare of some twelve thousand gawking murder inmates: like Argus, "watching that insult of a girl go by" (the girl bride on furlough who does not need to say in her letter that "she was wet all the way" [II 187]). In the retro style of Gradiva, like a passing angel, Julieta walks through the prison choral gaze as a 1970s afterimage of the surrealist celebrity-fetish identified in some French psychiatric circles during the 1930s as *erotomania*. During its Paris renascence in the 1960s, eroto-mania transposed the existence of the maternal phallus in male fetishism into a woman's "belief that she is the object of an omnipresent gaze which confers upon her the status of the desired one." (In his critical review of the term, David Macey situates the related *eroto-* and *nympho-* manias in the surrealist cult of convulsive beauty and female ecstasy whose afterlife in Lacan's doctrines leads to the notion of *jouissance*.)[6]

Julieta's sources for architectural *jouissance* and orgasmic *coloratura* place her golden aura in the shadows that surround the bedroom politics of politics. This has less to do with her apparent affair with Max Maduro (a *max-gold-ripe* "old-time Communist" boss) than with her gilded crust as a hidden treasure and would-be celebrity capable of scandalous intimacies. As much in sham as in shame, Julieta is where lovemaking lies all at once mocked and worshiped as it might in the actions of an automaton. Her nexus with automaton actions (*Weiderholungszwang* or *automatisme de répéti-tion*) triggers acts of surreal mimicry among her love objects. Her cuckold husband becomes a virtual marionette, while forsaken Infante is left to prowl the Avenue of the Presidents in the rain inside the plastic cage of a green transparent coat in which his mobile masturbations roam sheltered as he looks for a corresponding female sex vagabond. Communist blas-phemy is achieved as the sex automaton sees itself like Mornard-Jacson at midnight, "in search of a transvestite Trotsky to penetrate with [his] fever-ish icepick" (419/219).

CAIN'S LOT IN NOTHING

Ever since Gogol's famous story, the overcoat has enjoyed a life of its own in literary fetish animation. Traces of the accursed garment effect are felt as readers of Isaac Deutscher's *The Prophet Outcast* observe Leon Trotsky through the eyes of his wife, Natalya, as he feeds rabbits in the yard of his embattled Coyoacán outcast home in Mexico City. Natalya watches Leon next to the stranger named "Jacson" who lately visits them all too often and who on this mid-August occasion has brought the draft of an article for Leon to read. As she greets him, Jacson hugs "his over-coat to his body convulsively," and when asked why he is wearing it on such a sunny day, he says that it might rain (*POu* 503). Trotsky's head is struck as he reads Jacson's typescript: "'I had put my raincoat . . . on a piece of furniture . . . took out the ice-ax, and, closing my eyes, brought it down on his head with all my strength'" (504). Fallen and bleeding, Leon confessed to Natalya that the thought " 'this man could kill me' " had flashed across his mind just before the attack. (One wonders if it should be possible to slip or to stray across the line dividing murder victim from suicide in being so unshielded to contingency while being the prime target of Stalin's secret policy.) Are Trotsky's unguarded virtues, nobility, and intellectual absentmindedness, as pictured by Deutscher, suicidal tokens next to Mornard-Jacson's murderous-automaton filial mimicry at the service of Stalin's secret police? Is the Prophet's death (in Deutscher's tragic three-volume version of him as Armed-Unarmed-Outcast) the elongation, as if by anamorphosis, of Trotsky's lifelong suicidal project? And, if so, is Trotsky —as parody's main victim in Infante's fiction—the monstered proof itself of the incurable practice of parody as the joke-on-you-is-also-on-me rehearsal companion or bride of suicide?

Who knows? If only Leon (besides reading Gogol, as it boggles the mind to think he had not) had also dreamed The Overcoat, in Coyoacán itself. Then, like a well-groomed automaton of Dreamland, he would have perhaps cured himself of suicidal casualness and escaped Freud's suspicion of being—in the exercise of such casualness—a conspirator in his own annihilation. Trotsky would have scripted into his literary and political genes the story of how the automaton bureaucrat with the stuttering punning name "Akaky Akakievich" was killed by his brand-new, fetish-tailored overcoat turned into a target for theft. A different Trotsky (automaton of his ordinary claim to life and safety) might have then faced Jacson on that warm August afternoon in Coyoacán braced in wintry alertness. But such tender ironies are no match for the author of a serial ensemble of lampoon parodies on Trotsky's assassination in Tres Tristes Tigres, where obstinate parody makes the crime massively indebted to arcane ruminations in the voice of several Cuban writers. As a result, the knockabout rendition of the murder and its copious meanings murders yet again and repeatedly by grotesque comic means. At least once, in Lezama Lima's "I feel like one possessed who has just been penetrated bodily by a soft assegai" (TTT 229/241), corporeal consent impersonates suicidal surrender in the mocked victim's murdered (and buggered) and (all-willing) character.

Such meddling with unkind intent into someone else's suicide death wishes belongs to the armchair forensic art of character assassination, which is not all that consumes the passions of political revenge unleashed in "Between History and Nothingness: Notes on an Ideology of Suicide"— by now Mea Cuba's signature essay.[7] Insofar as the essay endeavors to certify the inevitable self-destruction of Communism as ruinously embodied in Communist lives, it builds upon the satirical celebrations and kaleidoscopic parodies of Trotsky's murder in *Tres Tristes Tigres*. The essay identifies in suicide not so much "an undefinable problem" as "an absolute ideology" at work in "the historical domain" (MC 188/166). (Which sounds like a denunciation-by-label of global Communism itself.) What could be labeled a worldwide suicidal *Trotskyistlichkeit* produces a brood of "fanatics of permanent revolution, the sons of Trotsky," for whom only one choice, a false one, is left standing: the choice between "choosing eternal history or nothingness" (MC 187/166). The manifesto essay argues that suicide's "absolute ideology" (grown on Cuba's soil) has grafted itself into the cell tissue of Trotsky's world revolution brainchild.

With serial-suicide-by-parody Trotsky on the masthead, eternally Infant Cain, son of the literature of power, cynical and sublime descendant of Europe's revolutionary Romanticism, soul brother of Thomas De Quincey, wants to commit the suicidal will to the power of actual suicide. Cain enforces suicide upon the suicidal. But, what if Trotsky were to tyranny what Cain is to murder? What if Leon's resistance to Stalin were like Cain's resistance to God—staged at the risk of political suicide? In scripture, Cain resists or dissembles or plain lies in answering God's voiceover question (Genesis 4.5–9) "Where is Abel your brother?" with "I do not know; am I my brother's keeper?" Might Cain mean: Are things rigged? Is something going on unbeknownst to THOU—to YOU? (After all, this is not Robert De Niro at the mirror asking Travis Bickle and himself "Are you talkin' to me?") Can the Absolute Questioner's tyrannous role ever be raised as an issue by Cain? Is such Total Power adroitly—and slyly—to be taken for granted by the brother with the blind courage to kill his God-favored brother? Is Cain's the first scripted case of Sartre's bad faith (*mauvaise foi*)? According to which, bad faith is not just hiding something from someone else (as when lying) but doing it to oneself (thus sparing oneself instead of wasting or doing oneself in). By which means, adds Peter Sloterdijk, "the duality of deceiver and deceived does not exist," and "the God of Cain would accordingly appear as the partner of a self-consciousness that can still deceive itself." What kind of God is it, asks Sloterdijk, "who treats people unequally and at the very least provokes them to crime, but then, with pretended innocence, asks questions about what has happened?"[8] The chief irony at work in "the first cynicism of the religious type" lies in God's becoming "pensive" as he grants Cain an injunction to last as long as it might take to reach the Day of Judgment and marks or tattoos him against blood revenge: "And the Lord put a mark on Cain, lest any who came upon him should kill him" (4.15). Power of such archaic sort stops short of dialogue and runs through all checkpoints. Power acting quicker than words, *non-dialogical* and brute, a carnival of One at one's own expense. At such a cynical angle, the difference between the chance to interact with God-the-Questioner and not to have the chance does not hold. To insist upon or to question such difference on behalf of genuine interaction would seem to mark for banishment or elimination the person who dares question back (as if by such subaltern questioning God had been turned political). The blame for politics lies with Man; that is why there is a God.[9]

King Claudius in *Hamlet* is one who cannot separate the primacy of politics from family ties. It is the king who mentions the "first corse" (1.2.105), implying (without wanting to) the corpse he made out of his brother's living body as the victim napped. Claudius is not one well fit to separate statecraft killing from hatred hatched inside family closets. A similar play between bodies familiar to each other's routines and their ultimate means against each other's lives comes up at the graveyard. Hamlet's punning banter with the grave-digger works by collapsing the murder weapon into the murderer's own bones—and creating a metonym kinship of sorts between killing tool and the killer's inner tooling. Hamlet says: "The skull had a tongue in it, and could sing once. How the knave jowls it to th' ground, as if 'twere Cain's jawbone, that did the first murder. This might be the pate of a politician which this ass now o'er-offices, one that would circumvent God, might it not?" (5.1.74–78). If, as Harold Jenkins points out, the bone in question should be "the ass's and not Cain's own," justice would still prevail, as he sees it: in "Cain's being in his turn jowled by an *ass*" (Cain thus *dashed* or *jawboned* by the clown—as the skull is upon the ground by the same ass person—as if by the clowning grace of punning).[10]

The time has come to turn to the *Cuba-Caín* nexus traced by suicide's uncanny and false zero-sum game as reviewed in the essay. *Cuba* is (just as *nada*) a four-letter word like *Caín*. In Hebrew, Cain is caught in wordplay as Eve declares: " 'I have added a life with the help of Yahweh' " (Gen. 4.1). Sound symbols link qayin as qny[ty] and qanah ("to acquire" or "to increase" or "create")—as if English *Cain* punned with *gain(ed)*. In the same context, Abel (in Hebrew assonance as *hevel*) means "puff," "vanity" or "vapour," "emptiness," "wraith." [11] It thus seems that *Cain* is to *gain* and *increase* what *Abel* is to *nothing* (provided *nothing* is less than *nothingness*). For, given that abstract nothingness may deflate itself to less than *nada*, plain˙ *nada* (as nothing but nothing or *nada más que nada*) could just as well spook Cain (as Abel's *puff* apparently does in Genesis). The murdered brother's ghost's plain-nothing *nada* puff (whether he was in fact murdered or never existed) *out-nothings* the swelled-up macho *la nada*–driven nothingness of Cain.

Accordingly, in the essay on suicide's modified title, "Between History and Nothing," *nada* would carry more of nothing than does "Nothingness" (there being nothing more annihilating in power than Lear's (or Cordelia's) "Nothing"—or Polixenes' jealous "nothings" squeezed by obsession in *The Winter's Tale*:

> . . . is this nothing?
> Why then all the world and all that's in't is nothing,
> The covering sky is nothing, Bohemia is nothing,
> My wife is nothing, nor nothing have these nothings,
> If this be nothing. (1.2.292–96)

Polixenes' obsessive harping on *nada* increases nothing into a vast something that in turn reduces him to nothing. His mushroom-size puff of royal jealousy puts Polixenes ("many-times-an-alien") in line with Cain's jealous inaugural blood feud.

The essay title's "Mea Cuba" puns *Mea Culpa* into *Cuba is my fault—Cuba is a fault of mine—I am at fault—my fault is mine as long as Cuba too is mine as faulted—in Me? CulpaCuba* or *CubaCulpa* joined, run together after breaking the hyphen's hymen *nada* that splits them like nothing. Caín's lot in nothing lies in his laying with Cuba in the incest bed of their joint guilt. There is no soil unsoiled by guilt. No Cuba holds without Caín's hold on Cuba.

TO DIE IN CUBA

In *Topaz* (1969) a Soviet defector's tip leads the Americans to Rico Parra, a revolutionary commander with the Cuban delegation visiting New York in October 1962, whose secretary, Uribe, is to be bribed in the attempt to photograph documents of a secret trade pact between Cuba and the Soviets. The French spy diplomat Andre Devereaux (Frederick Stafford), who is well connected with Cuba's underground, agrees to work for the Americans and soon enough obtains photos of the documents from a contact who enters the Theresa Hotel in Harlem where Parra and his gang of *rebeldes* are holed up.

Cuban revolutionary faces are first seen in drawings sketched by Devereaux's son-in-law, with Che Guevara's face at the center smoking a victory cigar (Guevara addressed the United Nations General Assembly not in 1962 but in December 1964) (Anderson 1997, 626–29). Call girls are shown escorted by Cubans on the floor *corridor* as they stare in passing at Rico Parra. He has that Castro look and wears the *Rhomb & Star* shoulder insignia as only Fidel could. Rico spits on the floor and leaves a half-eaten burger on top of a valued document. (Viewers have been warned by Devereaux's bubbly daughter that "the Cubans are wild.") Hernández, Parra's chief of security, evokes Che in unkind caricature, but his redhead pinkish looks supposedly translate those of guerrilla exporter and master spy Manuel Piñero Posada, a.k.a. Barbarroja, enlarged to thug dimensions and wearing lightly-rubbed reddish makeup and a wig. (The essay on suicide's English version notes the presence of Barbarroja and credits him with the banning of *Topaz* from Cuba.)

Devereaux flies to the island on October 22, 1962, to bring back photos of Soviet installations and to see Juanita de Córdoba, with whom he has been having an affair during visits there, "four or five times a year." (Photos of middle-range ballistic missile components scattered about a field at San Cristóbal in western Cuba had been taken by U-2 reconnaissance on October 14 and shown to Secretary of Defense Robert S. McNamara the following day [Blight, Allyn, and Welch 1993, 467].) A lethal dance between romance and politics ensues as Juanita is reunited in bed with Andre, the same bed where she honors her affair with Parra (her "landlord"). Rico tells Andre that Juanita is "a widow of a hero of the Revolution," that "she is loved and honored in this country." The Cuban heroine is thus carrying on with Andre (passionately) and Rico (dutifully) under the cinematic roof of a California mansion, which would have been, one presumes, heavily bugged in Cuba, though not in this film.

The film's romance banality allows the political character of each man's private use of Juanita to show, even while implying Parra's unawareness of what he would regard as her infidelity to him and to Cuba (or to Herself, since Juanita cannot but stand for the *Patria*'s female embodiment). In order to situate the film politically, one must take into account Rico's unknowing knowledge or disavowal of Juanita's love affair with Andre. *Topaz* accidentally situates in bedroom politics its hardest and most accurate look at the-end-justifies-the-means expediency in politically dealing with persons. But the film ignores the overriding likelihood of Parra's electronic knowledge of Juanita's romance with Andre and compounds the issue by suggesting Rico's unawareness of her sexual double-dealing. His bedroom surveillance is replaced instead by the scene in which, in prelude to lovemaking, Andre explains to Juanita the photographic spying gadgetry he has brought for her, and pauses to give her "a non-electronic present," a kiss, not quite French, before going on to show her how the Geiger counter works by placing it on the night table next to the alarm clock. The film's moral thinness allows the certainty of Rico's surveillance to come into view, even as it must avoid recognizing its probability on two counts: electronic ears would end the Cuban-French romance just as they would allow for the full deployment of Machiavellian cynicism on Parra's part. (That Rico would allow romance-under-surveillance to go on under his own roof in order to entrap Juanita and her underground network and compromise the Paris-Moscow Topaz conduit.)

The film's one memorable sequence begins with a closeup of Mrs. Mendoza's mouth after being tortured as she whispers into Parra's ear ("'Juaaniiitaaa de Coordobaaaa'"). This is followed by Rico's face staring in shock at the camera and then by a shot of his hands on both knees as he slowly goes upright and turns into focus from a midrange shot of his back to one of his face. But Muñoz, the army torturer, already knows of Juanita's involvement with the Mendoza couple as spies for the French and the Americans. Yet, Muñoz *orders* his superior, Parra, to learn by himself from Mrs. Mendoza who her underground leader is. Rico's stunned reaction comes from the double realization that he is a cuckold in both politics and sex and that his own torturer has gotten to the double-truth ahead of him. Parra then denies the torturer Muñoz any further knowledge of Juanita by shooting her while holding her tight as he utters in brooding tones: "the things that will be done to your body. . . . this body . . . [*gun shot*]." (In visual-opera style, Juanita's body swoons to the floor from an overhead shot as her gown spreads out "like a flower" pulled "by five strands of thread held by five men off camera.")[12] Rico Parra leaves the floor where his victim lies, a beaten man, dazed, but not before Muñoz answers Andre's call from the airport and tells him matter-of-fact that Juanita has been shot dead by Parra (this confirms Muñoz's role in tying together both male lovers in their ruinous joint knowledge of Juanita).

The sequence leading to Rico Parra's exit from *Topaz* could spell *castration* if such prime form of unmanning were to render him *castrated* as singularly *Castroed*. John Vernon's strong physical presence and dense voice intensify their combined effect in the last two scenes of his undoing. His left ear shot in closeup, his hands-on knees, his eyes with the automaton murder look, his death-warrant words to Juanita on her double betrayal ("to fool me, to work against me"), and her response justifying her own suicidal behavior against him: "because you made my country a prison." Vernon played the off-screen voice of Big Brother in a 1956 version of Orwell's 1984, but in *Topaz* he takes part in something quite different: the impersonation of tyrannous intimacy and the domestication of political murder. (In Cuban terms, Rico kills Juanita *Guantanamera* style: as if for the unseen audience.) Otherwise, Parra seems doomed and primed for suicide. Muñoz the torturer has got the beat on him. He is witness to Parra's murder of his lover, a revolutionary heroine widow and lover of a French double-spy working for the CIA. Rico's impersonation of Castro in sheer visual terms breaks up at the point where his *not* being Fidel should destroy him in the aftermath of his mishandling of Juanita's *ménage-à-trois* affair with himself linked to Devereaux's CIA adulterous romance.

On the fictional day in which Andre Devereaux flies to Cuba (October 22, 1962), Fidel Castro decreed a state of general mobilization and war alert throughout the island and JFK addressed his nation (at 7 P.M. EST) to announce the presence of nuclear missile sites there (Blight, Allyn, and Welch 1993, 467). The following day (in *Topaz* but not in history) a rally is held at the Plaza de la Revolución in Havana attended by Devereaux, who stands close enough to the speakers' platform to be spotted by Hernández the redhead, who remembers bumping into him three days before in front of the Theresa Hotel in Harlem while chasing the man who had photographed secret documents carried by Parra. Hernández informs Rico, who appears with Juanita in one of the shots edited into the newsreel footage of a mass rally in which Fidel is shown as he waves to the crowd next to President Dorticós and his wife. (If the brief shot of Che Guevara and Raul Castro comes from the same rally, it could not have been filmed later than 1964, the year in which Che left Cuba, never again to be seen in public while in the country during two short return visits, in mid-March 1965 and October 1966 [Anderson 1997, 626–29].) But the essay on suicide holds a different focal view of the rally's occurrence in film time during the October 1962 missile crisis.

In the essayist's view, someone named Javier de Varona can be seen in the edited newsreel shots. It is imagined that "Alfred Hitchcock makes his [de Varona's] shadow coincide for some historical seconds with an excessive and gesticulating Fidel Castro on the people's platform" (MC 175/154).

Yet Castro is only shown waving at the crowd and not speaking, just touching the mikes in pre-speech readiness. It is next fathomed by the essayist that a "sinister irony" manifests itself in having a "spirited" Javier de Varona and a "garrulous" Fidel Castro coincide in film space on the occasion when the challenge to go forth with a ten-million-tons sugar harvest is proclaimed by the "Maximum Leader" (MC 175/154). Most readers would share Hitchcock's unawareness of who is (or was) Javier de Varona and where he might appear in the edited newsreel. Perhaps he is the young man in front of whom Castro stops and blocks from view as he waves to the crowd. But it seems more likely that one is contemplating the impromptu mise-en-scène in which someone described in the essay as a direct suicide victim of Castro's personal tyranny is placed next to him for maximum effect.

Among the suicide cases discussed in the essay's hit-list of crumbled political lives, Javier de Varona's is the one that best combines self-abjection with the inability to escape murder by someone other than oneself. The essayist plays the role of post-suicide executioner, as if killing oneself were the incitement to being posthumously destroyed and surveyed in tabloid-style suicide gossip. In what seems hard to take if not as a poisoned-pen portrait, de Varona is depicted as a wealthy punk, a book thief, a prankster who would phone the poet Lezama Lima in the middle of the night to call him "old bugger," and who joined the Revolution's "extreme left" and became a State Security informer. (Knowledge of any such phone calls could come from Cabrera Infante's own share in the homophobic hazing of the poet Lezama Lima during the early years of the Revolution.) The document that is claimed brought about de Varona's downfall consisted of a lengthy analysis in which what everyone else already believed was exposed: that the ten-million-tons harvest fiasco was all Castro's fault.

As a sideline centerpiece of the essay's case-by-case demonstration, Javier de Varona's suicide is made to represent the writer's authorship shadow at its darkest. Authorship proves uselessly analytical and absurd in exposing what everyone already knows: "He arrived at the conclusion, already known by everyone without any analysis" (174/153). Yet, what is written proves usefully introspective—and lethal—to the writer. It exposes his own complicity in the failure being exposed: "What he wrote was his political testament. Naïve, as always, he thought that someone would publish it one day" (174/153). Without citing sources, it is said that "they [State Security] read the document, demented to them, and advised the widow to declare, for the good of all, that her husband had committed suicide because he knew that he was impotent. They did not say politically impotent" (*MC* 154/175). The defunct text is left untouched, except by his sudden widow, who reads and summons the suicide's surrogate executioners. This is how the doomed writer will rest: unread, embalmed, shelved. State Security will write the epitaph to authorship denying death any politics except in sex. The epitaph would read the same way in which the gist of de Varona's case reads in the essay's heartless summation. Such as: *a first-degree sexual impotent has died here his own filthy unpolitical death and left behind a written account soon to be shelved forever.* To which the essayist appends his own parody tombstone graffiti from the *Communist Manifesto*: "Communists of Cuba, commit suicide. You have nothing to lose but your life" (*MC* 175/167). (Although murder—officially accounted as suicide—has been mentioned in Javier de Varona's death, it seems well established that he took his own life.)

A Cuban journalist has recently credited de Varona himself with "the original idea" on suicide, similar but "not exactly the same" as the one illustrated in Cabrera Infante's essay: "I heard [the idea] argued (but not exactly as such) in Havana during the 1960s by a man of talent who in fact did not write much, Javier de Varona."[13] The essay's portrait of suicide as the result of the victim's sense of impotence and defeat (in consequence of revolutionary failure) is met by Rodríguez Rivera's silence on motives: "Indeed, Javier killed himself in 1970 [*en efecto, Javier se suicidó en 1970*]." Unless no motive needs mention when it comes to the one to whose credit goes the view of suicide in control of the essay: "He is mentioned [by Cabrera Infante] as a man of humor and a suicide [. . .] but not as a fundamental contributor to the ideas managed in his essay [*pero no como contribuyente fundamental a las ideas que su ensayo maneja*]." In the end, regardless of which desperate motives may have informed de Varona's death, or his own originality in rephrasing the sublime commonplaces of suicide, Cabrera Infante's essay remains invested in further victimizing the victim. It rightly denounces Police coercion and secrecy. Yet, the State's punishment in making de Varona's suicide abject, in sexual rather than political terms, is not so much deplored as it is exploited.

The essay exerts its own revenge. It finds the victim's guilt to be well deserved. Javier de Varona's self-annihilation shows in minimal local fashion the abject grandeur of Leon Trotsky's vast guilt, the reiterative homage-by-parody of whose death-by-murder turns (in *Tres Tristes Tigres*) into the burlesque demand for his (repeated) suicide by various serial hands.

THE AUTOMATON ALWAYS DIES LAST

The eye is the first circle; the horizon which it forms is the
second; and throughout nature this primary figure is repeated
without end.

Ralph Waldo Emerson

Prince of immediacy, he is even a sort of fetish, adored as such
by the workers of the earth.

Marcel Detienne, *Dionysus at Large*

Whether broken or intact, the heart knows of ligatures, and even though science has disowned the old notion that the end of its pulse signals the end of all the rest it thumped into animation, it is in the heart's silence where matters rest. Although neither a foe nor a friend of thought, the heart aids knowledge by resisting thought in such vaporous conceptions of human freedom as Emerson's in "Circles," where to the tendency of "each inert thought" ("as for instance, an empire, rules on an art, a local usage, a religious rite") to "heap itself on that ridge, and to solidify and hem in the life," the soul opposes its own conspiracy with the heart, which "refuses to be imprisoned," and "in its first and narrowest pulses, it already tends outward with a vast force, and to immense and innumerable expansions" (R. Emerson 1965, 303–4). It is just such a vast transpersonal and cordial force that is not taken into account by King Pentheus when, acting as a tyrant more than a ruler, he places the storm-hearted Maenads in shackles, until the god Bromios Dionysus, whom they worship, brings powers of instant self-release into the tools of ligation that bound them:

> As for those women you clapped in chains
> and sent to the dungeon, they're gone, clean away,
> went skipping off to the fields crying on their god
> Bromius. The chains on their legs snapped apart
> by themselves [*automata*]. Untouched by any human hand,
> the doors swung wide, opening to their own accord. (Euripides 1955,
>   lines 444–49)

Whether acting *to their own accord* (as wild women) or in a *sudden motion by itself* (as sheer force), what otherwise rests inanimate manifests automaton features in Dionysian epiphany. Dionysus's epiphany surge most often emanates from the heart's kindred affinity with the *phallos*: "For the phallus, too, moves without orders from the intellect. Its volume increases and diminishes. Made of tendon and cartilage, it can shrink or expand or fill with air" (Detienne 1989a, 61).

A similar though trickier concordance between vital sites occurs in the rhetorical figure of *Hypallage*. Sense organs and limbs are shown misaligning with their accustomed faculties; such as in Bottom's disoriented though sharply witted recollection of a dream where Scripture is copied in burlesque:

> The eye of man has not heard, the ear of man has not seen, man's hand is not able to taste, his tongue to conceive, nor his heart to report, what my dream was.[14]

Here the tongue's alignment with the mind in conceiving thoughts is driven home to the gross asinine phallic means that Bottom possessed in the dream he now strives to recollect once he is back in human shape (the heart's thumping "report" suggests the weapon in the tongue fastened to its phallic metonymic mate). Dealing with *hypallage*, a rhetorical figure akin to metonymy, George Puttenham nicknames its equivalent Latin "*Submutatio*" (which by common consent was known as "underchange") with the appropriately imagistic term *changeling* (for the ill-favored brat left by fairies in the cradle of the chosen child they steal). (As poets may use, he writes, "a wrong construction for a right, and an absurd for a sensible, by manner of exchange.")[15]

Something akin to such a rhetorical nexus in coupled disjointment occurs in physical and syllabic terms to Tristan's health and the untwisting of his birth name. Answering the challenge to win Isolde's hand, Tristan kills a dragon, cuts off its tongue, and puts it inside his armor and shirt, next to the heart, where it festers and fumes and threatens to rob him of his life. As a result of the nearly fatal harboring of the alien organ close to Tristan's heart, the evil Steward who aspires to earn Princess Isolde's hand will fail to show as winning proof the missing dragon tongue found hidden in Tristan's person when he was rescued and nursed with doses of theriac by the two Isoldes (queen and princess) and Brangane. The solution to a mystery lengthened by a fuming tongue bosomed next to a lover's heart clears up the hero's riddle as his twisted name turns back from *Tantris* to *Tristan*. As such, the *Tantris-to-Tristan/tongue-to-heart* chest metonym partakes of *hypallage*: an alien tongue resting out of place and contiguous to the heart it might thus mimic into death.

It was a species of changeling that eager eyes and ears and nostrils sought to detect inside the cabinet chest where Maelzel's automaton was supposed to have replaced human wit and toil with intelligent machine self-motion in a demonstration believed to have helped rehearse in Edgar Allan Poe's mind the writing of his trademark tales of detection.[16] Now, the last twist in the *Mammalian Chest Mystery* opened in chapter 8 is reached with the death of the automaton's last "director" (as Maelzel's man inside the chest is often called). For it turns out that the hidden player (the machine's heart and brain) was stricken with yellow fever in Havana during a trip to Cuba in early 1838. This was the show's second tour to the island. The year before, Maelzel had brought to Havana the exhibition that had already established itself in places like Baltimore, Chicago, and New Orleans. But spectators in Havana kept asking for the *Conflagration of Moscow*, the famous diorama that he had sold and which he now decided to build in painstaking detail and larger scale. After returning to Havana early in November 1837, the complete show ran during Carnival, from Christmas into February, with the *Conflagration* as its centerpiece. Then, troubles set in. Audiences dried out after Ash Wednesday in ritual penance and austerity; Maelzel's secretary, faithful companion, and surrogate son, William Schlumberger, caught yellow fever and died in April. Bereft of company and ruined, Maelzel lingered in Havana until mid-July, when he sailed for New York on loaned money, but, on the eighth day, after confinement in his cabin in chosen isolation, he was found dead and was consigned to the deep off the coast of Charleston (Standage 2002, 184–87).

The story told by Cabrera Infante in "Muerte de un autómata" unfolds in first-person monologue as a man lies dying in bed, in a hotel room, somewhere in the tropics, on an island, which in the closing third-person nonfiction pendant is identified as Cuba. The man misses his Maestro, he feels deserted and betrayed by Maelzel's failure to heed his warnings about the dire consequences of being unmasked by the Baltimore man whose text he memorized (in proper automaton fashion) and whom he finally addresses by the name of "Poe." Thus, "Death of an Automaton" appends itself to Poe's "Maelzel's Chess-Player" in the afterlife of the phrase in which the reader of the hybrid text (part story, part dissertation) is asked by Poe the writer to "imagine some *reversion*" wherein to grasp that "the Chess-player plays precisely as a man would not" (a forensic pirouette aimed at showing the automaton as nothing but an ordinary man, of the sort already spotted in the empirical environs of a Baltimore backstage by two nosy kids).[17]

But this reversion is in turn reversed in the mind of the haunted man dying of fever in Havana. For what he learns from the impact of Poe's text upon the audiences is that, ever since word of it got around, "no one has had any scruples in declaring that the automaton is just pure machine, insinuating already that I was inside without still saying so" (Cabrera Infante 1999, 141). The man who in the end invokes his own name to the writer, "Herr Schlumberger for you, Mr. Poe," is and is not pure machine. The main thrust behind the man's claim to personhood lies in the time-machine quality of the chest shelter and prison he continues to inhabit, even as he lies in bed.

The automaton is a man who cannot escape the artifact womb chest where his personal fate has forever tricked and locked itself into place. But such imprisonment testifies to exorbitance, as the man Schlumberger quotes the man JFK when he says, dying in Havana in April 1838: "Ich bin ein berliner" (Cabrera Infante 1999, 145). The insides of the chest beneath the Turk's chessboard in which the self-proclaimed Berliner operates in Havana in 1838 is a time-travel device inside which a writer (always the writer) impersonates a Trojan-Horse inmate Ulysses who returns to a city of compounded defunctness.

Just as Odysseus hid inside the wooden beast he himself had carpentered and held his breath while entangled inside with his best assault troops, the man automaton lies face up (like a dying sea turtle in the beach sand) as if he were still inside the chest cabinet where his labors became his best-known shelter from aimlessness. The city in 1838 is as eternal as the 1965 Havana of departure. The same city in either case, after never leaving it, unless in the afterlife of living in retro, exiled abroad, wombed, entombed, at home, alone at last in Havana.

part three

Cuban Afterlives

The story is told of an automaton constructed in such a way that it could play a winning game of chess, answering each move of an opponent with a countermove. A puppet in Turkish attire and with a hookah in its mouth sat before a chessboard placed on a large table. A system of mirrors created the illusion that this table was transparent from all sides. Actually, a little hunchback who was an expert chess player sat inside and guided the puppet's hand by means of strings. One can imagine a philosophical counterpart to this device. The puppet called "historical materialism" is to win all the time. It can easily be a match for everyone if it enlists the services of theology, which today, as we know, is wizened and has to keep out of sight.

WALTER BENJAMIN, Theses on the Philosophy of History

chapter eleven

Romantic Penmanship:
Friedrich Nietzsche and José Martí
in Brotherly Fashion

On the morning after this night, however, Zarathustra sprang
up from his bed, girded his loins, and emerged from his cave,
glowing and strong, like a morning sun emerging from behind
dark mountains.

FRIEDRICH NIETZSCHE, *Thus Spoke Zarathustra*

Friedrich Nietzsche was born October 15, 1844, and was nine years older than José Martí, who was born January 28, 1853. However, to say "older" implies a scope of chronological relatedness not at issue here. It is best then to sketch the biographic register, in Nietzsche's case, which will foreground the issue of authorship in his and Martí's lives as they intersect in the pages ahead and foreshadow themes of authorial responsibility as reflected in fictional character—mainly, how to account for character, not in the abstract, narratological sense, but in flash card or look-at-this-picture fashion.

For instance, given the fact that Infante could never emerge, chrysalis style, from inside the cocoon where his most devoted readership should want him kept buried and as defunct as ever, why not show him as pictured in someone else from elsewhere? Two cards are flashed. One shows N and the other M, two men recognized by some but not by too many as Nietzsche and Martí, or depending on when, where, and with whom, as N and someone else, or M and who knows who, etc. Or, who should Infante be, N or M? Or, better yet, who should Leonardo Padura's detective Mario Conde play, M or N? Meaning not to look like, but to be like. To be shown in some fashion. To be exposed, authored, as if besides oneself, madly other than oneself, Romantic other than oneself.

Now, looking at figures 4 and 5, one may ask, Where is M, where is Martí? Is M replaced by S in self-portrait? If so, in the M-and-N mirror play S is now facing us as if from where Schiele once gazed back at Schiele from mirror image to brush (occupying the place where Martí essayed self-

portraiture in one macabre erotic poem examined in this chapter). The place where what may be called the *once-a-spot* allows occupancy to the S of self-portraiture besides Schiele's self-portrait (the S where the signature *this is not me, this is not Schiele* bears witness to *this is me, Egon Schiele as Egon Schiele*). This place or site of occupancy may now be occupied by S mirrored and portrayed, touching himself in self-pointing, expressing perhaps *it's me*, as when me turns into you, or M into N, or S into both: adding itself to all of the above and yet to no one in particular. (It is thus, quite Romantically and ironically, that Infante and Conde occupy the spot of self-portraiture in defunct actuality besides M and N . . . as S.)

LOOK, THE MAN HIMSELF

"Who is my mother? Who are my brothers?" he said,
when he was told that they wished to speak to him.
Oscar Wilde, *The Soul of Man under Socialism*

For the moment, the question of authorship will face the labyrinthine implications in the subtitle to *Ecce Homo*, or in Nietzsche's last

FIGURE 5
Egon Schiele,
Self Portrait with
Head Inclined,
oil on wood
(*akg-images,*
London)

and briefest self-portrait: *How Does One Become What One Is.* In the first sentence after the preface, it is learned that becoming what one is may entail making significant others become, once again, in altered form, what they in some terminal fashion once were—to oneself. Namely, to the current or present author as ever under self-scrutiny. What Nietzsche writes next about his father and mother is meant here to inform the question of how, in their respective cases, he and Martí would relate to periods or occasions during a given year in their lives. Lives held for an instant in the combined spectrum of a single life. Lives-in-a-life in such fashion comparable on historical grounds otherwise mutually irrelevant. (Although the approach is thoroughly Nietzsche's, even a casual reading of Martí's poetry of passion and political prose should recognize the spectacle of lives combined in *la vida combinada*—Martí's maddest prophet's request to his listeners.)[1]

The opening section in *Ecce Homo* entitled "Why Am I So Wise" starts with: "The fortunateness of my existence, its uniqueness perhaps, lies in its fatality: to express it in the form of a riddle, as my father I have already died, as my mother I still live and grow old" (EH 8). The Nietzschean age of joint-life termination falls on the thirty-sixth year of his life: the father's following a fall, the son's upon surviving a near lethal season of migraine attacks in 1879. (Nietzsche had written *Human, All Too Human* in worsening health starting in the fall of 1876.) Ranked first among intended readers, Wagner became well aware that in that book, Schopenhauer's and his own intellectual and emotional tutelage over Nietzsche's authorship were laid to rest. He let it be known that his professed refusal to read it stemmed from compassion: "I have done him the kindness . . . of not reading his book, and my greatest wish and hope is that one day he will thank me for this" (EH xxvi). Wagner was born in 1813, the same year as Nietzsche's father, and in their intense friendship the younger man's religious bonding with *Tristan* and *Meistersinger* and his love for the composer and his wife, Cosima, are believed to have been touched by strong currents of filial affect. With this in mind, but in a spirit very much opposed to recent and perhaps fading trends in the legacies of repressed trauma, one observes the imprint of how, placed in the filial position, Nietzschean authorship becomes fated (and in the end fatal) in being so willed by the *lapsed* son (the father's) and yet still *current* son (the mother's) when grasped from the vantage point of what would become the author's autobiographic last will in *Ecce Homo*.[2]

So personified and signified by others—acting as hosts retroactively gathered into a sort of afterlife—authorship in Nietzsche may next find destination in one of Martí's Simple Verses, written in August 1890, in his thirty-seventh year, while in the Catskill Mountains recovering from exhaustion on doctor's orders. Martí's need to recover from what could well have worsened into a complete nervous breakdown nearly coincides (age-wise) with Nietzsche's far worse case of migraine sickness. However, Martí's ailing health and Catskills convalescence resulted from very different social demands and exertions from those endured by Nietzsche at Bayreuth in August 1876, at age thirty-two. In Nietzsche's case, external and internal stresses would prove inextricable from both his deepening illness and surging authorship, up through the thirty-sixth year of his life in 1879, a season of pain and creation in which later on he would situate, in the form of a riddle, the son's own age crisis-date linked to the father's kindred death.

By comparison, in Martí's case, age-passage through and beyond his thirty-sixth and thirty-seventh years (during 1888 and 1890) was fully occupied by his role as reporter and delegate at the Pan-American and International Monetary Conferences, his teaching and journalism, and his service as consul in New York for some South and Central American countries. At the time, among frequent public interventions, he wrote a letter to the editor of the *New York Evening Post* known to posterity as "A Vindication of Cuba." (It came in response to characterizations made in the press in opposition to Cuba's possible purchase by the United States in which colonized islanders and the enslaved blacks were portrayed as decadent, corrupt, and worthless).[3]

The question of authorship bifurcates in Nietzsche's and Martí's lives beyond the age framed by their respective (and here mutual) passage through the thirty-sixth year (marked in Nietzsche's life by serious illness and exuberant creative output and in Martí's by analogous though less severe health conditions and relentless engagement in highly public tasks). True, a writing of such power and imbued with anti-scriptural yet scriptural force as Nietzsche's defeats comparison. Yet, when grasped in the magnitude of its achievement and lack of readership, the work that encompasses *Human, All Too Human* and *Thus Spoke Zarathustra* allows for dialectical mutualness with Martí's — the wider apart the forking paths traced by their intimate and exposed lives become.[4]

Modern authorship is established and valued mostly as a matter of output and public success. In such terms, what Nietzsche accomplishes from the outburst of *Human, All Too Human* to the multiple compact lives sketched in *Ecce Homo* seems exorbitant in the antithesis it creates between ultimate ethical resonance and immediate public inconsequence. It starts by crossing the afterlife between his father's death and his own (in their joint terminal thirty-sixth year) and ends with the son's collapse at forty-five. At this point, Nietzsche's philosophical achievement crosses paths with (and bifurcates from) Martí's own political fate. But the bifurcation is best charted when held in the mirror of Zarathustra's teaching as the sovereign factor in the making of Nietzsche's own authorship as he intends to bequeath it to humanity envisioned beyond mundane politics.

Since all of Zarathustra's disciples proved failures, including himself in the role of his own nihilist shadow, authorship between Nietzsche and Martí entails the latter's defiant attempt to fail or to flunk Zarathustra. Practicing self-overcoming with and against Martí in the joint assumption of his colluding authorship with Zarathustra seems to pose a dual blas-phemy worth practicing (if anything in order to prove, in Nietzsche's face, what is impossible to prove before Zarathustra's: that the eternal return of the same or the identical is rendered impossible just as it becomes affirmed and activated through the assumption of past afterlives as Nietzsche's own authored life and Martí's). Martí would never create a character as exhaustive of (and faithful to) himself as Nietzsche's Zarathustra is to its author. Not any such character, as faithful and exhaustive of one's ethical and creative authorship, as Cuba's character is to Martí. Cuba, as akin in the worth and weight of its ultimate claim on life, as the construct he called *Our America* (*Thus Spoke Our America*).

Forking away from Zarathustra's Nietzsche, at age thirty-six, Martí achieves his widest hemispheric political task during the two conferences held in Washington and controlled by expansionist commercial interests bent on buying Cuba for the United States without there being an actual sale.[5] He crafts *Versos sencillos* at thirty-seven; leads the founding of the Cuban Revolutionary Party at thirty-nine; writes the *Montecristi Manifesto* in late March 1895; and is killed at forty-two, a few weeks later on May 19. But the forking paths in authorship follow a different course from the one marked by the otherwise trivial meaning in such aging dates. A gap in all appearance unnegotiable between Nietzsche's life and Martí's opens up in reading *How One Becomes What One Is* in *Ecce Homo*. The gap between Nietzsche's posthumous rank as the quintessential world-class thinker from modern to postmodern, in a role he would have despised, and Martí's own niche as the perfect local hero, even when elevated to hemispheric and in some designs universal status as a sublime speaker on behalf of common decencies and political virtues of the most practical sort.

Just as in the mirror of Zarathustra Nietzsche's authorship traverses eternally the reiteration of noontide, the meridian of Martí's rise to the tragic fate of being nationally authored originates, in his own poetic will, in verse 30 of *Versos sencillos*. (The version offered next attempts a stark fidelity to the original while not translating its poetic tones, in contrast with Esther Allen's more faithful and better creation.)

A flash ripped, blood colored,
through the clouded gloom:
by the boat's open gate
blacks came out bunched in hundreds.
The wind's fury broke trees in half;

row after row walked the naked blacks.
Swollen barracks shook in the wind,
a mother went by holding her baby in moans.
Red, as if over desert sands,
the Sun shone on the horizon
and beamed its rays upon a dead black body
hanging from a ceiba tree.
A child saw it,
he trembled out of passion for the groaning masses:
and, as he stood at the corpse's feet,
swore to wipe the crime clean with his life.[6]

Very close to Wordsworth's spots-of-times lyrical climate of sublime arrest at the site of primal violence, these lyrics are believed to respond to the dread and anger of a child of seven upon seeing a hanged slave, and his oath to what, even then, perhaps, and certainly now, at thirty-seven, must answer to the wedded duties to honor imposed by father-country and mother-land: by *país* and *patria*. The poet in Martí wills to himself in authorship terms what he wishes all patriots to regain. What is willed in the poem is a determined afterlife before death. A terminal life as determined in what amounts to a counter-suicide pact. It does, as it aims to turn the resolve to die—even in the certainty of death—into the antithesis of self-slaughter. (Which is far from—but quite close to—the sentimental patriotic way of recognizing in heated words lethal duties.) Authorship matures as the envisioned life comes to terms with the sworn assumption of patriotic duty in childhood. Such renewal of promised duty comes to Martí in the Catskill Mountains, where what he claims as a breakthrough into *simple poetry* dawns upon him and his fellow friends, who by force of immanent and enforced fraternization are tied to the renewed oath to liberate their homeland.

While being radically different in content and tenor from Nietzsche's writings, the vindication and renewal of patriotic duty in Martí's poem translates into mutual authorship with him, with the authored other rehearsed in the duties of a third author (such as the one prompted and promoted here). Such impossibly fraternal bond with the other seems destined in the prosecution of the father's living afterlife willed by Nietzsche next to the blasphemous shade of Pilate's *Ecce Homo* or "Behold the man!" handing-over of Jesus to the rabble. The patriot's nationalist destiny (so loathsome to Nietzsche throughout *Ecce Homo*'s concluding "Why Am I a Destiny") seems unequally destined as the instance itself of father-prosecution. For what is meant by "religion" and "holy" in Nietzsche's following abjuration implies "nation" in heightened status. He writes: "With all that there is nothing in me of a founder of a religion [. . .] I do not want 'believers,' I think I am too malicious to believe in myself, I never speak to masses[. . . .] I have a terrible fear I shall one day be pronounced holy" (EH 96). This is where, as considered next, Werner Hamacher's comments on *pèresécution* or *fathersecution* in Derrida's discussions of spectrality become relevant to the prosecutorial character of patriotic duty in Martí as destined in Nietzsche's afterlife.[7]

The oath-poem to the hanged slave would forfeit the mother-grounds of *patria* it reclaims unless it is prosecuted—followed to its full consequences —by the honor rules and father-duties to Nation. This other lament poem of love betrayed seems duty-bound to patriotic haunting (once again what is offered is a stark transcription of the lyrics' heavier diction):

> A dead friend of mine visits me often. He sits by my side and sings. What he sings hurts: "I once sailed like a bird in the blue skies, one of my wings was black and the other brown. My heart behaved like a madman who saw everything in two colors. Love was of two colors or it wasn't love. There was also a bad woman madder even than the madman and the wounded heart. She sucked all my blood and went away laughing. The mad heart went sailing off in the clouds like a drunken boat who knows where." (Ol 30–31)[8]

The author's implicit wish is to heal the wounded heart (in the chest) and departed (from the chest). He wishes to heal the heart of the returning friend who is also himself. He wants to heal a heart that cannot be not political. In the same voice, patriotic duty disturbs love's wounded intimate effusion already flown away. The author enforces upon himself, in prosecutorial fashion, a friend other than himself. He finds himself in his dead friend as other and besides himself. This other friend besides oneself is he who appears as one's dead and frequent visitor. He is fraternal and never to be severed from the figure of Nation as seen in the better known *Dos patrias* poem—to which it remains in umbilical poetic and patriotic bondage:

> I live in two countries, Cuba and the night, but they're only one. Just as the sun goes down, she shows up holding a flower in her trembling

hand, her mouth shut behind a veil, Cuba in pain, like a widow, goes by me. I have an empty chest where my heart once was. The time to die has come, no words can do what the world does best. I hear the battle cry, I feel trapped inside myself, and yet, plucking at her flower, and looking like a black cloud, Cuba, a widow, goes by. (Ol 85)

A *mise-en-abyme* tableau: one *patria* is in transit through the other, both a cosmos and a person, visible to the man whose own stolen love-heart, somehow, the war duties to which she summons him, in self-absorption, seem related. A hyphen ensues. It links *her-and-Her-before-me-and-Me-in-her* in spectral apparition: all in one bundle and enchained; akin to the *mère-sécution* discussed by Hamacher in reference to Derrida and the *mère sécutrice* figure in Jean Genet.

First, regarding Derrida's Genet, though incorporated in him, Martí's poem of the returning dead friend, fraternal and other in himself-as-oneself, binds together with his poem to the stolen heart and the two motherlands. The two poems fraternize and pass from amity into brotherhood as the requisitions of *patria* are jointly accepted and upheld, more so than ever where she seems wholly displaced, as when, in Genet's case as rephrased by Derrida, "she survives the interring of the one whose death she has foreseen," and by a logic of "obsequence" the "mother *secutrix* denounces, then lets the son die," "whom she transforms because of that into a daughter," and as such "leaves her," and "because of that makes her die and simulates, the divine whore, a suicide."[9] In Martí's joint poems, obsequence to *patria* or to the *mothered* land lies in the chest cavity from where the stolen love heart is taken. The gift is stolen by love's vampire *cupiditas*, but never by motherland's higher and truly sublime hunger. Patriots thus consent to *patria*'s gift-demands. These demands include the one to kidnap love from love lyrics and request its transformation into the love that kills in battle or endures enlisted in the struggle for independence.

Second, the Genet change into a daughter at mother's will, as alien as it seems to Martí's two poems (and ruling out the easy recourse to Freud's sense of *unmanning* by *heart-castration*), may involve the question of mother-tongue retention and loss (mother-tongue compounded by poetic idioms, becoming arch-female in transgendered virility). As seen by Hamacher, the second of the three spectral instances in Derrida embodies the "forgetting of the maternal" (*le oubli du maternel*) under stress from the linguistic demands of future-oriented revolutionary militancy. So, "revolutionary inheritance supposes," in this view, "forgetting the specter," that which lies in "the primitive or mother tongue," which is not "what one inherits but the pre-inheritance on the basis of which one inherits."[10] Yet, there is nothing primitive or spectral about the Spanish tongue inherited in infancy by José Julián Martí y Pérez. Nevertheless, in their various stripes, those in the habit of claiming or invoking the inheritance of Martí's authority should recognize a measure of resistance and embarrassment in the *literariness* of the authorship stamped on his political prose. (*Le oubli du maternel* or *olvido de lo maternal* is carried in the ink of literature's thickened blood.) Martí offered resistance and denseness of rhetorical craft when what mattered most was to send flying political and sentimental messages drawn from it. But rhetorical kinks and literary queerness would prove no match for the automaton-power of public discourse and its transformation of latent irony into sustainable kitsch.

Martí would be kept fresh: ironed-out and brought back from the distractions of figure. Assimilating the dated resistance of forms and discursive obsolescence creates message and soundbite at the expense of a more complex and compromised vision. Translating Martí—even when quoted verbatim—spirits away whatever the aging of prose and poetic diction teaches when properly heard and overheard in its dying echoes. Retranslating—beyond verbatim—what Martí never experienced may start by considering how the chance never came of saying about him what Nietzsche says about Wagner as he recalls the social spectacle of adulation at the first Bayreuth Festival in August 1876. "I hardly recognized Wagner" (he writes twelve years later in *Ecce Homo*); "Wagner had been translated into German! The Wagnerian had become master of Wagner!" (EH 60)— Wagner had become the automaton of his own triumph. The same would happen posthumously and in cycles and waves to Martí since not long after his death in May 1895. In all of its persuasions, the Apostle's nationalist cult remains oblivious to contingency—the exile province of learned fools, whether on home turf or abroad. The cult dismisses as blasphemous the unspeakable chance of Martí going Martí on himself as one may quiz the man's afterlife beyond his actual death to history, quizzed as in this blunt surmise and counterfact: the thought that he might have liquidated his anti-imperialism and sold out Cuba and himself even further to US commercial interests in expansion. Denying the Judas-like denial of the Apostle's bulletproof probity finds best support in the following passage from the *Montecristi Manifesto*, issued less than two months before he is killed: "The war of independence in Cuba, the knot that binds the sheaf of islands where shortly the commerce of the continents must pass through, is a far reaching human event and a timely service that the judicious heroism of the Antilles lends to the stability and just interaction of the American nations and the still unsteady equilibrium of the world" (SW 344). The denial of commitment to such global equilibrium in Martí's quizzed afterlife would copy what Wagner accomplished as he basked and profited in the worship he received from the wealthy and powerful against whom he had fought in the revolutions of 1848. Yet, the same worldliness and lofty speech-writing sublimity and idealism in Martí's words could be cynically read as if they could have, in the future he never lived, supported some NAFTA-type accommodation with the same USA commercial dominance.

Nietzsche saw virtual or figurative suicide in Wagner's surrender to vanity and glory beside affluence. Some among those who insist on Martí's suicidal rush to death in battle at Dos Ríos invent the actions of a Romantic automaton who chooses death above the perils and defeats of aging. They see the Romantic's will-to-death rejection of any future negotiations with the coming of age and the chance it may bring to accrue and to profit, negotiations which could entail the not-so-rare suicide variant of denying one's previous heroic life by embracing a second life of plenty. Behind the sly wisdom of ruling Martí's death a suicide lie resentment and sentimentality against the cult of national consensus (a cult implicitly accused of either one or both of these feelings by the accuser who himself suffers from them in cynical fashion). So: "Martí brought the Republic of Cuba to birth carrying a great cadaver around its neck. A dead weight who was, moreover, a hidden suicide, like a blot on the family: that one of which one must not speak. Poetic or political, the suicide of Martí was momentous. That is, disastrous" (MC 168/147). That is, the Apostle's timing was truly Romantic, except that it went too far. It made all-too-public what other Romantic poets had failed to convey, with such devastating force, to a suitable patriotic public they simply lacked.[11]

Another counterfactual aim would target the following injunction against despotism in Martí's 1884 letter to General Máximo Gómez: "A nation is not founded, General, as a military camp is commanded" (SW 258). The warning concerns the issue of tyranny and autocratic rule, regardless of a leader's political genius to command. For, as Martí writes in the same letter: "The *patria* belongs to no one, and if it does it will belong—and then only in spirit—to he who serves it with the greatest selflessness and intelligence" (259). Although it contradicts the spontaneous or intuitive sense of what superman or overman may mean in Zarathustra's teaching, the issue at the core of Martí's lessons to Cuba's leading General lies in what Nietzsche examines as self-overcoming (*Selbst-Ueberwindung*). Zarathustra reports hearing that "commanding is more difficult than obeying" and that (as implied in Martí's awareness of "selflessness and intelligence") "the Commander bears a burden" which "can easily crush him" (TSZ 137). The Commander faces extreme risk in self-overcoming: "He must become judge and avenger and victim of his own law" (137). It is not that the Commander may become his own worst enemy, but rather his worst best friend. Zarathustra's self-overcoming can be seen as the supreme suicide of the false will-to-power.

One last look at Martí's visiting *amigo muerto* requires a further glance at Nietzsche as the latter writes on friends as ghosts: "If we greatly transform ourselves, those friends of ours who have not been transformed become ghosts of our past: their voice comes across to us like the voice of a shade—as though we were hearing ourself, only younger, more severe, less mature" (HAH 2.242). The time frame present in the poem "Yo tengo un amigo muerto" does not allow for the friend's ghost to come from so far in the distance of early youth. The returning friend's affliction feels ever fresh and quite recent to the poet himself, yet it does answer Nietzsche's sense of great transformation as it applies, to the visited as well as the visiting friend, a strangeness grown and nursed in exile. When Hamacher discusses *frèresécution* or *brothersecution* as the third specter in Derrida, the bad brother syndrome appears as "a kind of ghost of himself [*une sorte de fantôme de lui-même*]" (1999, 185). The already mentioned prosecutorial effect cast by the father over the patriot creates agony: a turf of contingent friendship among patriots whose group friendship remains under threat from their own militant fraternization in revolution and war. When Zarathustra qualifies friendship, he hits the mark of such turf-agony:

> "At least be my enemy!"—thus speaks the true reverence, that does not venture to ask for friendship.
> If you want a friend, you must also be willing to wage war for him: and to wage war, you must be capable of being an enemy.
> (TSZ 82)

Martí's *amigo muerto* (in selfness and otherness) marks the spot occupied by the fraternal twin and the risk of his becoming his own birth enemy.

(It points from one friend to the other as each other's worst best friend. It points at the danger of friendship's talent to kill—even if by means other than the agencies of blood duty invoked in brother-love.)

Derrida brings to task commonplace appeals to "birth, to nature or the nation" in political discourse as inducing "fraternization" in either national or universal brotherhood. From both left and right, whether democratic or undemocratic, fraternal bonds bring politics into the grounded determination known as *autochthony* or *born-of-the-soil* (as when soul is soiled as if tattooed on birth grounds). He asks: "Has anyone ever met a brother? A uterine or consanguine (distantly related) brother? In nature?" (1997, 93). The answer could always be, "Who knows?" (If by "nature" is meant a realm so removed or out of reach from shared and constituted communal knowledge as to render its comprehension impossible—or the communication subsequent to meeting it inarticulate.) But what if the troubled answer should be "*Yes!*" (in response to the illusions of uncanny autochthony in Martí's oath poem to the hanged plantation slave), his posthumous oath to the absolute alien brought enchained from afar, from Africa, but nevertheless claimed as honored brother? It is as if the adult poet in the Catskills wanted to meet, in that hanging corpse grounded in the soil of childhood, the "autochtone venu d'ailleurs" (the earth-born [Cuban] brought from elsewhere).[12] *Cuban* only in the poet's desperate attempt to claim propel burial. A soil for the black corpse, now buried, yet a spore in flight. A body gone back to occupy the soil of its lost nation. A black soul hanged in the noon tempest, suspended by the oath to the burdens of honor and the patriotic exactions of fraternity.

HIC JACET: THE TRAINED HEART

Anyone knows English except the people in this hotel.
Guillermo Cabrera Infante,
"Muerte de un autómata"

The first death witnessed by Nietzsche's Zarathustra after his descent from the mountain where he primed himself in sabbatical exile for missions ahead results in his carrying away for burial the corpse of the tightrope walker, who falls to his death under the buffoon's verbal assault as he walks across two towers over the market square (TSZ 47–50). Besides the chance that the buffoon might represent Zarathustra's own mimicked agent as alter ego, in the eyes of the town's grave-diggers the intruding prophet is just " 'carrying a dead dog' " — even as he betrays his own cannibal affinities with ghouls: " 'Does Zarathustra want to rob the Devil of his morsel?' " (50). The fallen man-into-dog leftovers personify human fate as proclaimed in the earlier speech: "Man is a rope, fastened between animal and Superman — a rope over an abyss" (43). Now, a bit later, the prophet's nomadism has taken him a few rungs below the philosophical dog sloppiness performed by cynics on the town's square. He is neither a trained cynic nor a leper, like the *orisha* San Lázaro, Cuba's most popular sainthealer, on crutches and licked by his faithful dogs. No, at this point, Zarathustra dwells next to the itinerant wildness of the scavenger breed of dog he can if he so wishes clone. David Gordon White describes the ancient ascetic type of the "Dog-Cooker or Milker" who comes to work "within the social sphere, and even to live on its confines," and who resembles "the archetypal migrant worker, serving the inhabitants of the town even as he is excluded from social intercourse with them" (1991, 91). Like the barking wind in the ears of nonbeings at the edge of town, Nietzsche's founder of religious morals dwells.

Garbage-digger Zarathustra represents the pariah version of the automaton named Wilhelm Schlumberger who on a visit to Havana in 1838 dies of yellow fever, the last among the breed of actual individuals who lodged where Walter Benjamin places the "little hunchback" who impersonates for him the hidden hand of theology animating the chess-playing winning puppet of historical materialism. (Nothing is known of the drinking habits of the unbeatable hunchback, but Schlumberger's were such that on the rare occasions when he lost a game, he had nooked himself into his tiny workbox already drunk [G. Wood 2002, 91].)

Regardless of what the answer to Benjamin's first thesis on the philosophy of history might be, the irony of Schlumberger's captivity as theology's able hostage to historical materialism seems exquisite in fulfillment of Romantic cruelty. The German (on Cuban soil for the occasion) remains nameless and more adaptively contoured to the habitat of his labor than fatally crooked by the confining shape of his lair, the same way in which, in Hugo's Romantic conception, Quasimodo is framed by the vastness of his cathedral, as a snail might be by the hardened life-form that shelters it. Between the neighborly extremes of a monstrous prophetic outlaw milking or boiling dogs and a silent pariah hiding at the heart of chess play, the Romantic double-walking partnership known as *doppelganger* plays cat's cradle with the rubber band ligatures holding fast the living and the dead.

The neighborliness of the double-walker is where on this occasion the archaic beginnings of Romantic authorship might as well unquietly rest. One heart beating double in two places at once. The trained transient heart as *fugueur*. The escape artist already elsewhere and still talking to you in the mirror. The one believed buried alive reporting live for the camera.

The 1838 Havana yellow-fever experience transforms the cabinet curiosity of the beating heart hiding below the puppet Turk into the grotesque life terminal also reported by Poe: "To be buried while alive, is beyond question, the most terrific of these extremes which has ever fallen to the lot of mere mortality. That it has frequently, very frequently, so fallen will scarcely be denied by those who think. The boundaries which divide Life from Death, are at best shadowy and vague" (Poe 2000a, 955). Yet, a more genuine Romantic uncanny state of overlapped boundaries might be encountered on the same premises. It arises if and when one finds himself as buried alive while still dying exposed on bed sheets, adrift on a strange island, a guest in a weird hotel where no one speaks English. Alive still, unburied-yet-buried under the same weight laid upon the unsheltered tortoise once ripped from her shell, as Schlumberger is from the lair within which his materialist bondage to work found dialectical entombment.

The trained heart place-of-rest in double location is thus pinned down by work habits defined by their utter enslavement to creativity. Schlumberger's livelihood commitment to creation in its various ensemble forms is absolute (and needless to say suicidal). He knows chess well enough to recreate in hiding by means of magnets and mirrors what the boss's eagle look supplies him. The boss gives sight from outside the slot to the occupant hired to supply a measure of recreational catalepsy to the paying costumers. For the premature burial connection provided by the double beating-heart lies not in the theology of dread which locates the enthralled immobility of catalepsy in the body lying within the chest. (There is, after all, room for Romantic insight in the dungeons of the heart.) Catalepsy lies unburied in the audience of vampire materialists feeding on the show's routine fare while waiting for the fetish dessert served by the show's promised risk of failure.

Two main species of sublimity are thus found in Martí's Romantic penmanship with Nietzsche as brotherly partners in the art of writing. In one, the noontide experience recalled and summoned back from childhood soil in the poem about the hanged slave is overcome in Zarathustra's *Mittag* cusp:

That I may one day be ready and ripe in the great noontide: ready and
   ripe like glowing ore, like cloud heavy with lightning and like
   swelling milk-udder—
ready for myself and my most secret Will: a bow eager for its arrow,
   an arrow eager for its star—
a star, ready and ripe in its noontide, glowing, transpierced, blissful
   through annihilating sun-arrows—
a sun itself and inexorable sun—will, ready for annihilation in
   victory! (TSZ 231–32)

The upper limit and nomadic vortex point of convergence is thus reached
by chronotope, automaton, doppelganger, or any such enabling Romantic avatar of the ancient daimons and modern auxiliaries still at large among true
as well as sly believers. (Included among the former—and the latter—are
surviving Infante, his Defunct writing mate, and Leonardo Padura's detective Mario Conde.)

The second species of sublimity is harsh and as vulnerable to being mistaken as the previous one is invulnerable to any such pitfall in the exercise of judgment. Zarathustra's noontide vision is committed to (but quite
above) the common madness celebrated by De Quincey in the Literature
of Power (whose reach beyond literature in the narrower sense—as a practice of knowledge set in writing—seems exempt from truth trials). From
the truth on trial in Nietzsche:

Socialism is the fanciful younger brother of the almost expired despotism whose heir it wants to be; its endeavors are thus in the profound-
est sense reactionary. For it desires an abundance of state power such
as only despotism has ever had; indeed it outbids all the despotisms of
the past inasmuch as it expressly aspires to the annihilation of the individual, who appears to it like an unauthorized luxury of nature destined
to be improved into a useful organ of the community. (HAH 173)

Martí's reading of this passage and his judgment of it in writing mark
the breaking point in the spell of cordiality with Nietzsche created here.
The purpose has been not to betray the writer in either of these two false
brothers, nor to make them brotherly by ignoring their writings, abridged
here upon issues and images of ubiquity, of the heart doubled in two beating chests. At the end of the line, the request is made to read Martí beyond condescension and in character and as if he were as unavoidable in

one's reading life as Mario Conde and Infante remain in the posthumous and premature afterlives of their respective authors. M and N, M against N grain, whichever way, the unavoidable M&N message—a sort of commercial: that fictions of the literary brand lean on the truth that readership makes them bear.

chapter twelve

1989: The Year That Never Was

Author's Note: Events narrated in this novel are not real, although
they could well have been so, as reality itself has since shown.

    Any resemblance with events and real persons is, therefore,
nothing but sheer resemblance, the obstinate effect of reality.

    No one, therefore, should feel alluded to by this novel. Yet no
one, by the same token, should feel excluded from it, if somehow
it alluded to him/her.

    LEONARDO PADURA FUENTES, Pasado perfecto

I have endeavored as nearly as possible to represent the characters
as they probably were, and have sought to avoid the error of
making them actuated by my own conceptions of right and
wrong, false or true, thus under a thin veil converting the names
and actions of the sixteenth century into cold impersonations
of my own mind.

    PERCY BYSSHE SHELLEY, The Cenci

In 1921 Lenin set up economic policies whereby Communism
would take one step backward in order to move three steps forward (reculer
pour mieux sauter). The year 1989 started on Sunday, January 1 (not on Thursday, as it does in the opening date of Pasado perfecto as recorded in a Havana
police blotter). Therefore, there is a four-day lapse (counting 1988's leap-
year extra day) in which 1989 would have leaped or clicked backward by
three years to the previous Thursday in novel-time; or, as one may wish,
leaped forward to the following Thursday in novel-time, in which case by
nine years, since February 29's extra date in 1992 caused 1994's January 1
to skip from Thursday into Friday. What is being thus reckoned by following the week's wheel over two back-and-forth turns is not 1989's locked-
step relation to 1987 and 1998, the nearest years in which dates are set in
kindred Gregorian perpetuity. What really matters is the addition or sub-
traction in years lived by actual individuals in the balance, as it happens,
precarious, solid, or in-between, upon which their social circumstances

as determined by politics and policies would have placed them. (It is presumed that none of them would have enjoyed that "most ingenious paradox" which by the unquestioned authority of the Astronomer Royal in *The Pirates of Penzance* allows a chap of twenty-one to remain a child of four by virtue of his birth date on February 29.)

The existence of individuals in actual historical time brings up 1989's most notorious public and global person, Mikhail Gorbachev, prime minister of the Soviet Union and architect of those twin engines of deconstruction in trained political and bureaucratic lives, *glasnost* and *perestroika* (he visited Havana in April of that year). Something of Humpty Dumpty's sly regard for the eternal face in everyone (as when he tells Alice, " 'Your face is the same as everybody has—the two eyes . . . nose in the middle, mouth under. It's always the same' " [AA 276]) comes to mind when reading such phrases from practitioners of virtual history as: "Only crude determinism would insist that Gorbachev happened because Gorbachev had to happen."[1] Something like Humpty's recognition that the other's face is eternally about to slip into the other's other face, and the notion that such facial shift haunts the person to whom the same/other face might belong by turning it into one among a myriad of contingent factual outcomes. As when saying: *Only crude determinism would insist that Hurricane Felix did not happen to blow through Havana on October 9, 1989, just because it did not have to happen. But crude determinism melts in the mouth if it should be added that Felix did not happen, just as well as it might have happened, which is how it really happens in the last of the Four Seasons novels.*[2]

Such a harmless amendment is brought about by the "obstinate effect of reality," as avowed, with a touch of casuistry, in Padura's authorship disclaimer, where the ulterior effect of the *real* rises above the *ostinato* drone of ordinary events and becomes something unheard-of, noisily different yet mute, quite in one's face, but not felt, as when a mask is worn without knowing it. Something scandalous crops up, in the way in which it may seem misapplied or needless, as if Shelley's fear of customizing characters and motives from the Italian sixteenth century by means of his own "actuated" conceptions of right and wrong in *The Cenci* were to correspond to the minimalist anachronism of dealing, not with such distant historical and cultural times, but with the immediate, still presently *extant* epoch of just a year ago. Dealing precisely with last year with all the perfection achieved in the grammatical verbal modes of the past and future perfects.[3]

A MOST INGENIOUS PARADOX

Communism is an aspirin the size of the sun.

Leonardo Padura Fuentes, *Pasado perfecto*

The overarching plot of Padura's *Four Seasons* detective novels contains a minimalist alteration of calendar time not unrelated to (though on the whole very different from) Georg Lukács's notion of "necessary anachronism" and the parallax historiographic phenomenon which James Chandler calls "the calibration of uneven temporalities" in reference to Sir Walter Scott's *Waverley* novels.[4] What requires calibration are the different rates of speed and acceleration in one historical time-and-place development relative to another, as each unfolds in adjoining nations, such as England and Scotland, across the short but vast span of time, so reckoned, in the "'Tis Sixty Years Since" subtitle of Scott's *Waverley* (1814), recognized as the first self-conscious historical novel. (It was translated into Spanish and published in Mexico in 1833 as *Waverly o Ahora 60 años* by the poet, jurist, and historian José María Heredia y Heredia, then banished from the island of Cuba, charged with conspiring against Spain's colonial rule [JMH 90].)

Chandler refers to "time-place definitions mutually worked out between Scotland and England," together with Scott's division of Scotland into two "'chronotopic' zones" and the equivalent of roughly over a hundred years of English eighteenth-century development to about a single generation of Scottish development over the same period, as outlined in *Ivanhoe*'s preface. (Likewise, in *Waverley*'s postscript, a period of *two* generations lasting thirty years each is measured against two centuries of English development.)[5] Chandler considers how in *The Historical Novel* Lukács understands Scott's practice by relying on Hegel's concept of a given character's inner subjectivity and his or her rapport with the external aspects by which culture is rendered concrete and objective, both to that character and to his or her audience. Lukács finds in historicism a derivation of individual personality from the historical circumstances peculiar to the age in question. The notion of "necessary anachronism" entails translation, as Lukács emphasizes in quoting the "Dedicatory Epistle" to *Ivanhoe* (1819), in which Scott absolves himself of any wrongdoing as he finds it necessary "for exciting interest of any kind that the subject assumed [in his novels] should be, as it were, *translated* [Lukács's emphasis] into the manner, as well as the language, of the age we live in" (1963, 62). But Reverend Dryasdust (Scott) wryly admits the partial accuracy of the case brought against his practice (by "the severer antiquary"), namely: "that, by thus intermingling fiction and truth, I am polluting the well of history with modern inventions, and impressing upon the rising generations false ideas of the age which I describe. I cannot but in some sense admit the force of this reasoning" (1986, 526). In Lukács's view, "necessary anachronism" allows characters to "express feelings and thoughts about *real* [emphasis added] historical relationships in a much clearer way than the actual men and women of the time could have done" (1963, 63). The historical perspectives at issue in both Scott and Lukács translate into the paradoxical resemblance between fiction and the nonhistorical present as 1989 slips out of line with 1989 in Padura's *Four Seasons*.

The minimalist clue to necessary anachronism in *1989-as-it-never-was* concerns the mirage of instant obsolescence at a moment when little is changing in Cuba—though much is—as seen in the rearview mirror of the writing (in forward motion) of the *Four Seasons* during the 1990s, in Mantilla, a township on the southern outskirts of Havana.[6] The 1989 year current or in play as each novel unfolds recapitulates in foreshadowing fashion events and moods and human types lying just ahead in the nineties (1989 looks at itself as its own past through such modalities of near-future being). What may seem constitutive of the historical notion of culture, its *pastness*, turns into *presentness* in 1989. The thick-*ness* of essence becomes as "necessary" as anachronism does in Scott's *Waverley*—and just as the feared "actuated" force of the present upon the past does in the making of Shelley's *The Cenci*. As it unfolds unseen through the 1990–97 period of its writing, the *Four Seasons'* 1989 transforms past lives into the *pastness* and *posthumousness* of current ones (1989 *never was as it still never is in the current actuality of its own unnarrated future afterlives*).

The immediate past of the months just lived in 1989 informs the present of the lives emergent from that recent past just passed. These are the same lives whose humdrum or all-too-easy familiarity with their own recent past is thus rendered unfamiliar, but not by making the narrative of such a past strange or uncanny. Remaining all-too-familiar, recently past lives insist on their own remoteness, as if their presence in current lives needed reckoning. As if, in their posthumous character with respect to the present, these recent *afterlives* held the present responsible for the need to reflect hard on its own yet-to-be reckoned manner of being already-dead, to reflect as well on its dire need to, by such self-awareness, recover lost or wasted promises. As if ransomed by its own nearness to itself in the un-

finished recent past, the present encompasses in a crunch the two definitions of *afterlife* in the OED, noted by Robert Douglas-Fairhurst: "A subsequent or future life" and "a later period of one life," as he observes that
the "entry for 'afternoon' is approximately three times longer than that for
'afterlife,' a neglectful view," he adds, "given that there are readers who
believe that the afterlife will outlast an afternoon" (2002, 5–6). (The 1989
year that never was unfolds during the afternoon of an unfinished unending day in past perfect as future perfect.)

By way of setting aside any ready-made analogies between the hyper-
fictional 1989 at work in *Four Seasons* and the available hodgepodge of postmodern strategies, Padura's authorship claim upon the "obstinate effect
of reality" should be set in line with Lacan's notion of the real in relation
to a traumatic cause. At its most naively exposed, the residue of trauma
throughout *Four Seasons* resides in two connected bodies and persons: those
of Flaco Carlos, brotherly friend of police detective Mario Conde (*the-not-
anymore-skinny-Skinny-Carlos*, Angolan War vet crippled in combat in 1981
and now obese and confined to a wheelchair), and of his mother, Jose (with
her *bricolage* method of preparing lush meals out of some virtual cornu-
copia, invisibly flowing from the Land of Cockaigne).

Setting aside for now a deeper look into the question of individual and
generational trauma, the year that is 1989 (as it never was) *actuates* (as in
Shelley's fears of anachronism) that which is real in excess of itself, rep-
resenting, in Bruce Fink's words, "everything that has as yet to be sym-
bolized" (LS 27).[7] Everything that in trauma "implies fixation or blockage"
(26), and sheds off a surplus, refuse, "*residue*" or excluded pile, whose body
of numbers and symbols in Lacan's prestidigitation he himself names the
caput mortuum (borrowing a term from alchemy best known for its use in
Christian Rosencreutz's *Chymical Wedding*).[8] "One could go as far as to say,"
explains Fink, "that what, of necessity, remains outside the chain [of symbols and signification] *causes* what is inside; something must, structurally
speaking, be pushed outside for there to even be an inside" (LS 27). The
1989 that never was occupies this second-order or degree in *real-ness*: the
causative or *actuated* dimension with respect to the one year that was, but
that remains to be worked through, as it happens each time the year is sent
off with carousing noise, in deep and oftentimes drunken awareness that
its annual shedding is illusory. Thus:

$$Real_1\ 1989 >>>>> Symbolic >>>>> Real_2\ 1989$$

where the *causative/actuated* or second-order 1989 represents both itself, in such a determining role, and the residual of itself that each coming year will bring up as long as 1989 is looked upon as a significant past benchmark. (Such status typically swings both ways, as it does in *Four Seasons*: it extends itself unfinished into the future, as it looks back to the afterlives of some of its characters from before 1989 arrived on New Year's.)

This is where, to the anachronistic fluidity of the year that never is, that is never settled, as it shuttles back-and-forth between past and future, one adds the Lacanian question of *subjectification*: whose fantasies, whose subject's residual stuff, is causing all such movement? *Who* is 1989 as 1989? This brings matters one step closer to the issue of trauma as viewed by Lacan, or, in Fink's formula, closer to the operation of *"putting the I back in the traumatic cause"* (LS 63). Trauma is *traversed* by its own fantasy: "la traversée du fantasme" (61). The subject comes into being in self-defense, by absorbing into itself or *subjectifying* its encounter with trauma's encroachment. Even if one were to resist Lacan's notion of the child's encounter with the Other's desire as that of the *mOther*, the plot of *Four Seasons* would in turn resist such resistance. For throughout it, the ascendancy of Mario Conde's mother from within the plot's background goes hand-in-hand with the disclosure that the fiction being read is the one that Conde will write, and has in fact already started writing inside the plot. *Subjectification* and *Authorship* prove inalienable under a temporal regime in which mother turns into *mOther* by arriving late into itself as Conde's *Other*.

Before examining how *mother* waxes into *Other*, the issue of her not arriving all-at-once (or in one piece) must be understood in terms of *mOther* and its affinity with the year's peculiar mode of arrival. Lacan reshapes Freud's notion of deferred action or *Nachträglichkeit* in terms of the grammatical tense known as the future anterior or future perfect. Accordingly, a phrase's meaning is constituted retroactively by moving back from the end of the sentence to its beginning. The non-instantaneous creation of meaning requiring such retroactivity is well rendered by the future perfect's designation of an event-point yet to come, in reference to which another event-point will have occurred. Adapting the situation to 1989 and its arrival on the wrong day of the week, one may enunciate it in both the future perfect and the past perfect, given that the latter, after all, provides the ironic title (*Pasado perfecto*) for the first of the *Four Seasons*. In counterfactual terms, the disjointed event of the year's arrival and start is thus phrased *by the time it arrived, 1989 had already started* (past perfect) and *by then, just as it might have arrived, 1989 will have already started* (future perfect). In such terms, the *Subjectification effect* (Lacan's) may be adapted to the scheme in which signification, through delayed effect and retroactivity, is illustrated. In the scheme, E_1 stands for 1989 and its Gregorian calendar occurrence, while E_2 functions as its *subjectified* and retroactive signification:

a) 1989 $E_1 >>> E_2$

$<<<$

b) 1989_2 $E_1 >>> E_2$

(*signified/subjectified*) M.C. (Mario Conde$_2$)

Subjectification appears in a) as the second and altered signifier for 1989, and in b) in retro action with respect to the first, and in connection with Mario Conde's M.C. rubric as the subject in question.[9]

But it is one thing to discard the hodgepodge of postmodern fiction strategies as replacements for grand narrative schemes and another to trace in Mario Conde's authorship seizure of his own subjectivity a means to represent—as *openly historical*—current circumstances actuated by the imperative of *occultation*. Fredric Jameson considers "the mesmerizing new aesthetic mode" dominant in postmodernism as "an elaborated symptom of the waning of our historicity, of our lived possibility of experiencing history in some active way. It cannot therefore be said to produce this strange occultation of the present by its own formal powers but rather merely to demonstrate, through these inner contradictions, the enormity of a situation in which we seem increasingly incapable of fashioning representations of our current experience" (1991, 21). (Either this or its very opposite: the actuality of the historical as one works through and *actuates* such occult practices.)

For instance, police detective Conde identifies himself (along with Flaco Carlos and a small cluster of friends) with a "hidden generation" or *generación escondida* (VC 37; Po 249, 259), one of whose members, nicknamed *Conejo* (Rabbit), is "viscerally historical, always in need of reasons, causes, and consequences for the smallest of events" (Po 23). Rabbit practices virtual history with the best of them, as when he envisions the counterfactual "victory of the Arabs at Poitiers, Montezuma's over Cortés, or simply, the English staying in Havana after their conquest of the city in 1762" (VC 39). It is in connection with British Havana (and the lengthened Spanish rule over neighboring Florida) that the hidden generation's office of historian managed by Rabbit announces itself on the same page (and next to) the first third-person reference to internal authorship on Conde's part: "He [in self-reference] now thought that if he ever wrote the whole chronicle of love and hate, happiness and frustration, he would entitle it *Past Perfect*" (VC 28). Such counterfactual histories may seem a species of *rabbit dung* of the kind E. P. Thompson has branded *Geschichtswissenschlopff*—or unhistorical shit.[10] Yet, Rabbit's gesture in *Four Seasons* points at a target other than chaos. For nothing of the ordinary that happens in *Four Seasons* alters anything that might or could happen as such. Rather than counterfactual, Rabbit's historiography acts as a lure to envision factual alternatives to the plot's raw events as a reflection of what is going on all the time right under's Clio's nose, yet unremarked by the muse of history's long-range views and historical designs.

Buried in Rabbit-style new-historicist revisionism lies the worm or virus known as *literature*. This peculiar infection, as common as the common cold, dwells at the inner core of the hidden generation's closet bohemian choices side-by-side the routines of late adolescence. Literature has crept into a few lives through the chapter-at-a-time reading aloud during lit class of Julio Cortázar's *Rayuela* (1964) or *Hopscotch*. Such episodic audition of anti-literature as scripture (as if: *Bible-as-fun = literature*) leads to the publication of the first or *Zero Issue* of the journal *La Viboreña* (the title *Viper*— from the name of the school's barrio) in which the future police detective and *noir* novelist Mario Conde publishes *Domingos* (*Sundays*), a story of forbidden truancy from church in violation of his mother's rules, written in the *submerged* or *iceberg* style of Hemingway. The journal is suspended before it reaches the next issue beyond *Zero* when the school principal objects to its masthead caption—"Communism is an aspirin the size of the sun"— on grounds that it targets socialism as a headache. (It is further objected that all poems are about love and none about the Revolution or the life of one of its martyrs, that Conde's story does not attack the church's reactionary doctrines, that one poem praises a girl's love suicide.) The school principal demands that literature be addressed as Literature (as when 1989 should never turn into 1989 brought-back, intact, yet *redux*). He expects from writers a zero-sum game with fixed and equal amounts of winnings and losings balancing out to nothing left over, once the ideological inspection is finished.

Next to the official foreclosure apparatus, Rabbit's own gesture toward scrap histories lures the reader (in looking-glass fashion) toward the historical novel whose project the last of the *Four Seasons* foreshadows as the transformation of *noir* serial fiction into a double-layered narrative about the life of the Romantic poet José María Heredia (1803–39) and *La novela de mi vida* (*My Life's Novel*), the lost manuscript of the novel-within-a-novel inside the book published by Padura in 2002 under the same title.

In the most detailed chronology of Heredia's life thus far published, on the eve of the poet's second centenary, Padura registers his death on May 7, 1839, at the age of "thirty-five years, four months, and seven days" (he considers Heredia a contemporary in more ways than one, but none more important than his forced exile from Cuba, his *chosen* homeland or *patria*).[11] The key question posed by the poet's life and work is plainly this: "Why did Heredia decide that he ought to be [*debía ser*] Cuban?" After all, "he spent the thirty-five years of his life, give or take a few months, as follows: a little more than six years in Cuba (three of them in early childhood) [. . .] five and a half in Venezuela, two in Santo Domingo, a little over four on United States soil, and some sixteen years in Mexico, where he lived a long period of his expatriation and where he took part in the country's political, social, and literary life and was regarded as Mexican by many" (JMH 8–9). Banishment makes the homeland a choice beyond the accident of birth.

As mutual exiles, the lives of Heredia and José Martí run parallel. Martí's fulfills Heredia's in the Romantic mode of a parallelism of succession. Their lives run concurrently and yet in succession in Martí's desire to keep his own life unfulfilled as framed in Heredia's. Martí mentions how Heredia's "precocious" childhood reading of Plutarch taught him that, "as long as slaves went on living under the whip of impious masters in a land made for happiness, the book of the *Lives* would remain unfinished and the plan of the world unaccomplished" (a world in whose design "moral beauty belongs in the body, but just to warn about the imperative of a beautiful soul") (OI 318).[12] As he testifies to the unquestionable greatness of Heredia's poetry, Martí imagines him about to face banishment to Mexico, which he understands in terms of two kinds of moral choices available to Heredia. One is based on calculation, according to which "the passions are carefully ordered and virtue practiced as long as it may not bother life's pleasures," and another (the one chosen by Heredia), at first glance reckless, as "free range is given to the forces of the soul [*las fuerzas del alma*]," which being what they are, "must be allowed to exert themselves, as when falcons are released to the winds and then harnessed" (318). Such Emersonian residues in Martí's warmer urgencies create in him a vision of the precursor expatriate Heredia facing the Popocatépetl (soon to be addressed in a minor ode) and about to accept Mexico, "crying in fury upon seeing the country of snow where he shall live, on account of not knowing how to love in measured ways his own country of light [Cuba]" (318). Andrew Bush (whose understanding of Heredia's poetry dwarfs that of most others) recalls Jorge Mañach's assertion that great poetry is found, not in the rallying hymns of patriotic fervor, but in such poems as the "Descriptive Fragments of a Mexican Poem," written in December 1820 upon visiting the pyramid at Cholula, as Heredia neared the age of sixteen, and less than two months after his father's death. The greatness comes, in Mañach's view, because "Heredia is more a true poet when he signs, not what triumphs, but what dies," dies both in repeated sacrificial droves at the summit of the pyramid temple's "Colossal Phantom" and in the individual extinction of the father's royalist duty to Spanish colonial rule (Bush 2002, 254).

In Bush's reading, the poem's two successive selves enact a significant split mended in revision. While in the shadow of his father's death, the adolescent poet in Heredia incorporates his loss, "acting it out in the abrupt truncation of the poem's 1820 version" (Bush 2002, 256). But something quite larger unfolds in the poem's first life as occasioned by the trauma of paternal death. Heredia's poetic voice falls into silence and slumber; he "arrests and reverses the westward progress of poetry that aligns Spanish American historical consciousness with the masterplot of the Conquest." Bush further claims that "Heredia is not traveling the route of Cortés to the massacre at Cholula [. . .] but the diametrical opposite, the eastward route of Quetzalcoatl from Cholula to the sea and to his own embarkation with his family and his return to Cuba" (256). Quetzalcoatl's cyclical and calendrical demise is felt in the poem's dying breeze ("ligera brisa"), "folding wings in silence" ("las alas en silencio ya plegaba"); or in Bush's words:

Quetzalcoatl as Ehacatl, the wind god. Heredia atop the pyramid is cast in the role of the Enfermo [sick man] in its specifically pre-Columbian form: the human sacrifice—a death not his own . . . but of another he has incorporated: the death of his father, the death, too, of Quetzalcoatl, priest or god, culture hero, giver of arts and of agriculture. In this American version of the interstitial moment between death and life, dying breeze and rising star, human sacrifice atop the pyramid is a cosmic necessity, rather than a tragedy, a rebirth for which there is no mourning. (256)

As Bush sees it, *En el teocalli de Cholula* (the poem's augmented 1832 Mexican edition) represents the poet's awakening and recoil from the earlier absorption in the Aztec past. Heredia gains enlightened self-recognition of the awesome cruelties at the pyramid's summit, whose colossal shape had once cast its dark sublimity upon his mournful soul. The Spanish colonial government, at whose service Heredia's father had worked all his life, had just issued in Cuba the son's death sentence. Bush boldly insists that the revised 1832 poem's "modern" self-understanding, purged of the dark and stagnant melancholy of its earlier life, represents Heredia's "proleptic elegy for himself," as "though he could constitute his own burial society from beyond the grave" (257). In which case, José Martí, the man most responsible for eulogizing Heredia in the patriotic-poetic afterlife, institutes a measure of regression in the wake of such prolepsis.

The effect of Romantic parallel lives in succession takes place at two levels. In one, revision is achieved, when Martí ends one of his eulogies by placing Heredia's death beneath the Popocatépetl and the Iztaccihuatl volcanoes, but also at the top of "Mexico, immense temple built by Nature, so that, from the highest steps of its mountains, as of old, the sacrifices of the *teocalis* would consummate in themselves the final and terrible justice of American independence."[13] The precursor poet's death (Heredia's) is restored to the spot at Cholula where his earliest (at once gloomy, spooked, and majestic) encounter with *familiar strangeness* took place. (The Cholula *Unheimliche* is where the required union of territorial America under one *Patria* found articulate effusion in the 1820 elegy.) The "critical distance" achieved in the revised poem suggests to Bush the mapping of its own beginnings in the two great odes: "En una tempestad" (1822) and "Niagara" (1824), the latter written during Heredia's visit to the Falls (while seated "at the edge of the English cataract"). Indeed, two days later the poet wrote to his uncle Ignacio back in Cuba about the "torrent" spectacle and his own inner turmoil and asked: "Why is it that I cannot once and for all wake up from my slumber? Oh!, when will my life's novel end so that my own reality may begin?"[14] Whether or not Bush is correct in tying "En una tempestad" to one of Harold Bloom's instances of repression and poetic restitution, Heredia's "In a Tempest" heralds, on Cuban soil, in September 1822, the Niagara encounter lying less than two years ahead, once he reaches the northernmost point of exile. The twin odes celebrate the upheaval of confronting and absorbing onrushing energies whose ultimate fate remains political and by force violent, insofar as independence would not be won by peaceful means.

Such energies are *extraterritorial* with respect to the adopted homeland or *patria* (Cuba). Absorbed and released, sublime energies function in part as outlets for specific *territorial* political claims in the struggle for Spanish American independence. The other important poem of 1822 is "Oda a los habitantes de Anahuac," published anonymously under the signature of *Un Verdadero Americano (A Real American)* and secretly printed in Havana. The poem denounces Agustín de Iturbide's proclamation as Mexican emperor (1821) and his tyrannous dictatorship. Nothing less than Caesar's murder is demanded from the citizens of Mexico ("Is Brutus not breathing among you? / Are you without knives?"). A conspiracy (*breathing in unison*) gathers at poem's end led by the last three Aztec emperors, risen like furies from their "dusty graves" to encircle the tyrant in their revenge swarming. In Padura's comments, the "Anahuac Ode" meant "the definitive communion of Heredia with the ideals of independence" as he joined the Freemasons (Caballeros Racionales de Matanzas) and took part in the *Rayos y Soles de Bolívar* conspiracy, the uncovering of which led to his clandestine flight from Cuba aboard the *Galaxy* in November 1823.[15]

The second level of parallel lives in succession involves José Martí's return to Cuba in early April 1895 and his death in battle a few weeks later on May 19. On one hand, Martí's best-known eulogy places Heredia's death and remains back at Cholula, where the promise of independence stands in the idealized legacy of indigenous Mexico. On the other, the eastward voyage (Quetzalcoatl's and Heredia's) envisioned by Andrew Bush as the *meta-poetic* sequel of the first writing of the Cholula poem in late 1820 foreshadows the return back to the homeland, the disparate deaths of each poet, and passage into their joint afterlives.

The notion of afterlife finds sublime enunciation in Martí's 1897 anticipatory eulogy for Walt Whitman, when he writes, "Life is a hymn; death is an occult form of life," a compound state where both conditions are not only bound together but stand as that which renders possible the poet's life in both forms: in his own body and as the Over-Soul.[16] In the end, Emerson's transport into the ethos of Martí's cosmic patriotism requires unearthing and underlining, if anything because the *War Diaries* or *Diarios de campaña* (in which Emerson's, Whitman's, and Heredia's afterlives require no further utterance as they disappear behind other urgencies) seem, nevertheless, to summon a joint poetic imperative. When the poet José Lezama Lima considers the *Diaries* "the greatest poem ever written by a Cuban," a residue of Emerson's inclination to boundlessness reclaims in good faith what needs not be poetry in order to ring as true as the real circumstances that impregnated its heroic crafting beyond any ingenious or indigenous paradox.[17]

LEONARDO'S LEONARDO

I can paint false Picassos as well as anybody else.

Pablo Picasso, in Orson Welles, F *for Fake*

In each of the *Four Seasons* novels, a recent or distant crime that has ended in murder is inspected and solved in just a few days. In *Pasado perfecto*, a Ministry of Industries manager involved in corrupt dealings with Japanese companies is killed on New Year's Eve by a fellow bureaucrat and partner in crime whom he tried to blackmail in order to leave the island and escape prosecution. The case is solved by January 6 or *Día de Reyes*, of which no mention is made, since its celebration fell slowly out of fashion after the Revolution.[18] However, besides the homicide case being handled by Detective Conde, the now bygone tradition of giving toys to children on *Reyes* is evoked in the bicycle-theft murder of a boy. The person in charge of the investigation is Captain Jorrín, the oldest detective on the force, in whose "old wolf" grandfather voice the condemnation of increasing street violence and crime in Havana is heard. Jorrín's professional and ethical conscience relates to the parallel themes of school training and sentimental education among members of the hidden generation. But his voice speaks most directly to Mario Conde's family ancestry and his forsaken Catholic upbringing. Jorrín is the first among several representatives of patriarchal authority involved in Conde's life throughout 1989, as he nears with trepidation his thirty-sixth birthday. (Patriarchal origins are established in the figure of the Canarian great-grandfather who left Madrid to escape justice, changed his last name to Conde once in Cuba, and asked his many descendants to keep his patronymic, including the women as they married and became mothers.) Patriarchal authority in Mario Conde's life carries with it a Christian Catholic stamp put on him by his late mother. The lingering effect of this lost Catholic faith is first cued in the unnamed but implied presence of the extinct *Día de Reyes* in proximity to a murdered child and his stolen bicycle (the old Feast of Kings also marks an important debt to Afro-Cuban tradition).[19]

In *Vientos de Cuaresma* (*Winds of Lent*), a young math teacher, not much older than her high-school students, is strangled by one of them after she refuses to continue to give him advanced copies of exams. The case takes Detective Conde back to the prep school he first attended in 1972, which he now finds mired in corruption. (The murdered teacher was having sex with her students and with the principal, who falsifies the dates on his official account of the crime in need of keeping his wife in the dark about his affair with the victim.) The case is solved in a week, but the week in question involves counterfactual clues. The murder takes place past midnight on Ash Wednesday, in the wake of the victim's rum-and-marijuana wild party with a group of students and just after she had had sex and smoked grass with her killer. The dates marked as the 18th and 19th (with the latter identified as Ash Wednesday) are afterward situated in March, too late to allow for the start of Lent in accordance with the Catholic schedule of movable feasts. Moreover, once the case is solved and the March dates are set, it becomes possible to double-check that in 1989 the 18th and 19th of March fell on Easter Week. A murder committed at the start of Lent and solved in a week's time ends up virtually framed more than forty days later during Holy Week. During the period of Lent in question (as well as Easter), Conde carries on a carnal feast of his own with the wife of a physician on tour in Nicaragua. Their most passionate lovemaking (described as a "double suicide") would take place on the eve of Easter Sunday, the day Conde returns to the church where he took first communion at age seven.

The disjointment in movable feasts fits the pattern of recalling the spiritual incidents in Conde's life as it was once informed by the Catholic faith he now considers dead. He goes to the church on police business but conscious of having quit the faith in the same manner one might a ruling political party in a country such as Cuba: "his return to the parochial church almost thirty years after his *defection*" (VC 140, emphasis added). Quitting right after he takes first communion implies Conde's juvenile self-excommunication, as does now his running away in shame from the sermon about "fraternity" between God the Father and his Son Jesus: "When the worshipers stood up, feeling he brought profanity to the *Arcanum* to which he had renounced, Conde saw the chance and fled like a hunted man into the sunlight outside" (VC 141). The broken bonds of Christological brotherhood in Mario Conde's life contrast with the ties of Masonic solidarity present in José María Heredia's life as well as in the lives of the main characters of *La novela de mi vida* (a novel Padura dedicates to his father and to all of Cuba's Freemasons).

Conde is brought to the church by the need to see his friend and informant Candito Rojo, whose presence at mass surprises him. Candito the barrio tipster is Conde's opposite in family ties. The detective's ancestry goes back from grandfather to grandfather for over a century. Candito's family memory goes no further than the early death of his parents. Conde is an only son. Candito has a brother serving eight years in jail for armed theft. He has repeated the eleventh grade three times and never finished it. Conde graduated and is good at writing fiction. Both are divorced, but Conde lives the loner's life in the company of an occasional pet—tropical fish or dog. Candito "enjoys his homely expanse in the tame company of a younger brown woman [*mulatica dócil*]" (VC 58) in the midst of a crowded tenement. As the letters of their names indicate, the Conde/Candito resemblance operates as a decoy for their mutual split in collaborative contrast. Both men hustle in different though intertwined ways, one on a squalid detective's pay, the other "inventing a buck" (60) each day. Yet, the issue of honor creates a bond between them. Candito breaks the macho street code by supplying Conde with crime tips at the same time that he spells out the cardinal rule of Havana social existence in *Four Seasons*: "'There are two worlds here, Conde, daddy's kids' world and street people's world, like my own. And daddy's kids are the ones riding around in *Ladas* [official cars] and motorcycles'" (60). Such is the law that rules in the eyes of people-on-people surveillance as supplied to Conde by his candid-camera friend, Candito el R-ojo, whose name comes encrypted with the *eye* (*ojo*) and the *CDR* or *Committees for the Defense of the Revolution* initials, as if to mark off the shifting and treacherous boundaries between *socios* as social brothers.[20]

Enter *Hamlet*. Detective Conde and tipster Candito seem as nonfraternal as brothers may seem to each other in dreams of universal brotherhood. The bargains that on certain occasions unite Conde and Candito in the fight against crime, such as when busting the marijuana ring associated with the young teacher's murder, constitute a species of currency or fraternal exchange of the kind Prince Hamlet subjects to specular parody as he confronts Gertrude with "the counterfeit presentment of two brothers," in the picture of his murdered king father and his sibling murderer (3.4.54). For honor dwells in the maximum yet minimal *unlikeness* that binds Conde to Candito, as it does all through Four Seasons in remarkable kinship with Shakespeare.

Right from the start in Pasado perfecto, as the phone rings and Conde wakes up in hangover from the depths of sleep, the phrase "Dormir, tal vez soñar" ("To sleep, perchance to dream") lands him back on the desolate shore of the most famous and parroted inner/outer speech in world drama. Hamlet's words (3.1.65) translate into the cheap effect of the echoing "hammering phrase [frase machacona]" (Pp 13) uttered by Conde as he dragged himself into bed after vomiting in the toilet bowl. The hazardous passage from sleep and dreams into wakefulness marks the spot of soliloquy when it repeats itself at a moment of introspection near the start of Vientos de Cuaresma: "No one can imagine what a policeman's nights are like" (VC 24). The phrase opens up Conde's meditation on onerous duty very much in the style of a dramatic soliloquy. It is as if Hamlet's contemplation on suicide were like the scene of a crime revisited and further inspected, from the point where the phrase at the start of Four Seasons echoes in Conde's ears to the phrase that comes just before it in Hamlet ("To die, to sleep" [3.1.64]): "The murky waters of a policeman's nights: rotten smells, deaden colors. To sleep, perchance to dream! I have learned only one way to overcome my nights: unconsciousness, a bit like death each day, death itself each dawn, as the shining sun's presumed happiness tortures my eyes" (VC 24). While resting on the same phrase as before, Conde's inner speech has taken him one step back to the suicide/death point in Hamlet's speech. This is close to the well-known rhetorical use of hendiadys in Hamlet, when, instead of a noun modified by an adjective, a single complex idea is split into two nouns linked by "and" or another conjunction. The 1989/1989 reiterative ensemble of the same year altered represents a chronotopic hendiadys split between the melancholia of hangover and the masquerade of jubilation.[21]

Captain Jorrín's sudden death of a heart attack triggers a similar soliloquy-type reflection on defunctness and oblivion in which the graveyard scene in Hamlet is joined to the childhood moment when Conde heard the news of JFK's assassination: "'They killed Kennedy, they killed that son of a bitch'" (VC 184). From that moment on, at age ten, the child gained consciousness of death and of life being but "a brief stand between two nothingnesses" (184). The point of arrest encompasses the core of Conde's adult thoughts on the five-generation expanse of biographic memory required by his anguished sense of wanting to live far off into posthumousness. Thoughts of five past generations and five future ones bring Conde back to *Hamlet* and Yorick's skull: "Hamlet and myself before the same skull, it does not matter if its name is Yorick's, the jester's, or Jorrín's, or whether it might have belonged to a police captain or to Lissette Nuñez [the murdered math teacher], the happy slut at the end of the XX century" (185). Yet, Hamlet's age at Yorick's death is seven, as is Conde's when he takes his first communion from the hands of Father Mendoza and never sets foot in church for the next twenty-eight years. The soliloquy on his own paternal afterlives and dissension seems to gloss Hamlet's picture of death as "the undiscover'd country, from whose bourn / No traveler returns" (3.1.79–80): "I decided to abandon religion in favor of baseball on account of my doubts about his [Mendoza's] mystical explanation of death's boundaries: faith was not enough for me to accept the existence of a stacked-up eternal world: the blessed ones in heaven, the not-so-blessed in purgatory, the bad ones in hell, and the innocents going straight to limbo" (VC 184). Yet, this limbo occupies the contact zone of daily life in Havana as experienced in each of the *Four Seasons*.

In *Máscaras*, the third novel in the sequence, Conde visits Father Mendoza's parish seeking to learn about the transfiguration of Christ, observed on August 6, the day of the murder he has been trying to solve. He remembers that the sermon preached by the father on the day of his first and last communion was on Christ's transfiguration and wonders why. Mendoza now reveals to him that he had learned of Conde's father's death that very day, and because he felt fear upon the news, he spoke about Jesus' command to the apostles (in Matthew 17.7) to "'rise and have no fear'" (M 85). At this moment, Father Mendoza and Conde become retroactive communicants in dialogue across the interface between Church dogma and political heresy, religious heresy and Party dogma. Earlier, the police detective at the service of revolutionary justice referred to his abandonment of Catholic practice as a "defection" (140), a word loaded with political overtones in Cuba as elsewhere. Now, that same "remote Sunday of never recovered purity"—at the communion officiated by Father Mendoza —is thought by Conde to have involved "the priest and the dissident" (82). The detective's defection and dissidence from Catholicism become theological tokens which translate (in refracted form) the (unstated) political views and practices by ordinary citizens like himself in relation to the State apparatus. Such religious doctrinal beliefs of cryto-political significance are thus held in connotative limbo when seen in the mirror of theology under scrutiny by police work inside the detective's mind. In this regard, Conde's decision at the end of the fourth *Four Seasons* novel to quit police work and write detective fiction constitutes a dissident defection from a kind of social duty impossible to disassociate from State ideology.[22]

When Conde meets with Father Mendoza, he is working on the case of a gay man, Alexis Arayán, who, wearing a woman's dress, takes revenge upon his corrupt father, Faustino Arayán, a high government official, whom he lures into killing him in a crime staged on the date of Christ's transfiguration and enthronement in divine essence as the Son of God. A son's revenge-suicide is thus cross-dressed as symbolic parricide and political murder. Yet, Conde's police involvement with the Christological lore mimicked in the murder goes deeper than the garments of fiction worn by the murder victim and self-fashioned designer of his suicide at father's hands. For there is more in *Máscaras* than the red-herring glitter of cross-dressing simulation and the hollow politics of gender trouble. One is reminded of what Caryl Emerson was told while on a visit to the ex-Soviet Russia in the mid-1990s during the heyday of postmodern fashion. It was said that fiction could hardly match the routine scandal of a social situation in which Christ crawled out of the window as Lolita walked through the door. In the same historical time frame, but in anticipation of the end of Communism rather than in the wake of its presumed demise, it can be said that in Havana's *Máscaras* it happens as if Christ had left the building and then knocked at the door dressed as Lolita.[23]

One is lured into such views on pervasive (and exhausted) travesty by the learned pontificating on sexual camouflage found in the writings of the character called El Recio, a Paris-based Cuban gay essayist whose nickname (Headstrong-Hard) and cynical views on simulation, mimicry, and cross-dressing are borrowed from the work of late expatriate Cuban novelist, poet, painter, and art critic Severo Sarduy. Sarduy upheld a fetish-worship and phallicist admiration for the delights of entrapment he observed in sexual *travesty*, a name now largely shunned by political correctness in favor of cross-dressing. In Sarduy's gay politics of travesty and *transvestment*, harlotry masqueraded at the service of sexual predation as a sort of catch-me-if-you-can *cynegetics*. Of prime urgency in his views on sexual simulation was the winning of a trophy, a piece of work, a stolen favor often earned while engaged in the real or figurative practice of sex-work. In their Paris lives (often finished by the AIDS "plague") men *travestis* sex-worked and sweat-it-out in performance, but in Sarduy's theories these same men extracted a surplus of aesthetic joy from the labors of faking Woman.²⁴

The high point of survival *faking it* is reached when Conde's date (Poly) takes him to a hip party in Old Havana where every accommodation of desire to the devalued yet precious powers of Brechtian micro-politics is available at the drop of a hat or a wig:

> It dawned on Conde that in the Old-Havana living room these men and women were gathered as prime evidence of their being classifiable as [here follows Poly's chaotic list of all sorts of roles, jobs, and poses, ending simply in] . . . a heterosexual Stalinist macho.
>
> —Like me [answers Conde]. And cross-dressers [*travestis*]? Are there no cross-dressers here? he asked, glaring at her chest with the eyes of a vampire hunter.
>
> —Look [says Poly], standing by the balcony door is Victoria, who prefers to be called *Viki*, but whose real name is Victor Romillo. Isn't she cute. And the one with the dark mane over there, who looks like Annia Linares, in daytime he goes by *Steve* and in nighttime by *Star*, because she's the one who sings boleros.
>
> —Tell me something: I see some thirty people here, how can you get as many things from them as you tell me?
>
> —Poly beamed like clockwork.
>
> —That comes from practicing the *multi-job* [. . .] like the one standing next to *Star*, his name is *Free Willy*, but he is at least ten of the things I told you about. (M 143–44)

Stretched by cynicism to the breaking point, simulation remains nevertheless a replicant gesture fiercely and humorously trained on the fullness of life.

By whatever name, the impulse in question retains something akin to a religious spark or charisma, a sheer *want* (*Wunch/Wish*) to keep glowing at the heart of a culture grinding in bureaucratic routine and cynical unbelief. So many dissembling and shifting faces must be saying something about money, wealth, hustle, but also about spirit, memory energies, bodies-not-for-sale, even if at the always-on-sale point. Such is the lesson in ghoulish mask-reversal witnessed at the *multi-job* party and its *multi-employed-yet-unemployed* niche of pseudo-stars and gossip mythologies. Vampire masquerade heightens simulation, but for the sake of turning camouflage theatricalness into the allegory of ordinary living-in-stress as if being dressed in someone else's borrowed nakedness.

These counterfeit social actors are surveyed in a parody of police inspection at a moment in time, in August 1989, when the dollar or *fula* is not yet *depenalized* (as it was upon the announcement by Fidel Castro on July 26, 1993—a date in the near future incorporated or camouflaged into 1989 as-it-never-was). The first clue about the relevance of currency and exchange rates to the Arayán murder comes with the discovery that "dos pesos machos [two macho bucks]" (M 58) have been plugged into the victim's rectum. These two Cuban coins become false twin clues as the murder solution shoots through the inner space of arcane mystery. The money clues left by the father, as if deposited in the son's rectum, are meant to serve as tokens of gay homicide: "It occurred to him [the murderer] in haste, in order to mislead and make believe that it was a matter between homosexuals" (216). But motive falsification by the murdering father becomes an even truer fake when linked to the pair of coin-like medals in whose manipulation the crime's solution lies. The precious clues introduce maternal love tokens into the solution, since the pair of da Vinci gold medals engraved with "the figure of universal man" (the microcosmic emblem known as *Vitruvian Man*) were bought by the victim's mother at Leonardo's birthplace itself (161). She kept one medal (which was lost) and gave the other one to her son, who wore it around his neck as he was choked to death by his father. Thinking that his son would remain unidentified, Faustino Arayán brought the medal back home and placed it in a jewel box. But the medal had not been kept in the box by Alexis since he had left the house to live with his gay lover. (The paternal oversight about mistaken filial and maternal medals leads to Faustino's own demise.)

Not without a trace of humor, the nearness between two Cuban macho bucks (with a poor dollar exchange rate) and a pair of Leonardo gold-coin emblems of divine perfection begs for scrutiny. Arayán's revenge murder of his son comes in reaction to his being denounced by his son for having faked documents in 1959 in order to "jump on the revolutionary bandwagon" using the false testimony that he had fought against dictator Batista. When Faustino masquerades what amounts to political family revenge into a case of murder between gays, the *Little Faust* in him is also carrying through with the elimination of the *Mephisto* type of character which his own name projects back upon his son's sexual queerness as the reason for his paternal repudiation of him since childhood. This is the one stellar manner in which Severo Sarduy, the real-life Cuban and Parisian author (who in *Máscaras* becomes El Recio), imagined the specular force of mimicry at work in sexual simulation.

Although inspired by Roger Caillois's speculations on insect mimicry as defensive and predatory behavior, Sarduy's approach to human sexual capture involves retroactive actions similar to the ones present in André Gide's basic *mise-en-abyme* scenario. Gide stressed a mode of reciprocity based on male anger, whereby there could be "no action on an object without the corresponding retroaction on the agent," and, more important, without involving the effect of reciprocity: "not any longer in relation with other people but in relation with oneself" (Segal 1998, 190). Transvestite male-to-male sexual predation represents an instance of agony entrapped in *mise-en-abyme*. It is a manifestation of specular egotism based on the fetish object-transfer of phallic values and veiled attributes between enwrapped male actors.

Faustino Arayán—who was "Cuba's last representative at UNICEF" (M 62)—upholds in raw and prejudiced manner Freud's views on the mother-burdened etiology of male homosexuality, for which Leonardo da Vinci stands as the highest paragon. As examined by Freud, Leonardo, an illegitimate child, would have been taken away from his mother and brought to his father's household when he was younger than five. From then on he lived in separation from Ser Piero da Vinci during most of his childhood years and under the fading but latent memory of the lost mother's excessive love and the new mother's too-exclusive care (LV 30–31). Without any help from Freud, Faustino Arayán blames his son's queerness on a pair of nurturing women, his mother and the black maid María Antonia, whose loving care of Alexis occupied the void left by paternal rejection. As the maid-nanny tells Conde: "Faustino says that because of us he came out that way . . . the poor boy began to fear his father" (M 171). Female influence is minted in the numismatic filial bond between Alexis and his mother as invested in the "figure imprisoned within the circumference" (171) in Leonardo's drawing, the one which Mrs. Arayán inspects at Conde's request in search of proof that the medal taken from the crime scene and placed back in the jewel box is indeed not the one she lost.

As Alexis's mother identifies the difference that makes the medal *his* and not *hers*, the spotless frontal nudeness of Leonardo's geometrical male emblem of perfection comes to mind. Four arms and four legs extend from a single man's chest-trunk, shoulders, and head, as the horizontal and vertical arms and legs touch the lines of the square and the slightly raised arms and spread-out legs touch the circle. Freud ventures no comments on the *Vitruvian Man* drawing and its figure of a single male body joined to its own double-extended perfection. Yet, the drawing could have suggested to Freud's cast of mind that the chance of having the figure of one male body positioned *behind* another, upon the axis of the genitals, is annulled, as the lines that draw each pair of thighs are rendered visible, in a manner that enhances the single set of male reproductive organs as the common anatomical focal point of two bodies in one.

What Freud does offer, in a copious and expanded footnote to his 1910 study of Leonardo's artistic and research fantasies, is a set of complex and graphic comments on the master's drawing of "the sexual act seen in anatomical sagittal section" (LV 17). It is in the second 1919 edition of the *Leonardo* that Freud quotes at length in a footnote the substance of R. Reitler's 1917 application of his own views on da Vinci's withdrawn sexual involvement with women, or with the female figure, in actual or imaginary terms. Freud displays Leonardo's sagittal drawing overlaid with Reitler's forensic inspection, in which it becomes the written chimerical imbrication of male and female anatomical differences in transparent coital overlap. The unpolluted double frame of male perfection in *Vitruvian Man* is replaced by entanglement, by the inadequate or fend-off depiction of internal and external female organs and body parts, inlaid with adequate male elements, of which the genitals stand out, correctly traced, as Leonardo not only drew "the testis, but put in the epididymis" (LV 18). Yet, the defective drawing in the analyst's view does succeed in depicting the near caricature of a reluctant, wigged male, suggestive of wearing garments from the other sex, even as it appears in double nakedness, *his & hers*: "the features of a man with feminine head [writes Reitler as quoted by Freud] are marked by a resistance that is positively indignant" (LV 19). Two further related oddities are found in Reitler's Freud-influenced Leonardo chimera: "The male figure has a left foot and the female one a right foot" (a coupled oddity embroiled in the "almost grotesque way" in which coitus is "being performed standing up" [19]). It should be added that, in the first replay of the act of murder in *Máscaras*, the victim is imagined in genuflection and ready to service the client who strangles him/her from the rear, while in the second replay, visualized through the voice of Faustino's confession in Conde's mind, the scene is corrected: Alexis jumps back from the ground after being knocked down by his father and is suffocated by the bigger man while locked in a struggle with him.

With or without Freud, Arayán is entrapped by a son bent on murdering himself wearing a woman's red dress. Their physical struggle and brutally choreographed murder make up a theatrical scandal. A son's suicide at his own father's hands acts out a double substitution of Oedipal parricide. The father ruins himself by killing his son as their death duel mimics in spectral resemblance male-on-male sibling sex. (This is a reverse-angle shot of Freud's notion of male homosexual perversity in the son's repressed wishes to be possessed by the father.) Leonardo's (Padura's) Leonardo signature in *Máscaras* imprints the hardcore perverse interpretation of family murder in the aesthetics of travesty by two posthumous gay Cuban artists and one living: Severo Sarduy, Virgilio Piñera, and Virgilio's live fictional *revenant* in Alberto Marqués.

This is how, beyond the solution reached upon the father's confession, the murder scene remains open to revision, open to a type of mystery play that has in fact reinvented the murder and choreographed it in sartorial splendor. In researching the crime, Detective Conde has been assisted by the extravagant figure of the playwright Alberto Marqués, a victim of internal banishment in Cuba after his attempt to put on stage an adaptation of Virgilio Piñera's *Electra Garrigó* (inspired by Sophocles' *Electra*). Besides being two different persons, Marqués and Piñera are bound together into a single compound individual through their communicant afterlives as gay dramatists. In addition to Marqués's banned adaptation of *Electra Garrigó* in line with El Recio's (Sarduy's) gay aesthetics of travesty and simulation, Leonardo's universal male paragon should be held as the key evidence of being ideologically framed. Da Vinci's male human microcosm expresses both bound and unbound human freedom as it stands framed by circle and square. The emblematic male body retains its human figure as it is *circled* and *squared*. By contrast, artists like Piñera and his Alberto Marqués communicant afterlife were bound within parameters by their own fellow artists who acted in the name of the State and the Revolution. They were framed in the early 1970s and became known as *parametrados*—placed within parameters, their persons and their art kept in ostracism. It is in the stark nakedness of such historical truth that *Máscaras* performs its unmasking of political oppression and its shattering of postmodernist diddling in the pickpocket craft of unmarked quotations.

THE MISSING BUDDHA

The Buddha never quoted, in a land where
every leaf that trembled was a quotation.
    Roberto Calasso, *Ka*

On Thursday, August 17, 1989, a total lunar eclipse was observed in many parts of the earth, including Cuba. The event was governed, as it should be until the year 2566, by the *Saros 128* periodicity cycle, which measures approximately 6,585.3 days (18 years, 11 days, and 8 hours).[25] Reading over Mario Conde's shoulder into the pages of the daily "precious information treasure" best known as *Gramma (Official Organ of the Cuban Communist Party)*, one learns of the heavenly event still to come within a week, right on Flaco Carlos's birthday. Conde's quick glance over the international pages informs him that the "world is pretty fucked-up," except in the Socialist countries, where, "in spite of relentless external pressure, the staunch determination remains to never drift away from the ascending and victorious path of history" (M 153). The Arayán crime scene in The Forest of Havana is first visited by Conde on August 7, the morning after the murder. The following Sunday, the longest narrated day in the novel, the solution is delivered of its ephemeral mysteries.

Obstetrics correspond well with the observance of a hidden (and not-so-hidden) national birthday. The Sunday solution unfolds a week and one day after the observance of the transfiguration in which the willful murder victim executes his theological revenge travesty. Alberto Marqués is the midwife figure who assists Conde that Sunday afternoon in the combined task of absorbing the murder's implications and discussing the short story written by the detective and dated the previous Thursday, August 9. Marqués reads it on the spot and tells the author that he is in fact "a false policeman" engaged in a "different transvestite act," except that in his case the detective "has gone naked" and "revealed something else" (M 219). The story appears in italics (185–93), not long after Conde watches a bus driver as he hesitates on whether to open the door and allow a pleading woman on board. The text is written in a trance. Its first readers besides the author himself are Flaco Carlos and his mother, Jose. When taken to Marqués for a second opinion, the story still lacks a title. Citing Camus' *L'etranger* as precedent, Marqués suggests the title *La muerte en el alma* (*Death in the Soul*) and praises how the story withholds judgment on the afflicted lives it briefly surveys, in a manner, he elaborates, that would have drawn official fire during "another epoch" for "assuming bourgeois anti-Marxist aesthetic postures" (M 219), because it does not pass judgment on the social ills it should expose, mirrored in what Marqués tells Conde are his own and Virgilio Piñera's troubles as *parametrados* guilty of improper conduct during the early 1970s. Thus, the communicant voices of Marqués and Piñera are joined in the afterlife of a private literary *seance* with Detective Conde. The seance is held on the second Sunday in August, which in the year 1989 that was, and the one that never was, *came* and *comes* on the thirteenth day, on Fidel Castro's birthday.

The seldom-heard noun *ephemeris* refers to calendars and book charts for the tracking of heavenly bodies as well as for logging daily events and marking the almanac dates of important celebrations. The story written by Conde is punctuated by eight Tuesdays and a fatal Thursday in the lives of a bus driver and the woman he chances to meet in early August and kills for no stated motive in late October. The plot constitutes a private almanac of eight weeks charted by the joint-lives and intersecting routines of two social robots. Besides marking dates with such emphasis (as well as itineraries, schedules, automaton bus-work routes, the victim's schedule of classes, and the driver's married-life habits), the detective's story avoids any solution and limits itself to narrating the crime. It simply lets the case tell itself and closes it without any further concern for mysteries, motives, or solutions behind the killer's actions or the victim's possible collaborative role in her own undoing. As it leaves behind the case to be solved or not by police work, the story seems to turn its back on the need to confront crime, just as it disavows in minimalist fashion the chance to explain the questions unrelated to criminal actions and motives posed by the case. The story posits—without addressing questions to it—a realm of intelligible motives at stake either above or below the rationale and rationality of both the criminal mind and its surveillance and capture by law enforcement. Flaco Carlos, the story's first non- or post-authorial reader, calls it "squalid" (in homage, no doubt, to J. D. Salinger and quoting from the story "For Esmé—with Love and Squalor": "This is the squalid, or moving, part of the story, and the scene changes").[26] Flaco Carlos knows much about wounds marked by squalor, by the shark-sharp (*squalus*) asperities of life before and after combat. For, when it comes to afterlives, Flaco's life in *Four Seasons* marks the meridian of no return between the split second in which the spine-shattering bullet hits him and the perpetual aftermath of recovery, in contagious guilt, held together by the bonds of generational friendship.

The *Four Seasons* serial plot lies within the compass first opened in *Pasado perfecto* as one learns that Carlos never knew what hit him; that the group calling itself the *hidden generation* is united (in Conde's authorship's design) by Flaco's Angola War maiming: "Conde was convinced that it had been his own war, even though he had never held a rifle in his hands, and the enemy's face was obvious: Flaco laying in bed"; and, ever since that moment, "the clean, unworried, happy friendship of old, was sullied by a feeling of guilt that Conde could never exorcize" (Pp 157). The compass opened by trauma begins to close in *Paisaje de otoño* at the point where Mario Conde's Flaco novel appears as work-in-progress printed in italics over a page of unmarked citation. It ends in lapidary tones: "*He had received that bullet without sender, guided by a faceless man, shot by a kind of hatred that he had never felt nor shared*" (Po 159). The victim in question is the maimed friend-of-friends, Flaco, but between him and the writer in Conde's authorship design stands the "X" of Salinger's squalor. It is the same "X" assigned to the staff sergeant who "several weeks after V-E Day" shares a room somewhere in Bavaria with nine other American soldiers in Salinger's "For Esmé—with Love and Squalor." The soldiers' wounded afterlives exist in the "'Dear God, life is hell'" (NS 105) shell-shocked aftermath of massive combat. Corporal "Z" tells "X" (who is trying to light a cigarette with shaky hands) that he "goddam near fainted" when he first saw him at the hospital: "You looked like a goddam *corpse*. How much weight ya lose? How many pounds ya know?" (NS 107–8). Five straight campaigns of warfare after D Day turned Salinger's shell-shocked "X" into a skinny *flaco* sack of bones in the eyes of Corporal Z, his jeep partner throughout the ordeal. Their bond makes them war relatives of Flaco's Angola veteran physical ordeal. Clay (as Corporal Z is named) "was a huge, photogenic young man of twenty-four," who during the war had been photographed by a national magazine in the Hürtgen Forest "with a Thanksgiving turkey in each hand" (NS 106). (One may envision a similar picture of Conde's Flaco friend in the Angolan bush, as yet unhurt, a lost image in the spiritual wars of visual memory.)

The observance of the ephemeris on F. C.'s birth date in *Máscaras* trails off into *Paisaje de otoño* when, for the first time in *Four Seasons*—and from then on until the end—Flaco's name is written with a lowercase *f* for the nickname: "flaco Carlos" (Po 24). An F to *f*-related "X" may be said to mark

Flaco's birthday as a hidden and unclaimed Cuban ephemeris: a blank-yet-engraved date standing just one step away from where combat death rests in the Unknown Soldier's missing dog tag. In the maimed body and restless soul of Conde's best friend lie the afterlives of the war dead. Also, on August 17, four days removed from August 13, F. C.'s birthday quotes and iterates (like a blank or muted hendiadys) the other *F. C.* of the *Fidel Castro* birth date. The "X" of squalor marks unknowingness in the face of uncertain fate. But it also marks knowingness in opposing such uncertainty. *"X" points at nothing in particular on behalf of no one in particular, no one except the utmost particular singularity wherein character claims itself as memorable, unsoiled and as soulful as squalid, and, in thus claiming itself as unfading, it stands menaced by what it wishes to overcome.*

It seems typical in such claims to honor and posterity to wish oneself memorable and unsoiled. But, *squalid*? The squalid condition would seem all the more odd in association with posterity, unless it implied a moral fiber at whose core the material conditions that define squalor were spiritually reversed into the wealth of friendship. Hence, when two Army Intelligence officers investigate corruption in Conde's headquarters detective unit and his name comes up, Chief of Squad Major Rangel dumbfounds them by declaring that the lieutenant likes to write about "squalid and moving things" (M 127). He might as well have said *miserable* things in his efforts to perplex the investigators with things not worth their time in being of material insignificance to an inquest aimed at uncovering the flow of stolen goods and illegal currency, but an inquest also aimed at *not* allowing such criminal police wrongdoing to highlight miserable zones of squalor in the social fabric whose protection and surveillance it is supposed to control.

Squalor is found transformed into sustainable wretchedness in the Old San Isidro barrio bordering the docks. It is at the heart of it, where prostitutes once labored in droves, that matters of honor, occupation, and self-knowledge converge on Conde's work well beyond crime. He goes to San Isidro working on the last murder case which he must solve in just three days before making good on his promise to quit the force. Havana's "alien" borderland and "most ignoble stretch" of dock-life and beehive tenement sex cells bring up the old question of what makes a man a *whoreson* or *hijo de puta* (Po 118). The question lies in whether the whore's condition is perpetual and her son's fate forever *bewhor'd* even if his birth comes after she quits her kind of work. It was at the "port's most mythic" Two Brothers

Bar that Conde's friend Andrés, while drunk, told his buddies that having a *puta* for a mother does not a whoreson make, even when born at the time of her trade (Po 119). (A matter of honor to which police lieutenant Fabricio, Conde's nemesis, applies his jealous scorn.)

The lieutenant (whose last name is never given) treats Conde with insolence and triggers his homophobic rage. Fabricio's presumed lack of manliness comes up when Conde remembers his grandfather Rufino, around whose cockfighting pit he learned that real men do not have to brag about their manhood or *hombría*. Things come to a boiling point upon "Old Wolf" Jorrín's sudden death. The two enemies get into a brawl outside the funeral home. Himself blinded by rage, Conde is hit smack in the face with a blind man's buff from the back of Fabricio's hand. "Coño, qué *galletaza*! [What a fucking slap!]" (VC 188) is the phrase heard from the school kids, already experienced machos who are well aware of the extra insult lugged by the itchy unmanly *galleta* slap (in fitting response to Conde's earlier promise to Fabricio that he would "rub his itch" anytime and anywhere he wanted to).

The brawl comes on the heels of the scene already discussed in which Jorrín's death prompts thoughts of transience and oblivion at Yorick's grave site. In *Hamlet* a "whoreson dead body" is all that is left of the king's jester in the grave-digger's contemptuous memory of an old buddy of his as he hands the skull over to the prince: "A whoreson mad fellow's it was" (5.1.166, 170). As observed by William Kerrigan, in Hamlet's world, "to call a woman a 'whore' or 'bawd' is not to call her a prostitute," as when the prince says of Claudius: "[he] that killed my king and whor'd my mother" (5.2.64), meaning that she has received gifts from a traitor and usurper.[27] The same applies to Conde and Fabricio as they face off in the role of specular whoresons at San Isidro's Two Brothers or Dos Hermanos Bar. Fabricio has been kicked out of the force; he is drunk and beaten as he persists in asking Conde if the slap he landed on him still itches. The corrupt dealings that led to Fabricio's purge along with four other detectives also caused Major Rangel's firing, even though he was innocent of any wrongdoing. (Rangel is the clean cop in charge and Fabricio the rotten subaltern who insists on diminishing the major's former rank by suggesting with sexual innuendos that Rangel and Conde were cronies.) Yet, even if Conde is right when he puts Fabricio among "policías hijos de puta como tú [whoreson cops like you]" and calls him "un chivato y un puta mala [a squealer and bad whore]" (Po 123), it seems that his unquestioned accuracy in banishing his nemesis off the plot with such a tongue-lashing involves him in righteous scapegoating. The term for scapegoat in Spanish is *chivo expiatorio*. The Cuban slang noun *chivato* means "squealer" and the verb *chivar* means to "pester" or to "trouble" someone. The twin roles of squealer and scapegoat are embodied in Fabricio's person as the conjured object of Mario Conde's avenging wrath.[28]

There is no better place in which to consider scapegoating than barrio San Isidro. It is there that the voice of Calvert Casey utters its aberrant homily of nocturnal atonement and incorporation aimed at (and infused with) "three long ages of weariness" and "stale commercial coitus."[29] The pleading voice pleads for its own "swollen, rotten body" to be plunged into the black waters assigned in the "old bay" to the chimerical "mother, father San Isidro," a "sublime toothless faggot," so that the putative son may lick "the pus of [their] ancient flank" (CS 16). A species of filial lust implores attachment to the phantasmagoria of combined parenthood into which the load of evil usually at issue in scapegoating is dumped. The "mournful semen of twenty despairing generations" has fed venereal juices into the "tender, rheumy-eyed great mother" from whom the voice's plead for atonement begs Her to rock and to nurse the body it mouths: "Rock me in your great leprous arms, pus-smeared lover; feed me from the great raw pustules of your breasts" (16). It is hard not to think of the "leperous distilment" venom dropped into King Hamlet's ear, but more so of Prince Hamlet's "'mobbled queen'" Hecuba (with her "bisson [blinding] rheum" [2.2.499–502]) and her abject affinity with such an infected nurturer of filth as San Isidro. Hecuba's figure suggests itself prompted by "rheumy-eyed" in place of the more patently venereal "blenorrágica" in the original Spanish. (Shedding off the chimeric pun *blenoTrragic*: tragic waste rendered routine at San Isidro distills *Cuba* down to Her filthy essence.) In all of this, the foul sterility crammed into San Isidro's venereal district in Casey's voice of atonement seeks fecundity beyond sexual means. The incestuous communion between scapegoating and atonement seems implicit in the wish to feed from filth and through such feeding serve in turn as food for self-defilement. As it swells and rots its way into the corresponding infections in the bay's waters, the body in question evokes Hamlet's "convocation of politic worms" as the fat substance of the king's body travels by earthworm's bait and fish's mouth until it reaches "progress through the guts of a beggar" (4.3.19–31). Hamlet entertains such thoughts of transpersonal interspecies and digestive and excretory traces right on the eve of his trip to England and what should turn out to be his last departure from Danish soil, to which he, however, returns for a brief though much fulfilled afterlife.

Hamlet succeeds in his round-trip home by means of forgery. First, he opens the commission given by the king to Rosencrantz and Gildenstern and finds that it orders his own beheading. He promptly forges a second letter requesting that its bearers be put to death and seals it with his dead father's signet. With this in mind, as if standing next to the wayfarer prince back on native soil, the Four Seasons endgame is reached.

Conde's last case can be briefly inspected by looking into its cast of characters and occupations:

Major Rangel: Chief of police force detectives unit. Fired after an Army Intelligence investigation on grounds that he failed to prevent corruption in the ranks.

Lieutenant Mario Conde: Working on the case on a terminal three-day deadline after resigning from the force on news of Rangel's removal.

Colonel Alberto Molina: Analyst on transfer from Army Intelligence as Rangel's replacement.

Lieutenant Fabricio: One of five detectives removed from the force charged with corruption. Conde's nemesis.

Miguel Forcade Mier: Ex-head of the Expropriation Bureau at the National Institute of Urban Reform and Economic Planning. Returns to Cuba after years in Miami (murder victim).

Miriam Bodes: Victim's wife and younger than him by more than twenty years (accomplice to murder suspect).

Gerardo Gómez de la Peña: Former head of Economic Planning. Served time for embezzlement and falsification of documents. Victim's ex-boss. Swindled by him. Owner of a fake Matisse (murder suspect).

Rolando Fermín Bodes Alvarez: Bureaucrat. Served time for embezzlement. Miriam's brother (murder suspect).

Adrián Riverón: Municipal director of the Office of Control and Distribution of Supplies in charge of food distribution in urban sectors. Miriam's ex-boyfriend and current lover (murderer).

Panchín Bodes: Bureaucrat. Serial monogamist. Miriam's father.

Dr. Alfonso Forcade: Botanist, spiritualist, telepathist. Victim's father.

Fernando García Abreu: Expert forger of paintings (including the early Matisse masterpiece *Autumn Landscape*).

Juan Emilio Friguens: Art historian and curator. Expert in lost paintings and forgeries.

Andrés: Physician. Member of Conde's *hidden generation* group. Has filed a formal request to migrate from Cuba.

Basura: Stray dog named Trash rescued and kept by Conde.

Felix: Hurricane.

Miguel Forcade Mier's castrated body is found at the sewage wasteland seashore of Playa del Chivo or Goat Beach, its head cracked, probably by a vintage baseball bat made of mahogany. The victim's return to Cuba is caused by the hidden purpose of recovering and taking out of the island on a fast boat the statue of a golden Buddha buried in his father's botanical garden. (The thirty-pound gold figure represents in legend shape a huge fifteen-centuries-old Chinese *MacGuffin* buried on Cuban soil, in homage to Dashiell Hammett's *Maltese Falcon*, beneath a tangled web of private forgeries, official fraud, and embezzlement.)

Before defecting in 1978 and moving to Miami, Forcade Mier made enemies selling the confiscated art and furniture assets of the families who had left the island. Taking advantage of his charge to issue official certificates, he sold to his own boss (Gómez de la Peña) the fake Matisse left at home by the García Abreu clan. It was painted by Abreu Jr. with the authenticating rubric decoy of a missing yellow dog, a doubtless mark of fraud quickly noted by curator and forgery expert Juan Emilio Friguens when asked by Conde to inspect the canvas. The accursed and genuine golden Buddha buried in the garden and the worthless Matisse hanging like a trophy in someone's living room are juggled by Forcade Mier in his doomed attempt to abandon Cuba once again and for good without leaving behind the statue. For which purpose he alerts his elderly father—to whom he had long ago entrusted the secret—that the missing Buddha had in fact been found by him and buried in the hallowed grounds of the botanist's garden, instead of a dog named Buddha, as he first had told him.

Wanting to help Conde crack the case, Forcade breaks the promise made to his son not to tell anyone about the Buddha. The fabulous tale he weaves about fifteen centuries in the life of the statue puts the old man in meteorological and telepathic alignment with Conde, whose certainty about the coming of Hurricane Felix he shares and endorses more than anyone else in the story, just as he proves at one point capable of reading the detective's thoughts. With a hint at those "charms" which at the end of *The Tempest* Prospero declares "all o'erthrown" (5.318), Forcade reveals that, more than a century ago, a tempest like the one now approaching caused the Buddha's disappearance from Cuba. (It seems that, just as the Tempest may be summoned by privileged charms to shipwreck people upon an Island, with a bit of luck and good timing, a random storm may be met as if by chance at the mouth of a bay on Cuba's northern coast to cloak in shipwreck the escape for parts unknown of two thieves with a golden Buddha.) In coordination across time, the successful theft of the Buddha under high winds in 1870 matches the lethal failure of Forcade's son to remove it from the island yet again in early October 1989. Detective Conde understands that the dead son lived only for the statue's sake, in which he saw "sufficient splendor to change his karma" (Po 194), and thus died murdered and ignorant of what his own father learned from the Buddha's gold-shaped smile, that truth lies beyond all realms: "its ultimate spiritual essence wholly afar from the earthly world, untouched beyond the kingdom of appearances" (197). Yet, beyond all smiles, a cruel joke attends the Forcade father-son karma unplugging.

As explained by Roberto Calasso, originally, during a long early time when all actions were applied to sacrifice, the term *karman* related to all endeavors, but it went on to gain autonomy, as a "neutral, generic word to indicate all actions," so that, by the time of Buddha's teachings and his many silences and studious omissions, any given action would be implicitly unbound from its knotted duty to ancient sacrifice. On the Buddha's effects on *karman* and ritual offerings Calasso writes: "The Buddha undid the knot that tied the victim to the sacrificial pole. But at the very moment he was undoing it, he explained that everything is a knot. From their vantage point in the heavens, the spies of Varuna, god of knots, were watching" (Calasso 1998, 366–67). While growing up in his father's secluded park, Siddhartha was prevented from seeing the spectacle of old age and death. Later on, the Buddha would love the solace found in parks near towns; his "wanderings were punctuated by the rests he took in these parks" (367). Therein lies a link with Forcade's garden and the burial implantation on its soil of a Buddhist token of joyful wisdom turned into a golden fetish of greed and lust.

Forcade's botanical enclosure represents the navel of the story on Cuban soil in converse association with the wandering whirlwind of Hurricane Felix. While much feared, the storm's harm is as certain to be overcome as is the awareness that this hurricane is and is not. For, besides the switched coordinates of latitude which would put it somewhere near the Arctic Circle, the Caribbean Tempest's actuality over the roofs of Havana defies refutation—just as it happens with Prospero's charmed weather magic in The Tempest. ("There's no harm done . . ." not so much perdition as an hair," is Prospero's phrase to Miranda [1.2.26, 30].) And yet, harm does come to Forcade and his falsely prodigal son from kindred and mightier sources of energy, honor, and disgrace overcharged with religious wisdom.

Old Forcade dwells inside a locked garden or *hortus conclusus* in which various elements of theological and poetic lore are clustered. The association in medieval learning between the locked garden and the Virgin's chaste fertility finds itself represented in the altar which in Forcade's patio gathers the "crowned Virgen de la Caridad del Cobre" (Cuba's highest sacred figure) who is "flanked by St. Lazarus the leper with his dogs, and the very black Virgen de Regla" (Po 174). Turning to Chaucer's use of the locked garden motif in the "Merchant's Tale," one finds that, like old January, Forcade's son Miguel marries a much younger woman. In Miguel's case, as in January's, cuckoldry is not prevented, but whereas old January builds a walled garden in which to keep his youthful May bride safe from the sweet harms brought by young intruders, Miguel's wife poses a bit more complex danger.

The Song of Solomon phrase on which the medieval locked garden tradition rests makes one single body out of the bride and her enclosure: "hortus conclusus soror mea sponsa / hortus conclusus fons signatus [a garden locked is my sister, my bride / a garden locked, a fountain sealed]." [30] By contrast, Forcade's garden is more like the graveyard of his son's wasted karma, his Inferno. The Buddha's burial site being dug up by Conde (as it continues "without giving birth" to the statue) has "in fact been Miguel Forcade's life's entombment," from a distance in his Miami exile (Po 195). Then, even if one is to believe that the unearthed statue is pure gold, as reported, there is no doubt that its carnal clone in Miriam's false blonde hair shows, in the intimate parts of her body, all the rank genuineness of those precious jewels in whose adulterous pursuit young squires like Chaucer's Damyan breached locked gardens. In this instance the Chaucer connection follows a crooked path, as when Conde uncovers an extra gift besides the unburied Buddha. He finds the "shining" clue of Miriam's adultery with her husband's killer in a photo dedicated to her lover Adrián Riverón hidden at the bottom of a drawer. She poses naked, legs slightly open in full depth, showing dark instead of gold, and inscribing the promise: "UNTIL YOU SHALL HAVE ME AGAIN, IN FLESH AND BONE. YOUR MIRIAM. 7-12-84" (Po 212–13).

But besides such chthonic and venereal wealth there is also vision-in-blindness next to the Buddha buried in old Forcade's garden. (In Chaucer's tale, merchant January goes suddenly blind, so comedy may profit from his not learning of his cuckoldry, even as he regains his sight but also gains forgetfulness of what he has seen with the combined help of Pluto and Proserpine.) The elder Forcade is not blind, but, since first met at the garden, his eyes appear "lined in live red, as if the tired flesh around them refused to keep them there any longer" (Po 175). His are *rheumy eyes* blinded in tears like Hecuba's in "bisson rheum": "It's a bad day of the year," he tells Conde, as "his tears are swallowed into the bloody well of his eyes" (175). Figural blindness enables sublime vision in Forcade's role as Magus. His suffering and custody of the plants he considers himself to have "fathered" and which he is convinced will in many cases not survive his death are purgatorial. His figure inspires comparison with Time itself as the Old Man staring at the moon in the middle sector of Coleridge's "Limbo":

> But that is lovely—looks like human Time,—
> An Old Man with a steady look sublime,
> That stops his earthly task to watch the skies;
> But he is blind—a statue has such eyes;—
> Yet having moonward turned his face by chance,
> Gazes the orb with moon-like countenance,
> With scant white hairs, with foretop bald and high,
> He gazes still,—his eyeless face all eye;—
> As 'twere an organ full of silent sight,
> His whole face seemed to rejoice in light!
> Lip touching lip, all moveless, bust and limb—
> He seems to gaze at that which seems to gaze on him![31]

The sublime ability to commune with the moon and with nature at large through blindness is what justifies the allegorical comparison between Coleridge's blind visionary Old Man and Padura's Magus planted on Cuba's open yet locked-in garden.

The microcosmic garden is kept open only as the object of illusion whose fulfillment remains barred by the collapse of patriarchal love into melancholia. Conde's success in sharing telepathic images with Forcade by opening his own endopsychic projections to his communicant mastery is correlative with the patriarch's son's blocked access to his own father, except to try to steal back the golden idol. Parental melancholia harbored in the father locks out the false return of a prodigal son who is back in Cuba just to flee once again seeking to achieve his dreams of plutocracy.

ONE WITH THE TEMPEST

Within the scope of harvesting Shakespeare's *The Tempest* in search of political symbols of resistance against colonialism, Dr. Alfonso Forcade's life-work is a colossal ruin. Botanist, spiritualist, telepathist. But as such "a prophet devalued by memory and time" (Po 145), father of a recurrent crook who profited from State business affairs and who mastered Socialist and state-capitalist government shenanigans. Forcade may combine both Prospero and Caliban. It seems about time for the huge though intimate difference which has split these twin characters in the modern history of Latin American intellectual politics to vanish, vanish as if it lacked in color separation inside the spectrum of fading dreams. In truer Caliban fashion, rather than the bipolar split ruled by political propaganda, their combined figures should now stand in solitary observance of the wretched absence of prosperity. If one was taught how to curse by the other, by now and for the foreseeable future their common though disparately held stocks lie in the accursed share of arrest in growth and diminished Cuban dreams placed on hold.

Were it still possible to affirm hope through such joint ventures, these two-characters-in-one would have to disclose their mutual differences through acts utterly open to chance; insofar as chance may offer the chance to oppose closure, locked-in-step policies, slogans. Thus, Dr. Forcade, standing at the forking paths of his Garden, could be played, with some applied cosmetics and the right garments, by Jack Birkett, in the afterlife of his impersonation of Caliban in Derek Jarman's 1979 free version of *The Tempest*. Rather than speculating on the results of such combined mimicry, it should suffice to observe, in order to leave matters quite open, that in their learned *Shakespeare's Caliban: A Cultural History*, Alden and Virginia Mason Vaughan allow blind man to escape the more than twenty identities listed in their index for the remarkable person whose dramatist inventor plainly calls "a savage and deformed slave," and whose uncanny performance by Birkett the authors examine at some length. For Jack Birkett, as his eyes might or might not let the viewer know, is and was blind, though, in acting up Caliban, he singularly acts not in blindness.³²

Music is the memory of what never happened.
JACK GILBERT, *The Great Fires*

Detective and writer Mario Conde's professional fate in *Four Seasons* takes a Romantic path to closure and to any foreseeable reopening of hopes made tangible. He summons a hurricane named Felix and addresses its landfall intoning Heredia's farewell to the World and greetings to the Tempest:

At last, fatal world, we stand severed,
the Hurricane and I in ourselves alone.³³

At his birthday party, on October 9, 1989, after listening to Andrés and his cathartic biography of separation and current wish to leave Cuba, Conde goes home in high winds and declines to spend the night with his old flame and current lover, Tamara. The abstention may seem definitive, for, beginning with the writing undertaken that same night, literature has come to occupy Conde's first life-choice in the afterlife of being a cop. Even the clues left behind for his own benefit—in possibly coming back to Tamara —require passage through the ordeals of narration and symbol. His earnest insistence on calling the business and office of narration in print "moving and squalid" is foxy and unsentimental, but deeply Romantic in the irony that sustains it. There are base alchemy elements in the cynical irony infused in Conde's charms, as witnessed by the companionship of Basura (the dog named Trash adopted from the raging Tempest). Trash is the third dog in the story. The first one is removed from the Matisse canvas to cue an act of forgery; the second is buried in fake replacement of the missing Buddha; the third is adopted as a token and street-smart fetish of the trashing about in the authorship of detective novels for ulterior and as yet unknown involved readings.

In the end, the Tempest signature in *Four Seasons* belongs to a pair of paired twin sets. One set is truly identical and female; the other is mirrored in the likeness of male friendship. It so happens that, once upon a time, Flaco and Conde fell in love with the same identical twin named Tamara but had to settle for the dream of sharing and switching her in the shape of her twin Aymara, after the one sister they both loved picked another boyfriend. Everything in Flaco and Conde's dream Wonderland seemed *jima-gua* or twin-like (houses, spouses, children born in twin sets on the same date). They fulfilled their twin brotherhood in sororal and tribal fashion. Even their mothers would become umbilically attached in mutual after-lives. Doña Jose supports her invalid son Flaco with love and convivial excess. Conde attends her miraculous banquets as if to nurse (rather than just feed) himself from their bountifulness. In the end, a share of the lust invested and satisfied in these instances of *Agape* is present in the scene of *Eros* at the morgue as Conde cleans, caresses, and kisses his mother's body in a moment of sublime *necrofiliation*.

As discussed above in reference to Martí's *patriotic-erotic* poetry of *adel-phofilia* or brotherly mourning, the lost friend returns as sibling—as if borrowed back from the dead. The bosom from which the returned issue issues forth bears the mother's seal, her imprint, her life-and-death birth-mark stamp, on whose surface the *philéo-* of suspended hyphenation in *I love* seeks free passage through love, exemption for any further debt even as owed to her. If the conjured-up Tempest of happy Felix should evoke in the conjurer the intense love for the lost twin, the mother's mark marks the navel spot of such love-dream of twinhood.

Yoruba beliefs brought to Cuba, fostered among Afro-Cubans, the worship of twin *orishas* known as *jimaguas* or *Abeyí*, who in the eyes of Fernando Ortiz were like the *Dioscuri*: sons of Zeus and brothers of Helen by the same mother, Leda, and confederates of Venus as the Gemini in dichotomous sky nexus. As such, the celestial *jimaguas* are related to "snakes, medicine, sex, fertility, tempests, thunder, and rain" (Hu 467). The *jimaguas* are commonly seen as the least touched-up among the *orishas*. Unlike others, which were dressed in Catholic hybrid shapes, these two *orishas* remained stark and idol-like, as if begging unembarrassed recognition in the redeemed colonialist slur of *fetiches*: "the idols in this case are united in a single shape, the more so since the doll is meant to be wrapped up leaving unwrapped only the twin heads: the twins united in one piece issuing perhaps from the carving of the idol in wood rather than from any given symbolic purpose."[34] This early instance of *jimagua* lore in Ortiz's work is followed by a closeup taken from the investigative work and press sensationalism during the breakout of *negros brujos* witch-hunting in late 1904: "Inside the wrapping, in the hollow part of the *jimaguas*, were found human remains, horns, roots, dirt, nails, stones, as well as other trash soaked in blood. These *jimaguas*, so prepared, were recently found in the hamlet of Abreus"

(1995b, 75). Tied together in one bundle and grounded in stormy October, Mario Conde's *jimagua* brotherhood with flaco Carlos (and with el Flaco Carlos and Leonardo Padura Fuentes) takes effect in meteorological fashion across the yearly round of cyclone culture in Cuba. But their fraternal knotted soul should also be placed against the darker background of the first genuinely *noir* case in Cuban modern history: the *negros brujos* inquest that led to the execution by *garrotte* in January 1906 of Victor Molina and the ex-slave and healer Domingo Boucourt.

The indelible stain of scapegoating rests not so much on the journalistic rush to find witchcraft motives for rural child murder as on what it yielded as scientific trophies in the pair of "criminal brains" displayed at the University of Havana's Museo Antrológico Montané. Perhaps, rummaging through papers in the near future at the National Archive, at the heart of San Isidro, ex-detective-turned-novelist Mario Conde could find clues and energies to reopen that remote *noir* season in the darkest colors of his people's history.

notes

INTRODUCTION

1 A second edition of *La isla que se repite* was published in 1998 in which the chapters added to the second of two editions in English are incorporated. See *RI*.

2 The opening pages of "The Poetry of Pope," published in the *North British Review* of August 1848, have achieved unique status and are often reprinted as "The Literature of Knowledge and the Literature of Power"; see *Conf* 329–34.

CHAPTER ONE

1 Menstrual taboos are discussed in GB 686–705.

2 John Bodel, "Trimalchio's Underworld" (Tatum 1994, 243, 256 n. 37).

3 Virgil 1894–1900, book 6, 17–18; and Virgil 1977, 147.

4 Although the title is often cited without initial capital letters after the first word, as is the norm in Spanish, Cabrera Infante has consistently adopted the capitalized spelling followed here.

5 These views are articulated in the essay frequently excerpted as "The Literature of Knowledge and the Literature of Power," which the author took from an 1848 review he wrote on the works of Alexander Pope. De Quincey 2000, 16:340.

6 "Italian opera is paradigmatic of power because, for De Quincey—who does not understand Italian—it has absolutely no ideational content. Opera thus reduces language to a series of semiotically opaque but immediately affecting musical sounds in which emotions and images are excited, but not necessarily shared with another mind" (Rzepka 1995, 34–35).

7 Jackson Lears writes: "Outside the orbit of industrial capitalism, according to Marxian tradition, products became animated by embodying the beliefs and practices of their particular social milieu; they epitomized a sense of intimate relatedness to the material world. Under industrial capitalism, in contrast, production was severed from consumption, and an atomistic, dualistic worldview prevailed; things were isolated from their origins and seemed to move mysteriously on their own: a different sort of fetishism was born" (1994, 5).

CHAPTER TWO

1 The title "Weariness of Work Inextricable" is taken from W. F. Jackson Knight's translation of the labyrinth reference ("hic labor ille domus et inextricabilis error") in Virgil's lines (1894–1900, book 6, 16–19): "hic crudelis amor tauri suppostaque furto / Pasiphae mixtumque genus prolesque biformis / Minotaurus inest, Veneris monimenta nefandae; hic labor ille domus et inextricabilis error [In it, that bull-love, love callous; Pasiphae, bride in secrecy; and there, record how wicked love can be, hybrid procreation, two shapes in one, Mino-

taur in the midst; and all the old wandering ways of the house that was there]"
(Jackson Knight 1967, 142).

2 "La voz de la tortuga," Vt 51–58.

3 *Caguama* (a name of indigenous Caribbean origin) is interchangeably used for either the green or loggerhead sea turtles. (Professor Ernst discussed *caguama* mating habits by mail and confirmed—in reference to the tale—that "mating could never take place in this fashion.")

4 *New Oxford Annotated Bible* 1977 (Song of Solomon 2.12). The biblical phrase is noted by Raymond D. Souza but without reference to its possible source in Carroll's *Alice*, even though elsewhere he mentions Cabrera Infante's confessed indebtedness to Martin Gardner: "He has remarked [. . .] that the novel [*Tres Tristes Tigres*] owes more to Martin Gardner's *The Annotated Alice* than to Lewis Carroll's work" (*GCI* 97). Martin Gardner (*AA* 139 n. 6) discusses the connection in the King James text.

5 "La vieron los dos al mismo tiempo y al mismo tiempo pensaron lo mismo. Los dos muchachos eran de veras muy parecidos, sólo que uno era bien parecido y el otro no. Pero los dos eran igualmente fuertes y a menudo pulsaban con brazos idénticos[. . . .] Eran, de hecho, los muchachos más fuertes del pueblo, sólo que uno era listo y el otro no. Ahora el más listo de los muchachos concibió una idea que no tuvo que decir a su amigo (a menudo los dos pensaban lo mismo al mismo tiempo)" (Vt 11–12).

6 "Un muchacho del pueblo se había enamorado de una belleza local y ella también se enamoró. Querían casarse, pero él era muy pobre. Ella también era pobre. Todo el mundo en el pueblo era pobre" (Vt 10).

7 See IS 321–446 and HC 209–44. In a visit to the keys recorded in "Crónica de un mundo que se acaba [Chronicle of a world coming to an end]," Leonardo Padura Fuentes writes: "We found something unexpected: a *tinglado*, the famous black turtle, laying face up on deck, teary eyes, heavy breathing, legs tied over the chest . . . now and then it lets go a deep accusatory sigh" (1994, 152).

8 "En medio de estos manglares / que se columpian gentiles, / brillan conchas y reptiles / y cacuamas de los mares," by folk poet Juan Cristobal Nápoles Fajardo, el *Cucalambé* (quoted in Ortiz 1985, 105).

9 "El huracán y los simbolismos del caracol y el tabaco" (Hu 538–93).

10 Hu 540, 553–55, and CC 121.

11 Hu 555. But Carl O. Sauer among others has identified the narcotic mixed with tobacco snuff as the plant *Piptadenia peregrina*, introduced into the Caribbean from South America and mentioned by Fray Ramón Pané in his *Relación* (Account) of the indigenous people of Hispaniola and Cuba: "La cual cohoba es un cierto polvo, que ellos toman a veces para purgarse y para otros efectos [Cohoba is a certain powder that they take at times to purge themselves and for other effects]" (*AAI* 15–16/R 30).

CHAPTER THREE

1 The title "A Fallen-from-Use Path Taken on the Outskirts of Town" translates "un paseo desusado por las afueras del pueblo" (Gg 137), the topographical verbal marker of passionate family murder in the banquet speech examined at length in this chapter.

2 The sense of caricature, character, and cinematic pastiche informing this chapter benefits from Lynch's "Fleshing Out Characters" (1998, 23–79).

3 "La cebada tostada y reducida a harina en un molinillo de piedra, puesto en movimiento con la mano por medio de un pequeño hueso de cabra, era el alimento sano y sabroso que llamaban gofio o ahorén, del cual usaban como de pan cotidiano" (Viera y Clavijo 1981, 1:69).

4 Souza's biographical account, based on the author's own testimony, differs importantly from the published speech's text, as it places the son's birth before the "visit" to the Canary Islands: "Shortly after the birth of Guillermo senior, Francisco Cabrera returned to his native country with his Cuban wife and new son for a visit" (GCI 7). (It remains to be seen whether shifting the birth of the son from Cuba to the Canary Islands results from the author's memory lapse or from the speaker's wish to offer his father's Canarian birth to his host Tenerife audience and the talk's sponsors.)

5 "Pero mi padre no era un hombreriego sino una mujeriego que, como Descartes, avanzaba enmascarado hacia cada Cristina, su larva oculta tras la máscara del pudor político: un comunista no puede ser libertario ni libertino" (Gg 140, emphasis added).

6 Masson 1969, 21. In his Garbo biography, Barry Paris relies on Sven Stolpe's *Christina of Sweden* (New York, 1966) in declaring the queen a pseudo-hermaphrodite, with internal reproductive organs of one sex and external organs of another (G 290–92). However, in his "Queen Christina of Sweden, A Medical/Anthropological Investigation of Her Remains in Rome," Carl Hermann Hjortssjö's osteological analysis of the royal bones revealed their conformance to a "typically female" structure. See QC 300.

7 "Latin: Larva, espectro, fantasma, máscara fantasmal . . . larvado, disfrazado [in disguise]" (Bde).

8 "Por quién doblan [dub/toll] las películas," (Cs 67–79).

9 Bergstrom 1999, 89. Geoffrey O'Brien becomes the Proust of cinephilia in *The Phantom Empire: Movies in the Mind of the Twentieth Century* (New York, 1995).

10 "This young Queen's face changed so suddenly according to the motions of her soul that from one moment to another she became unrecognizable" (Baillet 1985, 303).

CHAPTER FOUR

1 The title "Talking about Beauty and the Beast, She's Both" quotes Deckard (Harrison Ford) as he speaks about Zhora, the replicant Snake Woman (Joanna Cassidy), in Ridley Scott's *Blade Runner* (1984). The film is reviewed in *Cine o sar-*

dina by Cabrera Infante as "La caza del facsímil" (*Cs* 430–36) in unspecified reference to Lewis Carroll's poem *The Hunting of the Snark*.

2 Kurt Nimuendajú collected the existing version of Monmanéki's story, which he first wrote in Portuguese in compliance with the Brazilian government's ban during World War II on any writings or publications in German (see Lowie 1952, 151–53).

3 The stories are examined in *AP* 63–65, 178–82, and 191–92.

4 Mark A. Schneider offers a sympathetic but sharp critique of the "sentimental appeal" found by Lévi-Strauss in Monmanéki's fivefold serial monogamy. He responds to the presumed moral issue raised by the lack of attractiveness among Tukuna women by pointing out that "in tribal societies the frequent conjunction of preferential female infanticide, polygamy, and the status gain to be had upon marriage seem to overcome the reservations of most prospective husbands, so there isn't much reason to see the issue [wives' good looks] as having salience in the life of primitive communities" (Schneider 1993, 105).

5 For the susceptible ferryman as tortoise, see *OTM* 444–57.

6 See J. J. Arrom's comments on the twins' cosmological associations (*AAI* 13 n. 56/R 66 n. 56).

7 The connection between Pané's account of the turtle's birth, Arrom's photographed artifact of a turtle glued to a man's back, and the clinging woman in Lévi-Strauss is made in López-Baralt 1985, 51–52.

CHAPTER FIVE

1 *Ody* 12.355–65, 395–96; and Jean-Pierre Vernant, "Food in the Countries of the Sun" (Detienne and Vernant 1989, 164–69).

2 As the result of digging and decipherment work by J. F. Champollion and J. B. Greene in Egypt during the 1820s and 1830s, The People of the Sea were first shown in a relief at Medinet Habu, manacled and branded and brought as prisoners of war to Pharaoh Rameses III after a naval battle around 1186 BCE. They are believed to have lost the battle in the Nile Delta during " 'the Great Sea and Land Raids,' " in which "the foreign countries [Sea People] . . . made a conspiracy in their islands" and " 'all the lands were on the move, scattered in war' " (Sandars 1978, 9–10).

3 Perry Meisel, *The Myth of the Modern: A Study in British Literature and Criticism after 1859*, 145 (quoted in Rickard 1999, 220).

4 One is well aware of the civil wars fought on the psychoanalytic battlefield of pre-Oedipal theories. As understood here, *wordplay* is in regressive and tacit rapport with *aggression* or *aggressivity*, regardless of the spin or accent put on either concept by way of Melanie Klein or Lacan, just to mention two obvious tendencies of enormous consequence. See Sánchez-Pardo 2003, indexed under "Aggression."

5 For a *mise-en-abyme* view of the reading face mirrored in the beloved's buttocks, see González 2004, 930–49.

6 According to Pierre Vidal-Naquet in "Land and Sacrifice in the Odyssey," Alcinous's palace "constitutes the perfect *oikos* [homestead]" (see Gordon 1981, 93–94). Utopia is also implicit in M. I. Finley's summation: "The Homeric city is utterly 'faceless,' most obviously in Scheria. [. . .] Not a word is said about its residential quarters, streets or terraces of houses[. . . .] What matters most about the Phaeacians [. . .] is their unreality, their position halfway between the world of fantasy Odysseus was finally leaving and the real world to which he was soon to return" (1965, 155–56).

7 When Aeolus discovers incest between his youngest children, he throws their offspring to the dogs and orders the mother to kill herself. After tolerating the other sibling-unions for some time, he breaks them up and scatters his own brood into exile (Graves 1990, 1:160). Vidal-Naquet concedes the likelihood of interpolation in the Homeric incest genealogy of Alcinous and Arete but points out further common traits between the known insular affairs of Aeolia and Phaeacia (Gordon 1981, 93).

8 Plutarch's *Moralia* 139a, quoted in Faraone 1999, 113.

9 For parallels with Shakespeare's *The Tempest* and the Nausicaa episode in the *Odyssey*, see Barton 1992, 33–41.

10 From hereafter, page numbers in parentheses divided by a slash refer to the Seix Barral 1979 first edition of *La Habana Para un Infante Difunto* and to the 1984 translation of it as *Infante's Inferno* (II). When quoted separately (abbreviated as HID), my own translation of the original 1979 edition text is provided instead of the freewheeling (and often self-engrossed) American-English version, brilliantly done by Suzanne Jill Levine with the author's many extravagant additions and occasional cuts. The Spanish text is quoted only when given peculiar emphasis.

11 See Souza's account (GCI 79–83) of the last sojourn in Ithaca-Havana and his brief discussion of the unpublished manuscript of "Ithaca Revisited," an autobiographical work yet to emerge from limbo into posthumous light and at this writing already announced for publication in the near future.

12 Quoted in Anderson 1997, 673.

CHAPTER SIX

1 About Anne of Oxford, De Quincey wrote: "If she is now living, she is probably a mother, with children of her own; but, as I have said, I could never trace her[. . . .] This person was a young woman, and one of the unhappy class who subsist under the wages of prostitution." He goes on to credit his own survival to her: "To whose bounty and compassion I owe it that I am at this time alive" (*Conf* 20–19).

2 The survey of movie houses is found in HID 203–6 and II 93–95.

3 On the mermaid as soul-sucker, see Doniger 1999, 193–94. Myths spinning the uses and misuses of proper canoeing are discussed by Lévi-Strauss in "The Canoe Journey of the Moon and the Sun" (OTM 133–97).

4 Max Friedländer describes "a grotesquely mis-shapen woman in ostentatiously

rich and fanciful attire, of a kind calculated to accent feminine charm [. . .] used
for the brazen display of repulsive decay and monstrous malformation [. . .] an
apparition, a nightmare, presented with punctilious realism, elaborated with
pedantic technique and thoroughness" (1984, 34). The portrait is believed to
match another one known as *Old Man*, most likely based on a Leonardo drawing not yet identified. Although seldom observed, the comically attired woman
holds a withered rosebud in her right hand, as a gift to the old man, who in the
other portrait raises his right hand in refusal (see Silver 1984, plates 123 and
124).

5 See Gardner (AA 82 n. 1) for comments on Alice's nemesis in the Duchess.

CHAPTER SEVEN

1 *Asinus Aureus* (4.31), quoted in Winkler 1985, 90 n. 53.

2 David Rollo explains in graphic detail the wordplay on phallic mysteries at work
in the snake fears implanted by the scheming sisters in Psyche's maiden soul,
which is to say, on the unravished Soul itself (or herself). See "From Apuleius's
Psyche to Chrétien's Erec and Enide" in Tatum 1994, 351. John Winkler remarks
that "the dragon wants both a consort and a meal, and for that he needs Psyche's limited cooperation; after nine months he can stop telling lover's lies"
(1985, 92).

3 The specular seizure borne in the gaze's internalized object of desire is discussed and illustrated by Lacan in "The Gaze as Object Petit a" (1978, 67–122).
Ken Dowden examines the allegory of the soul's possession by a *daimon* as Psyche's pregnant fate of illumination. See "The Roman Audience of The Golden
Ass" in Tatum 1994, 428.

4 Ethnographic instances of such fears or compulsory aversions abound, as in
this Amazonian Mehinaku story: "Each month the piranha bite the women and
make them bleed. Sometimes, the women can feel the piranha bite and tell their
husbands, 'soon I am going to have my period,'" which Thomas Gregor explains as "an anxious fantasy about women's anatomy" and female genitalia in
association with "injury and danger," as well as with the origins of menstrual
blood in a "wound" (AP 142).

5 The death of Hymenaeus (Hymen) during the marriage rite of passage for whose
origins he is credited could signify the end of "the testing period in the lives of
young men," which in ancient Greece took place during the aristocratic young
man's prior life as the lover of an older man. The death of Hymen, who is often
depicted as a pederastic young lover, implies his rebirth into eternal youth and
the cyclic renewal of premarital love with men (see Sergent 1986, 110).

6 The English version's itch for farcical excess adds to the chop-chop show: "A
thigh is not a thigh: a thigh without a hip is only a sigh for me. Now about her
hip. Her hip, her only hip for me, was high and round: it was the hip of nothing
less than a full woman[. . . .] She could be a gallery of women, all the women
in the love museum put together[. . . .] Her naked neck and fully lighted face,
topping off her divined body divine, from lips to labia" (II, 336, 337).

7 See "Love and Psychoanalysis," 14 (booklet excerpt from Brill's *Hitchcock's Romance: Spellbound Criterion Collection DVD*).

8 Ibid., 13.

9 Appignanesi and Forrester 1992, 273. Also "Lou Andreas-Salomé: 'The Fortunate Animal'" and "Anna Freud: The Dutiful Daughter" (ibid., 240–307).

10 Points of interest in Keane's commentary are found in the following chapter numbers of the *Spellbound Criterion Collection DVD*: 3, "Authorship/Hitchcockian Lines (The New Chief)"; 17, "The Other Author (All That We See or Seem)"; 22 "Confrontation of Authorship (The Angry Proprietor)."

11 Spoto 1993, 274. Peter Conrad provides a witty summary of the novel's twisted account of psychoanalytic methods in which one is informed that Beeding's Dr. Murchison (who is no killer) "has been highly spoken of by Freud" (HM 244).

12 Dedier Anzieu's monumental *L'auto-analyse de Freud et la découverte de la psychanalyse* (1975) or *Freud's Self-Analysis* (1986) is now supplemented by Alexander Welsh's sharply observed *Freud's Wishful Dream Book* (1994).

13 Sulloway 1992, 390. See also 390–93 for a summary of the so-called phylogenetic scenario or the "phylogenetic-historical conception of sexuality." The five Freud books in question are *Totem and Taboo* (1912–12), *Group Psychology and the Analysis of the Ego* (1921), *The Future of an Illusion* (1927), *Civilization and Its Discontents* (1930), and *Moses and Monotheism* (1939).

CHAPTER EIGHT

1 "The Drying Up of the Breast" and "Vampires, Breast-Feeding, and Anxiety" (Copjec 1994, 129–30). In his review of the restored *Vertigo*, Peter Wollen asserts that the film's closest counterpart in Hitchcock's work is *Rebecca* (1997, 14). Jonathan Freedman observes that *Vertigo*'s villain (Kevin Elster) "seems to have seen Hitchcock's Rebecca one too many times" (Freedman and Millington 1999, 95).

2 See Mabbott's notes to "Morella" (Poe 2000a, 236 n. 1) and "Von Kempelen and His Discovery" (Poe 2000b, 1355–67).

3 "Berenicë" (Poe 2000a, 219). Maurice Schérer (Eric Rohmer) published "A qui la faute?" in the Hitchcock issue of *Cahiers du Cinéma* 7.39 (October 1954): 6–10, with emphasis on "the ascendancy of one conscience over another, of one soul over another soul" (quoted in Sloan 1995, 372).

4 Quotations from *The Symposium* are from R. E. Allen's 1991 edition.

5 The foremost Platonic account of successive incarnations is found in the allegory of the charioteer and his horses given by Socrates in *Phaedrus* (Plato 1973, 246–50), whose climactic ending should vibrate in the reader of "Morella" (in sublime reversal of the story's dismal gloom): "Pure was the light and pure were we from the pollution of the walking sepulchre which we call a body, to which we are bound like an oyster to its shell" (250c).

6 Jonathan Lear finds it tragic "when there is a recognition that neither Eros nor any other being can perform the task that Diotima assigns to it," in which mun-

dane life can gain access to infinite value aided by love, instead of love being, as pictured by Aristophanes, "a distraction from, indeed a retribution for, trying to ascend to a higher level of existence." See "Eros and Unknowing: The Psychoanalytic Significance of Plato's Symposium" (Lear 1998, 151–52). The pursuit of "primordial wholeness" (Symp 192e) includes a list of "fragmented descendants" in whom Aristophanes recognizes, in G. R. F. Ferrari's words, "adulterers, Lesbians, eagerly passive homosexuals destined to a career in politics," but not, for instance, "married couples or modest boys"; by choosing such examples, he adds, "from among social deviants, but betraying not a hint of censure," and by going as far as to defend "the passive homosexuals whom he satirized in his plays," Aristophanes "subordinates 'good' and 'bad' in love to the universal desire revealed in his allegorical depth psychology." See Ferrari 1992, 252.

7 The translation of these passages for *Infante's Inferno* (made by Suzanne Jill Levine with Cabrera Infante) is avoided here due to the farcical elements with which their joint effort all but overwhelms the original. In the wake of Romanticism, tales of carnal and spiritual romance (before ending in catastrophe) tend to portray the erasure of body boundaries between lovers and the birth of a single crystallized erotic subject in whom prior selves remain breached and on hold and menaced by dissolution. These are not particularly comic themes, though they are made ripe for comic lampooning and parody, which is what the original *amazona* story endures in this translation, a text in which the ghost of Nabokov (so improbably at home in the younger version) gets trampled by English wordplay run amok.

8 Cabrera Infante married his first wife, Marta Calvo, on August 15, 1953. Their first daughter, Ana, was born on September 28, 1954. See Calvo's interview in Hurtado 2000. The Amazon-Infante affair starts some three months after his wedding and ends not too long after the first daughter's birth.

9 "A propos de Vertigo ou Hitchcock contre Tristan" (Sloan 1995, 381 and entry 275).

10 "Debreasting, Disarming, Beheading: Some Sacrificial Practices in the Scyths and Amazons" (Lincoln 1991, 199).

11 "Maelzel's Chess-Player" (Poe 1902, 14:24).

12 Quoted by Charles Barr (V 70).

13 See interview in <http://www.Londondance.com> under *Talk to Her*. All further quotations are taken from *Hable con ella* DVD: *Special Features Comments* by Pedro Almodóvar and Geraldine Chaplin.

14 Cabrera Infante reviewed *Hable con ella* for El País (June 6, 2004). He asks who the real protagonist is: "The still [motionless or stiff: yerta] woman or the agonizing woman?" (*Yerta* comes from *erguir*, for "to set aright" or "erect.") The prone and comatose woman in this case would be *stiff-erect*. Calling it "Almodóvar's most delicate film," the reviewer recognizes the rape and rules out the agony. Benigno takes Pygmalion's actions with the beloved statue to extremes in bringing back to life the stiff woman by making her pregnant.

CHAPTER NINE

1 "Hitchcock's Trilogy: A Logic of Mise en Scène" (Bergstrom 1999, 221).

2 It is been said of Phaedrus that his "very shortcomings make of him an ideal character," ideal in his unfitness to philosophically unravel the intricacies of knowing oneself while taking part in "a dialogue between someone who possesses a knowledge of his own ignorance [Socrates] and someone who is ignorant of even his own ignorance [Phaedrus]" (Griswold 1986, 18).

3 Walter Hamilton comments on *Phaedrus* (Plato 1973, 12).

4 Bury is quoted by R. E. Allen in his comments to *Symp.* 178a–80b.

5 Robert Alter, "Sodom as Nexus" (Goldberg 1994, 33).

6 "¿Quién será su héroe? ¿Ohdiseo o Judises?" The required y for i in "Odysseus" for "Odiseo" yields "Judy" in English. This is trivial, but not perhaps the festive recognition of God's carnal signature in the grandchildren's flesh—the sons of one of the two daughters taken by the Lot-Odysseus figure out of Cuba in October 1965. The oldest chronological passage in reference to Lot appears in *Tres Tristes Tigres*. It involves two brothers and their mother in a nightmare of apocalyptic nuclear annihilation. The dreamer sees himself seated on the Malecón seawall in Havana with his back to the water, gazing in double vision at the sea and the city. Under a blazing sun, a woman in black next to him appears stripped of the beauty she once had. The sea turns as white as the beach sands while the entire shore rises and folds back upon itself. Her black dress now ablaze, the woman's "invisible face is black and white and ashes all at once" as the dreamer jumps off the seawall and runs toward the beach now transformed into a prairie of ashes. Everyone is in flight, except her, who remains at the wall, burning to ashes. A mother leaves her two boys behind as she runs with the crowd seeking shelter under the huge umbrella that the beach has now become, but which in the end (under "the murderous light") turns into a mushroom. The dreamer goes on running. "'It's the myth of Lot in the light of present-day science,'" Silvestre tells Arsenio, who responds, "'or of its dangers'" (TTT, 313–14/339–40; page numbers divided by a slash refer to the 1967 Spanish edition of *Tres Tristes Tigres* and the 1971 English edition, *Three Trapped Tigers*). Given the amount and intensity of work done between 1965 and 1966 in revising the manuscript of the award-winning novel ("He began work intensely on the revision of his manuscript in Madrid, and [as] he experienced a burst of creativity [the book] grew by leaps and bounds" [GCI 84], it is possible that the Lot dream passage might have been revisited and reworked *after* the death of Zoila, Cabrera Infante's mother, whose illness had prompted his return to Havana in June 1965, too late to see her still alive. One way or the other, Zoila and her two sons appear seared and sired in Lot's flight from Sodom, caught in retroaction by the grandsons' circumcision.

7 Details in the sequence of lectures about the "multiple legends of the alter ego" run as follows: (a) the two blonde Isoldes (blond Helen and her phantom double in Stesichorus's *palinode* and Euripides' *Helen*); (b) Phaedrus's "argument" in the *Symposium* about Orpheus being presented by the gods with a phantom of

Euridyce; (c) Hitchcock's "suffering from the blondes superstition" (including a list of ten blonde actresses that ends with "twice-a-blonde Kim Novak") (*Atn* 114).

8 R. E. Allen comments that "Phaedrus's attitude toward Orpheus is dismissive, mere upper-class prejudice against musicians" (Plato 1991, 13). On the conception of the bridal journey in *Alcestis* as a journey to Hades, see Seaford 1986.

9 *Alcestis* (Euripides 1995, 3).

10 "Admetus, literally 'the untamable,' is none other than Hades, an anthropomorphization or hypostasis of the god of the underworld" (Sergent 1986, 225).

11 *The Bacchae*, line 100 (Euripides 1979, 36).

12 "Spurts and Leaps" (Detienne 1989a, 55). The fighting bulls known in Spain as *toros de lidia* are bred to be fierce. But they are not as such wild animals. For it is their breeding that is supposed to preserve their wild fury. The "sacrificed" bull's ears and tail are awarded as trophies on occasions (which for purists nowadays come all too often, just as the fierceness of the beasts fought is perceived in decline). The bull's meat is sold and consumed. Testicles are considered a delicacy. Trueno, the bull who kills Lydia, would have been fought by the next torero in line until being successfully *ajusticiado* or brought to justice, the routine term for the kill. The edible parts of the carcass would have been sold as meat. (Thanks are due to José Domínguez Búrdalo for lively information on such matters.)

13 In *The Cult of Pan in Ancient Greece*, Philippe Borgeaud writes: "Being possessed by the nymphs, since it was a form of inspiration, could confer the gift of divination. Nympholepsy probably had a role at certain prophetic sanctuaries" (1988, 105).

14 At this point in time, and particularly among readers concerned with social affairs in the United States, where Almodóvar's movies have been so well received, *Talk to Her*'s story of pastoral enchantment, erotic melancholy, suicide, emergence from coma, and possible nuptials between Alicia and Marco can hardly escape polemical comparison with the issues raised and exploited in Terri Schiavo's case and its dismal climax in the spring of 2005.

CHAPTER TEN

1 Souza writes that "Cabrera Infante received eighteen applications of this treatment [electroshock therapy][. . . .] During a five-year period, he also went through a series of five different antidepressive medications" (*GCI* 119). The script for *Under the Volcano* had come up "three times longer than a normal screenplay" and was caught in production conflicts, which led to the film's French backers' demand that their advance to Cabrera Infante be returned on breach-of-contract grounds. The stress of writing what amounted to a double-task in translation (from English into Spanish and from Lowry's dense prose into film script) had caused "periods of intense agitation and suspicion accompanied by hallucinations" (117). In Souza's view, scriptwriter and protagonist had collapsed into one burdened mind: "It was as if a symbiotic relationship were developing between the Consul and Cabrera Infante" (117).

2 "La visión del mirón miope" (*HID* 395–415), "Vigil of the Naked Eye" (*II* 206–17).

3 Goya's caption "Ni por esas (Que tiranía)" implies that "not even by such means" (as the huge keys) can the tyranny of the belt achieve its purpose (Bihalji-Merin, Lafuente Ferrari, and Seidel 1983, plates 9 and 189).

4 "El autor como político, el político como autor" ("Actors and Sinners"). Page references to *Mea Cuba* (MC) in Spanish and English are given in parentheses separated by a slash.

5 Hudson recalls how the press claimed that "the girl was undoubtedly a North American tourist since no one of that age living in the tropics could be so undeveloped physically[. . . .] She was not an American tourist, though; and it turned out that she had developed whatever attractions she had in the tropics" (*IS* 240).

6 The phrase from Piera Aulagnier-Spairani's paper on femininity is quoted in Macey 1988, 184. The materials from which Lacan drew his 1932 doctoral thesis (*De La Psychose paranoïaque dans ses raport avec la personalité*) dealt with the writings of a schoolteacher woman inmate at the Clinique psychiatrique diagnosed as suffering from erotomania, paranoid delusions, and mental automatism, disorders related by Lacan to the fashionable surrealist experiments in automatic writing (Macey 1988, 182–83).

7 "Entre la historia y la nada (Notas sobre una ideología del suicidio) [Between History and Nothingness: Notes on an Ideology of Suicide]" (*MC* 166–94/138–72). Any serious dealings with the question of suicide in the history of Cuba and the diaspora will be indebted to Louis A. Pérez Jr.'s *To Die in Cuba: Suicide and Society* (2005).

8 Sloterdijk 1987, 300 n. 29, 281, who quotes and considers Sartre's *Le'Etre et le néant*.

9 Hyam Maccoby considers Cain's role as that of a professional killer entrusted by tribal (Kenite) law with human sacrifice. Cain is no "petty-minded villain" who compounds "stinginess with violence" and who murders out of brotherly envy. In Cain's banishment by God under terms of protection, traces are found of his role as "Sacred Executioner" (Maccoby 1982, 24, 28, 33).

10 *Hamlet* (Shakespeare 1982) (Jenkins comments on 5.1.74–79).

11 See E. A. Speiser's notes to Gen. 4.1, 30 n. 2, in the *Anchor Bible* (1964).

12 Hitchcock's description of the shot (Spoto 1993, 502).

13 "La idea original no es suya [Cabrera Infante's], por cierto. Se la escuché argumentada—no exactamente así—en La Habana de los años 60 a un hombre de talento que en verdad escribió muy poco: Javier de Varona" (Antonio Rodríguez Rivera, "Los cubanos por los caminos del mar," <http://cubahora.cip.cu/sociedad/2000/febrero/29>).

14 *A Midsummer Night's Dream* (4.1.211–14), taken as a parody on 1 Corinthians 2.9.

15 *The Art of English Poesie*, Electronic Text Center, University of Virginia, <http://etext.lib.virginia.edu>. For instance, in *A Midsummer Night's Dream*: "For Oberon is passing fell and wrath, / Because that she as her attendant hath / A lovely boy,

stol'n from an Indian king— / She never had so sweet a changeling" (2.1.20–23).

16 "Poe's line of argument [in "Maelzel's Chess-Player] prefigures the way in which the analytic powers of the Dupin stories will take itself as the most natural, not to say inevitable, object of its own analysis" (Irwin 1994, 105).

17 Poe 1902, 14:37. *The Baltimore Gazette* of June 1, 1827, reported: "Two boys who were said to have found out the Turk's secret [. . .] on a hot day in the last week of May [. . .] had climbed onto the roof of a shed next to the exhibition hall and saw Maelzel opening the top of the Turk's cabinet after one of the exhibitions—whereupon a man climbed out" (Standage 2002, 166).

CHAPTER ELEVEN

1 Salient incidents in each life are respectively itemized in R. J. Hollingdale's "Chronology of Nietzsche's Life" (EH xx–xxx), Esther Allen's Martí "Chronology" (SW xxvii–xxxii), and Cintio Vitier's "Cronología" (Martí 1978, 418–86).

2 Besides Nietzsche's own writings on the Wagners, their cult, and the music, see Fischer-Dieskau (1976) and Hollinrake (1982).

3 See Martí's letter and the anonymous *New York Evening Post*'s "A Protectionist View of Cuban Annexation" and the anti-annexionist article in a Philadelphia paper to which it responds (SW 261–67).

4 R. J. Hollingdale considers the body of aphoristic work written from *Human, All Too Human* (1876–80) to *Dawn* (1881) "the most thorough course in skepticism produced in the nineteenth century" (TSZ 12). Yet, Richard Schacht remarks that "*The Birth of Tragedy* sold modestly well, and attracted a good deal of attention—even if much of it was hostile. But the same cannot be said of any of Nietzsche's subsequent books, during his sentient life. Prior to his collapse, none of them sold more than a few hundred copies, and few of them attracted any attention whatsoever" (HAH xii).

5 For a detailed economic and political history of the period from a Marxist perspective, see *The Roots of the Modern American Empire* (Williams 1969) and *Comercio y poder* (Zanetti Lecuona 1998).

6 See SW 280–81 for Allen's original facing translation.

7 See "Lingua Amissa: The Messianism of Commodity-Language and Derrida's *Specters of Marx*" (Hamacher 1999, 183).

8 The eighth among *Versos sencillos* is rendered here in prose and reduced to basic meaning at the expense of poetic effect. It is thus updated and imperfectly anglicized. *Yo tengo un amigo muerto/que suele venirme a ver* is chosen by the Cuban poet César López as epigraph for his sequence of elegies in *Consideraciones*, two of which are written in memory of Frank País, a recognized *mártir* in the struggle against Batista and hero of the Revolution, murdered and mutilated by the Santiago de Cuba police on July 30, 1957. The first elegy, *No puedo hablar de él como no era* (I cannot speak of him as he was not), is haunted by Martí's poem.

9 Derrida 1986, 117; Derrida 1974, 116.

10 Derrida 1994, 110; Hamacher 1999, 84.

11 In his essay on Cuba's suicide syndrome, Guillermo Cabrera Infante writes: "Martí, retarded Romantic, chose one of the deaths possible for the poets of the 19th century. Reader, take your cure for sinners [a list of suicidal behaviors ending in death follows: Keats's (who did not kill himself and died of tuberculosis), Coleridge's, Baudelaire's, etc.]." "Each poet has the right to no more than one death," but Martí achieves "the reverse of such private deaths" by placing his albatross corpse around the young Republic's neck (MC 167–68/147). While documenting Martí's elevation of "sacrifice [death] to near mystical heights" and surveying the assessment of his death by leading biographers and writers ever since, Louis Pérez Jr. makes a point about exemplariness which Cabrera Infante's suicide reductionism rejects as being in essence stupid: "The death of Martí at Dos Ríos, whether by choice or by chance, served as exemplary inspiration, one to which Cubans then and thereafter would refer to as the measure of duty required as a function of nationality" (2005, 82).

12 The phrase concerns the ironic reversal of the rules of Athenian autochthony in Euripides' Ion, written "sur le thème de l'autochtone venu d'ailleurs" (Detienne 2003, 58).

CHAPTER TWELVE

1 Mark Almond, "1989 Without Gorbachev: What If Communism Had Not Collapsed" (Ferguson 1997, 394).

2 Leonardo Padura Fuentes (henceforth Padura) wrote Las cuatro estaciones between 1990 and the fall of 1997. Pasado perfecto (Pp) was first published in Mexico (1992) and then Havana (1995) in a revised version; Vientos de Cuaresma (VC) in Havana (1994) and Madrid (2001); Máscaras (M) in Havana and Madrid (1997); and Paisaje de otoño (Po) in Madrid (1998) and Havana (1999). Quotations refer to the Madrid TusQuets four-volume edition. All translations of Padura's writings are mine as authorized by the author, except in the case of Máscaras, which has just been released in translation as Havana Red.

3 In "The Play's the Thing: Casuistry in The Cenci," James Chandler analyzes Shelley's anxieties regarding the perils of anachronism in the representation of distant historical characters as reflected in "the casuistical tendencies of the play's characters" (1998, 497–507).

4 Chandler's exposition of Lukács's thesis on necessary historicist anachronism is followed here in what it represents of a significant update and critique of Romantic literary regional mappings involving related national spheres (1998, 109–10, 132–36, 500–502).

5 In "A Postscript, Which Should Have Been a Preface," Scott sees in "the present [1814] people of Scotland a class of beings as different from their grandfathers, as the existing English are from those of Queen Elizabeth's time" (1998, 340). Hence the one-Scottish-generation-to-one-English-century ratio between matched histories and developments. In the "Dedicatory Epistle" Scott writes, in the pen of Rev. Dr. Dryasdust: "Even within these thirty years, such an infinite change has taken place in the manners of Scotland, that men look

back upon the habits of society proper to their immediate ancestors, as we do on those of the reign of Queen Anne, or even the period of the Revolution" (1986, 522). See Chandler's analysis of these views (1998, 134–35).

6 Padura remembers the town's past with Hawthorne-vintage sly antiquarian nostalgia: "Mantilla was so young and so poor that it had no legends, ghosts or old stories. It had no cemetery suitable for the dead to reappear, and the church's saint never performed a miracle worth remembering. We never had anything resembling a wealthy lady of indispensable neurotic habits who in dark nights of wantonness would play forbidden games and give birth to voluptuous rumors" ("Una cacería de fantasmas [A hunt for ghosts]" [1994, 69]).

7 Access to Lacan on this matter is obtained through Fink's "Trauma" and "Subjectifying the Cause: A Temporal Conundrum" (LS 26–28, 63–66).

8 "The caput mortuum or caput corvi is the head of the black Osiris or Ethiopian, and also of the 'Moor' in the Chymical Wedding. The head was boiled in a pot and the broth poured into a golden ball" (Jung 1976, 513).

9 Fink discusses the illustrated scheme of signification (LS, figure 5.6, 64), adapted here to the related subjectifying cause and its retroactive temporality: "In the statement 'By the time you get back, I will have already left,' my departure is retroactively determined as prior. Without your return, it would have no such status. It takes two moments [two 1989s and a retro-actuated Conde M.C.] to create a before and after. The signification of the first moment changes in accordance with what comes afterwards" (LS 64).

10 Quoted by Niall Ferguson, "Virtual History: Towards a 'Chaotic' Theory of the Past" (Ferguson 1997, 5).

11 "Heredia was our contemporary. Although he lived in the early nineteenth century, and lived the life of a Romantic poet, a revolutionary, a man of his time, his life included many substantive elements of being Cuban [la cubanía or Cubanness] which hold true even to this day. Fundamentally one element: exile" (Ríos Jáuregui 2003, 38). The chronology appears in JMH 100), together with Padura's biographical sketch and a selection of the major lyrics.

12 "Heredia" (first published in El Economista Americano, New York, July 1888).

13 Quoted by Augier in Heredia 1993, 33.

14 The letter is quoted by Padura (JMH 73).

15 "Oda a los habitantes de Anahuac" and "En una tempestad" (JMH 119–27).

16 "El poeta Walt Whitman" (Martí 1978, 269). Esther Allen translates "oculta" as "secret" (SW 187), but occult seems to better resonate with the spiritualist currents common at the time. The triumph of Whitman's anticipated death comes in words Martí borrows from him: "Having revealed to the world a sincere, loving, and resonant man, [Whitman] awaits the happy hour when material existence withdraws from him and, abandoned to the purifying air, he becomes blossom and fragrance on its swells: 'disembodied, triumphant, dead'" (SW 194).

17 Lezama Lima's phrase is quoted by Esther Allen (SW 350).

18 By the early 1970s, gifts for children were given at a date in July, at the end

of the school year. Three kinds of toys, ranging from small to large (of lesser, medium, and higher value), were offered as well as raffled. The bicycle would rank at the top of the list of such gifts. The practice ended during the years of economic crisis in the early 1990s known as *el período especial* or special period.

19 In Catholic liturgy, the Adoration of the Magi is observed on January 6. The *Día de Reyes* befits Fernando Ortiz's concept of transculturation in colonial Afro-Cuban life. Slaves and free blacks celebrated the carnival in the streets of Havana on that date until the festivities were banned in 1880 upon the abolition of slavery. Ortiz recreates the harlequinade of dancing devils or *diablitos* in a 1920 article republished in 1960 as "La antigua fiesta afrocubana del Día de Reyes." He claims that "the Afro-Cuban *Día de Reyes* amalgamated and regrouped on Cuban soil a host of scenes and rituals of African as well as universal origin[. . . .] It was The Blacks' Carnival, in the mystical sense in which such an expression finds support in a deliberate and authorized scientific explanation" (1984, 72).

20 The implicit relevance of CDR surveillance in Conde's world is among the issues perceptively examined by Manuel Fernández, who concentrates on Candito Rojo's clandestine economic activities. See "La figura del mimo en *Máscaras* de Leonardo Padura Fuentes," *Ciberletras* 7 (July 2000): <http://www.lehman.cuny.edu/ciberletras/v07/fernandez.html>.

21 See William Kerrigan's analysis of hendiadys in the play's patterns of repetition, "ubiquitous doubling," and "the doubleness of woman" (1994, 79–80).

22 Manuel Fernández discusses the doctrine aimed at erasing the practical distinction between common and political crimes outlined by Cristobal Pérez, whose 1982 *Por la novela policial* he quotes: "In a socialist society, common delinquency confronts the revolutionary state, the people in power. Counterrevolutionary delinquency aims directly at the destruction of the new type of state. This is why both types of delinquency coincide[. . . .] In practice, it can be said that a common crime is also a counterrevolutionary manifestation." See "El género policial y la lucha de clases: Un reto para los escritores revolucionarios" ("La figura del mimo"): <http://www.lehman.cuny.edu/ciberletras/v07/fernandez.html>.

23 Caryl Emerson considers claims that literature had undergone a sort of stagflation in its talents to shock and teach. The Russian market was suddenly flooded with redesigned foreign imports, ranging from the Talmud to Henry Miller: "In a culture accustomed to a great deal of regimentation from above and a quasi-religious mission attached to literature from below, this overload temporarily paralyzed and disoriented their readers. It resembled Bakhtin's carnival — but with a difference: there was no promise of any reimposition of the hierarchy, nothing stable in the background that might reassert traditional order and thus guarantee participants the recurrent pleasure of violating it" (C. Emerson 1997, 11).

24 Although in *La simulación* (1982) Sarduy examines men's tactics of lure-and-disguise, his main source was not Jean Baudrillard but Roger Caillois's older work on insect mimicry, mainly in *Méduse et Cie* (1960), where evasion, capture, consumption, and luxurious display are the key phenomena.

25 See <http://www.phys.uu.nl/~vgent/calendar/eclipsecycles.htm>.

26 NS 87–114. One of the two epigraphs for *Paisaje de otoño* quotes Esmé's phrase to the American soldier who narrates the story: "Squalor. I am extremely interested in squalor" (Po 101). Padura dedicates to his wife, Lucía, two books in the name of the same phrase ("con amor y escualidez"): *Adios, Hemingway* (2002) and *Un camino de medio siglo: Alejo Carpentier y la narrativa de lo real maravilloso* (2002). In a passage from a work-in-progress (received from Padura in December 2004), Mario Conde encounters the living ghost of J. D. Salinger in circumstances in which his own life seems in danger of joining the other's limbo in a single afterlives twinship. The story is part of the forthcoming novel *La neblina del ayer* (Madrid, 2005). "Conde returns, almost 40 [*sic*—50] in 2003 as buyer-seller of old books [. . .] who starts looking for a beautiful singer of *boleros* from the 1950s after finding a note inside a book[. . . .] It is a novel about the *bolero*" (author's e-mail).

27 Kerrigan 1994, 83.

28 Scapegoating is thought to rest on the so-called *pars pro toto* (small loss in exchange for greater good) rationale for sacrifice put in practice during times of extreme crisis and in further association with acts of atonement. The phenomenon is studied at length by Walter Burkert all through *Homo Necans* (1972/1983) and, succinctly but with undiminished comparative range, in "Transformations of the Scapegoat" (1979, 59–77) and "Scapegoats" (1996, 51–53).

29 "In San Isidro" (CS 13). "En San Isidro" was first published in *Ciclón* (1959).

30 Weber 1969 (*Canticum Canticorum*) and *New Oxford Annotated Bible* (Song of Solomon 4.12).

31 Coleridge 1996, 214; commentary, 332. Thanks are due to Jerry Christensen for reference to this poem.

32 A. and V. Vaughan 1991, 285–86, under "Caliban as:," and 209–10 for a view of the film much focused on Birkett.

33 José María Heredia, "En una tempestad" (JMH 127).

34 Ortiz 1995b, 75. For an inquiry into the social and historical backgrounds of Ortiz's Lombrosian study of the black criminal mind, see Bronfman 2002, 549–87.

bibliography

WORKS OF LITERATURE, PHILOSOPHY, AND FILM

Almodóvar, Pedro, dir. 2003. *Hable con ella.*

Apuleius. 1931. *Apuleius Metamorphoseon Libri XI.* Rodolph Helm, ed. Leipzig.

———. 1998. *The Golden Ass.* E. J. Kenney, trans. London.

Benítez Rojo, Antonio. [1992] 1996. *The Repeating Island: The Caribbean and the Postmodern Perspective.* Durham.

———. 2000. *Mujer en traje de batalla.* Madrid.

Benjamin, Walter. 1969. "Theses on the Philosophy of History." *Illuminations.* Harry Zohn, trans. New York.

———. 1999. *The Arcades Project.* Cambridge, Mass.

Byron, Lord. 1986. *Don Juan.* T. G. Steffan, E. Steffan, and W. W. Pratt, eds. London.

Cabrera Infante, Guillermo. 1967. *Tres Tristes Tigres.* Barcelona.

———. 1971. *Three Trapped Tigers.* New York.

———. 1973. *Un oficio del siglo XX.* Barcelona.

———. 1979. *La Habana Para un Infante Difunto.* Barcelona.

———. 1984a. "Del gofio al golfo." *Jornadas de Estudios Canarias-Americas* 1.4.

———. 1984b. *Infante's Inferno.* New York.

———. 1985. *Holy Smoke.* New York.

———. 1992. *Mea Cuba.* Barcelona.

———. 1994. *Mea Cuba.* New York.

———. 1995. *Arcadia todas las noches.* Madrid.

———. 1997. *Cine o sardina.* Madrid.

———. 1998. "Cronología a la manera de Laurence Sterne . . . o no." *La Gaceta del Fondo de Cultura Económica* (Oct.): 12–18.

———. 1999. *Todo está hecho con espejos: Cuentos completos.* Madrid.

Carpentier, Alejo. [1962] 1989. *El siglo de las luces.* Madrid.

Carroll, Lewis. 1960. *The Annotated Alice.* Martin Gardner, ed. New York.

Casey, Calvert. 1998. *The Collected Stories.* Durham.

Chaucer, Geoffrey. 1977. *The Canterbury Tales.* Middlesex.

Coleridge, Samuel Taylor. 1996. *Coleridge: Selected Poems.* Richard Holmes, ed. London.

De Quincey, Thomas. 1966. *Confessions of an English Opium Eater and Other Writings.* Aileen Ward, ed. New York.

———. [1821–45] 1985. *Confessions of an English Opium Eater and Other Writings.* Grevel Lindop, ed. Oxford.

———. 2000. *The Works of Thomas De Quincey.* Vols. 3 and 16. Grevel Lindop, ed. London.

Derrida, Jacques. 1974. *Glas.* Paris.

———. 1986. *Glas*. John P. Laevey Jr. and Richard Rand, trans. Lincoln.

———. 1994. *Specters of Marx: The State of the Debt, the Work of Mourning, and the New International*. Peggy Kamuf, trans. London.

———. 1997. *Politics of Friendship*. London.

Descartes, René. 1966. *Discourse on Method and Other Writings*. Middlesex.

Du Maurier, Daphne. [1938] 1971. *Rebecca*. New York.

Emerson, Ralph Waldo. 1965. *Selected Writings*. William H. Gilman, ed. New York.

Estévez, Abilio. 2002. *Los palacios distantes*. Barcelona.

Euripides. 1955. *Euripides I. The Complete Greek Tragedies*. Richmond Lattimore, trans. Chicago.

———. [1970] 1979. *The Bacchae of Euripides*. G. S. Kirk, trans. Cambridge.

Hemingway, Ernest. [1952] 1995. *The Old Man and the Sea*. New York.

———. [1970] 1997. *Islands in the Stream*. New York.

Heredia, José María. 1993. *José María Heredia: Obra poética*. Angel Augier, ed. Havana.

Hesiod. 1914. *Shield of Heracles; Theogogy; Works and Days*. Hugh G. Evelyn-White, trans. Cambridge.

Hitchcock, Alfred, dir. 1945. *Spellbound*.

———. 1954. *Rear Window*.

———. 1958. *Vertigo*.

———. 1959. *North by Northwest*.

———. 1969. *Topaz*.

Hoffmann, E. T. A. 1969. "The Sandman." In *Tales of E. T. A Hoffmann*, Leonard J. Kent and Elizabeth T. Knight, trans. Chicago.

Homer. 1965. *The Odyssey of Homer*. Richmond Lattimore, trans. New York.

Joyce, James. [1922] 1993. *Ulysses*. New York.

López, César. 1993. *Consideraciones, algunas elegías*. Havana.

Mamoulian, Rouben, dir. 1933. *Queen Christina*.

Martí, José. 1963. *Obras completas*. Havana.

———. 1978. *Obra literaria*. Cintio Vitier, ed. Caracas.

———. 2002. *José Martí: Selected Writings*. Esther Allen, ed. and trans. New York.

Marx, Karl. [1852] 1963. *The Eighteenth Brumaire of Louis Bonaparte*. New York.

Nietzsche, Friedrich. 1954. *Thus Spoke Zarathustra: A Book for All and None. The Portable Nietzsche*. Walter Kaufmann, trans. New York.

———. [1883–85, 1892] 1968. *Also sprach Zarathustra. Ein Buch für Alle und Keinen. Nietzsche Werke VI. Kritische Gesamtausgabe*. Berlin.

———. 1969. *Thus Spoke Zarathustra: A Book for Everyone and No One*. R. J. Hollingdale, trans. London.

———. [1888–1909] 1992. *Ecce Homo*. R. J. Hollingdale, trans. Michael Tanner, ed. London.

———. [1871] 1993. *The Birth of Tragedy Out of the Spirit of Music*. Shaun Whiteside, trans. Michael Tanner, ed. London.

———. [1878] 1996. *Human, All Too Human: A Book for Free Spirits*. R. J. Hollingdale, trans. Cambridge.

———. [1878] 1997. *Human, All Too Human (I): A Book For Free Spirits*. Gary Handwerk, trans. Stanford.

Novás Calvo, Lino. [1933] 1990. *Pedro Blanco, el negrero: Biografía novelada*. In *Obra literaria*, Jesús Díaz, ed. Havana.

Ortiz, Fernando. 1949. *El huracán: Su mitología y sus símbolos*. Mexico City.

———. 1984. *Ensayos etnográficos*. Miguel Barnet and Angel Fernández, eds. Havana.

———. 1985. *Nuevo catauro de cubanismos*. Havana.

———. 1995a. *Cuban Counterpoint: Tobacco and Sugar*. Durham.

———. [1906] 1995b. *Los negros brujos*. Havana.

———. [1940] 2002. *Contrapunteo cubano del tabaco y el azúcar*. Enrico Mario Santí, ed. Madrid.

Padura Fuentes, Leonardo. 1994. *El viaje más largo*. Havana.

———. 1997. *Máscaras*. Madrid.

———. 1998. *Paisaje de otoño*. Madrid.

———. 2000. *Pasado perfecto*. Madrid.

———. 2001a. *Adios Hemingway/La cola de la serpiente*. Havana.

———. 2001b. *Vientos de Cuaresma*. Madrid.

———. 2002. *La novela de mi vida*. Madrid.

———. 2003. *José María Heredia: La patria y la vida*. Havana.

———. 2005. *Havana Red*. Peter Bush, trans. London.

Plato. 1973. *Phaedrus and Letters VII and VIII*. Walter Hamilton, trans. New York.

———. 1991. *The Symposium*. R. E. Allen, ed. New Haven.

Poe, Edgar Allan. 1902. *The Complete Works of Edgar Allan Poe*. James A. Harrison, ed. New York.

———. 2000a. *Tales and Sketches: Vol. 1, 1831–1842*. Thomas Ollive Mabbott, ed. Urbana, Ill.

———. 2000b. *Tales and Sketches: Vol. 2, 1843–1849*. Thomas Ollive Mabbott, ed. Urbana, Ill.

Scott, Sir Walter. [1819] 1986. *Ivanhoe*. New York.

———. [1814] 1998. *Waverley*. New York.

Shakespeare, William. 1979. *A Midsummer Night's Dream*. The Arden Shakespeare. Harold F. Brooks, ed. London.

———. 1982. *Hamlet*. The Arden Shakespeare. Harold Jenkins, ed. London.

———. 1987. *The Tempest*. The Oxford Shakespeare. Stephen Orgel, ed. New York.

Sophocles. 1994. *Ajax—Electra—Oedipus Tyranus*. Cambridge.

Strassburg, Gottfried von. 1965. *Tristan*. A. T. Hatto, trans. Middlesex.

Virgil. 1894–1900. *The Aeneid of Virgil*. 2 vols. T. E. Page, ed. London.

———. [1959] 1977. *Virgil: The Aeneid*. W. F. Jackson Knight, trans. Middlesex.

OTHER WORKS

Åkerman, Susanna. 1991. *Queen Christina of Sweden and Her Circle: The Transformation of a Seventeenth-Century Philosophical Libertine*. Leiden.

The Anchor Bible. 1964. Garden City.

Anderson, John Lee. 1997. *Che: A Revolutionary Life*. New York.

Anzieu, Dedier. 1995. *Freud's Self-Analysis*. London.

Appignanesi, Lisa, and John Forrester. 1992. *Freud's Women*. New York.

Baillet, Adrien. [1691] 1985. *La vie de Monsieur Descartes*. New York.

Barr, Charles. 2002. *Vertigo*. London.

Barthes, Roland. 1964. *On Racine*. New York.

Barton, Anne. 1992. *Byron: Don Juan*. Cambridge.

Bennington, Geoffrey. 1993. *Jacques Derrida*. Chicago.

Bérard, Victor. 1927. *Les Navigations d'Ulysse I*. Paris.

Bergstrom, Janet. 1999. *Endless Night: Cinema and Psychoanalysis, Parallel Histories*. Berkeley.

Bhabha, Homi K. 1994. *The Location of Culture*. London.

Bihalji-Merin, Oto, Enrique Lafuente Ferrari, and Max Seidel. 1983. *Goya. Los Caprichos. Su verdad escondida*. Madrid.

Blight, James G., Bruce J. Allyn, and David A. Welch. 1993. *Cuba on the Brink: Castro, the Missile Crisis, and the Soviet Collapse*. New York.

Blumenberg, Hans. 1985. *Work on Myth*. Cambridge.

Borgeaud, Philippe. 1988. *The Cult of Pan in Ancient Greece*. Chicago.

Boureau, Alian. 1998. *The Lord's First Night: The Myth of le droit de cuissage*. Chicago.

Brill, Lesley. 1988. *The Hitchcock Romance: Love and Irony in Hitchcock's Films*. Princeton.

Bronfman, Alejandra. 2002. "'En plena libertad y democracia': Negros Brujos and the Social Question." *Hispanic American Historical Review* (Aug.): 549–87.

Burkert, Walter. 1979. *Structure and History in Greek Mythology and Ritual*. Berkeley.

———. [1972] 1983. *Homo Necans: The Anthropology of Ancient Greek Sacrificial Ritual and Myth*. Berkeley.

———. 1987. *Ancient Mystery Cults*. Cambridge.

———. 1996. *Creation of the Sacred: Tracks of Biology in Early Religions*. Cambridge.

Bush, Andrew. 2002. *The Routes of Modernity: Spanish American Poetry from the Early Eighteenth Century to the Mid-Nineteenth Century*. London.

Calasso, Roberto. 1998. *Ka: Stories of the Mind and Gods of India*. New York.

Carr, Archie. 1952. *Handbook of Turtles: The Turtles of the US, Canada, and Baja California*. Ithaca.

Carson, Anne. 1989. *Eros the Bittersweet*. Princeton.

Chandler, James. 1998. *England in 1819: The Politics of Literary Culture and the Case of Romantic Historicism*. Chicago.

Conrad, Peter. 2000. *The Hitchcock Murders*. New York.

Copjec, Joan, ed. 1993. *Shades of Noir*. London.

———. 1994. *Read My Desire: Lacan against the Historicists*. Boston.

Corominas, Joan. 1967. *Breve diccionario etimológico de la lengua castellana*. Madrid.

Cottom, Daniel. 1991. *Abyss of Reason: Cultural Movements, Revelations, and Betrayals*. New York.

David, Gregson. 1997. *Aimé Césaire*. Cambridge.

Deleuze, Gilles, and Félix Guattari. [1980] 1987. *A Thousand Plateaus: Capitalism and Schizophrenia 2*. Minneapolis.

Detienne, Marcel. [1977] 1979. *Dionysos Slain*. Baltimore.

———. [1986] 1989a. *Dionysus at Large*. Cambridge.

———. 1989b. *L'écriture d'Orphée*. Paris.

———. 2003. *The Writing of Orpheus*. Baltimore.

Detienne, Marcel, and Jean-Pierre Vernant. [1979] 1989. *The Cuisine of Sacrifice among the Greeks*. Chicago.

———. [1974] 1991. *Cunning Intelligence in Greek Culture and Society*. Chicago.

———. 1998. *Apollon le couteau à la main. Une approche expérimentale du polythéisme grec*. Paris.

———. 2003. *Comment être autochtone: Du pur Athénien au Français raciné*. Paris.

Deutscher, Isaac. 1963. *The Prophet Outcast: Trotsky, 1929–1940*. New York.

Doniger, Wendy. 1999. *Splitting the Difference: Gender and Myth in Ancient Greece and India*. Chicago.

Douglas-Fairhurst, Robert. 2002. *Victorian Afterlives: The Shaping of Influence in Nineteenth-Century Literature*. Oxford.

Emerson, Caryl. 1997. *The First Hundred Years of Mikhail Bakhtin*. Princeton.

Ernst, Carl H., and Roger W. Barbour. 1989. *Turtles of the World*. Washington.

Evans, Dylan. 1996. *An Introductory Dictionary of Lacanian Psychoanalysis*. London.

Faraone, Christopher A. 1999. *Ancient Greek Love Magic*. Cambridge.

Feldman, Richard, Bruce Fink, and Marie Jaanus, eds. 1995. *Reading Seminar XI: Lacan's Four Fundamental Concepts of Psychoanalysis*. Albany.

Ferguson, Niall, ed. 1997. *Virtual History: Alternatives and Counterfactuals*. London.

Ferrari, G. R. F. 1992. "Platonic Love." In *The Cambridge Companion to Plato*. Cambridge.

Fink, Bruce. 1995. *The Lacanian Subject: Between Language and Jouissance*. Princeton.

Finley, M. I. [1954] 1965. *The World of Odysseus*. New York.

Fischer-Dieskau, Dietrich. 1976. *Wagner and Nietzsche*. New York.

Forsyth, Neil. 1987. *The Old Enemy: Satan and the Combat Myth*. Princeton.

Frazer, Sir George James. [1906–15] 1994. *The Golden Bough: A Study in Magic and Religion*. London.

Freedman, Jonathan, and Richard Milington. 1999. *Hitchcock's America*. New York.

Freud, Sigmund. [1917–18] 1962. "The Taboo of Virginity (Contributions to the Psychology of Love III)." In *The Complete Psychological Works of Sigmund Freud*, vol. 11. London.

———. [1905–12] 1989a. *Jokes and Their Relations to the Unconscious*. New York.

———. [1910–19] 1989b. *Leonardo da Vinci and a Memory of His Childhood*. New York.

———. [1919] 1995. "The Uncanny." In *Psychological Writings and Letters*. New York.

Friedländer, Max. 1984. *Early Netherlandish Painting VIII: Quentin Massys*. London.

Fuentes, Norberto. 1984. *Hemingway in Cuba*. New York.

Gantz, Timothy. 1993. *Early Greek Myth*. Baltimore.

Geertz, Clifford. 1973. *The Interpretation of Cultures*. New York.

Gilbert, Stuart. [1930] 1952. *James Joyce's "Ulysses."* New York.

Glaukroger, Stephen. 1991. *Descartes: An Intellectual Biography*. Oxford.

Goldberg, Jonathan, ed. 1994. *Reclaiming Sodom*. New York.

González, Eduardo. 1992. *The Monstered Self: Narratives of Death and Performance in Latin American Fiction*. Durham.

————. 2004. "Odysseus' Bed and Cleopatra's Mattress (69)." *MLN* 119.5: 930–48.

Goodwing-Williams, Robert. 2001. *Zarathustra's Dionysian Modernism*. Stanford.

Gordon, R. G. A., ed. 1981. *Myth, Religion, and Society*. Cambridge.

Goytisolo, Juan. 1977. *Disidencias*. Barcelona.

Graves, Robert. 1990. *The Greek Myths 1 and 2*. London.

Gregor, Thomas. 1985. *Anxious Pleasures: The Sexual Lives of an Amazonian People*. Chicago.

Griswold, Charles, Jr. 1986. *Self-Knowledge in Plato's Phaedrus*. New Haven.

Gruzinski, Serge. 2001. *Images of War: Mexico from Columbus to Blade Runner (1492–2019)*. Durham.

Hamacher, Werner. 1999. "Lingua Amissa: The Messianism of Commodity-Language and Derrida's Specters of Marx." In *Ghostly Demarcations: A Symposium on Jacques Derrida's Specters of Marx*, Michael Sprinker, ed. New York.

Higgins, Kathleen Marie. 1987. *Nietzsche's Zarathustra*. Philadelphia.

Hjortssjö, Carl Hermann. "Queen Christina of Sweden, A Medical/Anthropological Investigation of Her Remains in Rome." *Acta Universitatis Ludensis* 11.9 (1966).

Hollinrake, Roger. 1982. *Nietzsche, Wagner, and the Philosophy of Pessimism*. London.

Hulme, Peter. 1986. *Colonial Encounters: Europe and the Native Caribbean, 1492–1797*. London.

Hulme, Peter, and William H. Sherman. 2000. *The Tempest and Its Travels*. London.

Hurtado, Fabio. 2000. "Intimidad de un tigre: Entrevista a Marta Calvo, primera esposa de Guillermo Cabrera Infante." *Suplemento Cultural Espacios, 3*.

Irwin, John T. 1983. *American Hieroglyphics: The Symbol of the Egyptian Hieroglyphics in the American Renaissance*. Baltimore.

————. 1994. *The Mystery to a Solution: Poe, Borges, and the Analytic Detective Story*. Baltimore.

Jackson Knight, W. F. 1967. "Cumaean Gates." In *Virgil: Epic and Anthropology*. London.

Jameson, Fred. 1991. *Postmodernism, or, the Cultural Logic of Late Capitalism*. Durham.

Jung, C. G. [1956] 1976. *Mysterium Coniunctionis*. Princeton.

Kerrigan, William. 1994. *Hamlet's Perfection*. Baltimore.

Kittler, Friedrich A. [1987] 1990. *Discourse Networks: 1800/1900*. Stanford.

Klein, Norman M. [1993] 1998. *Seven Minutes: The Life and Death of the American Animated Cartoon*. New York.

Köhler, Joachim. [1989] 2002. *Zarathustra's Secret*. Ronald Taylor, trans. New Haven.

Kraut, Richard, ed. 1992. *The Cambridge Companion to Plato*. Cambridge.

Lacan, Jacques. 1966. *Écrits*. Paris.

———. 1978. *The Four Fundamental Concepts of Psycho-Analysis*. New York.

Lampert, Laurence. 1986. *Nietzsche's Teaching: An Interpretation of "Thus Spoke Zarathustra."* New Haven.

Lear, Jonathan. 1998. *Open Minded: Working Out the Logic of the Soul*. Cambridge.

Lears, Jackson. 1994. *Fables of Abundance: A Cultural History of Advertising in America*. New York.

Lévi-Strauss, Claude. [1949] 1969. *The Elementary Structures of Kinship*. Boston.

———. [1966] 1973. *From Honey to Ashes: Introduction to a Science of Mythology: 2*. New York.

———. [1968] 1978. *The Origins of Table Manners: Introduction to a Science of Mythology: 3*. Chicago.

———. [1971] 1981. *The Naked Man: Introduction to a Science of Mythology: 4*. New York.

———. [1985] 1988. *The Jealous Potter*. Chicago.

———. [1988] 1992. *The View from Afar*. Chicago.

———. 1995. *The Story of Lynx*. Chicago.

Lincoln, Bruce. 1980. *Priests, Warriors, and Cattle: A Study in the Ecology of Religions*. Chicago.

———. 1991. *Death, War, and Sacrifice: Studies in Ideology and Practice*. Chicago.

López-Baralt, Mercedes. 1985. *El mito taíno: Lévi-Strauss en las antillas*. Puerto Rico.

Lowie, Robert. 1952. *The Tukuna*. University of California Publications in American Archeology, vol. 45.

Lukács, George. 1963. *The Historical Novel*. Boston.

Lynch, Deidre Shauna. 1998. *The Economy of Character: Novels, Market Culture, and the Business of Inner Meaning*. Chicago.

Maccoby, Hyam. 1982. *The Sacred Executioner*. New York.

Macey, David. 1988. *Lacan in Context*. London.

Mailer, Norman. 1973. *Marilyn, a Biography: Pictures by the World's Foremost Photographers*. New York.

Masson, Georgina. 1969. *Queen Christina*. New York.

Needham, Rodney. 1978. *Primordial Characters*. Charlottesville.

The New Oxford Annotated Bible with the Apocrypha. 1977. Herbert G. May and Bruce M. Metzger, eds. Oxford.

The Oxford English Dictionary. 1989. 2nd ed. J. A. Simpson and E. C. S. Weiner, eds. Oxford.

Pané, Fray Ramón. 1974. *Relación acerca de las antigüedades de los indios*. Mexico City.

———. 1999. *An Account of the Antiquities of the Indians*. Durham.

Paris, Barry. 1994. *Garbo: A Biography*. New York.

Pérez, Louis A., Jr. 2005. *To Die in Cuba: Suicide and Society*. Chapel Hill.

Pérez-Firmat, Gustavo. 2003. *Tongue Ties: Logo-Eroticism in Anglo-Hispanic Literature.* New York.

Pucci, Piero. 1987. *Odysseus Pulotropos: Intertextual Readings in "The Odyssey" and "The Iliad."* Ithaca.

Reynolds, Michael. 1999. *Hemingway: The Final Years.* New York.

Rickard, John S. 1999. *Joyce's Book of Memory: The Mnemotechnic of "Ulysses."* Durham.

Ríos Jáuregui, Anett. 2003. "Leonardo Padura y la novela de su vida." *La Gaceta de Cuba* 2:38.

Royle, Nicholas. 2003. *The Uncanny.* New York.

Rzepka, Charles J. 1995. *Sacramental Commodities: Gift, Text, and the Sublime in De Quincey.* Amherst.

Salinger, J. D. [1953] 1991. *Nine Stories.* Boston.

Sánchez-Pardo, Esther. 2003. *Cultures of the Death Drive: Melanie Klein and Modernist Melancholia.* Durham.

Sandars, N. K. 1978. *The Sea Peoples: Warriors of the Ancient Mediterranean, 1250–1150 BC.* London.

Schneider, Mark A. 1993. *Culture and Enchantment.* Chicago.

Seaford, Richard. 1986. "Wedding Ritual and Textual Criticism." *Hermes* 107:106–30.

Segal, Naomi. 1998. *André Gide: Pederasty and Pedagogy.* Oxford.

Sergent, Bernard. 1986. *Homosexuality in Greek Myth.* Boston.

Silver, Larry. 1984. *The Paintings of Quentin Massys.* London.

Sloan, Jane E. 1995. *Alfred Hitchcock: The Definitive Filmography.* Berkeley.

Sloterdijk, Peter. 1987. *Critique of Cynical Reason.* Minneapolis.

Souza, Raymond D. 1996. *Guillermo Cabrera Infante: Two Islands, Many Worlds.* Austin.

Spoto, Donald. [1983] 1993. *The Dark Side of Genius: The Life of Alfred Hitchcock.* New York.

Standage, Tom. 2002. *The Turk: The Life and Times of the Famous Eighteenth-Century Chess-Playing Machine.* New York.

Stanford, W. B. 1992. *The Ulysses Theme: A Study in the Adaptability of a Traditional Hero.* Dallas.

Strong, Tracy. [1975] 1988. *Friedrich Nietzsche and the Politics of Transfiguration.* Berkeley.

Sulloway, Frank. 1992. *Freud: Biologist of the Mind.* New York.

Tatum, James, ed. 1994. *The Search for the Ancient Novel.* Baltimore.

Vaughan, Alden, and Virginia Mason Vaughan. 1991. *Shakespeare's Caliban: A Cultural History.* Cambridge.

Vernant, J.-P. 1981. "The Myth of Prometheus in Hesiod." In *Myth, Religion, and Society,* R. L. Gordon, ed. Cambridge.

Viera y Clavijo, José de. 1981. *Historia de Canarias.* Vol. 1. Canary Islands.

Weber, Robertus, ed. 1969. *Biblia Sacra. Iuxta Vulgatam Versionem.* Stuttgart.

Welsh, Alexander. 1994. *Freud's Wishful Dream Book.* Princeton.

White, David Gordon. 1991. *Myths of the Dog-Man.* Chicago.

Williams, William Appleman. 1969. *The Roots of the Modern American Empire.* New York.

Winkler, John J. 1985. *Auctor and Actor: A Narratological Reading of Apuleius' "The Golden Ass."* Berkeley.

————. 1990. *The Constraints of Desire.* New York.

Wollen, Peter. 1997. "Compulsion." *Sight and Sound* (April): 14–18.

Wood, Gaby. 2002. *Edison's Eve: A Magical History of the Quest for Mechanical Life.* New York.

Wood, Robin. [1965] 1989. *Hitchcock's Films Revisited.* New York.

Zanetti Lecuona, Oscar. 1998. *Comercio y poder: Relaciones cubano-hispano-norteamericanas en torno a 1898.* Havana.

Zeitlin, Froma. 1996. *Playing the Other: Gender and Society in Classical Greek Literature.* Chicago.

Žižek, Slavoj. 1992. *Enjoy Your Symptom! Jack Lacan in Hollywood and Out.* London.

index

Note: Modifications throughout the index are arranged in thematic order by the title of the work discussed as listed alphabetically by author. Modifications under themes listed separately follow ascending page order.

purity, 41; *La Habana Para un Infante Difunto (Infante's Inferno)*, and role of *Defunct (Difunto) Infant (Infante)* fictional *persona*, 4, 10–14; and *Defunct-Infant* temporal dialectic in reference to Joyce's *Ulysses*, 14; in referenceto De Quincey, 61–62; in referenceto Faust, 15; in relation to fetishism and question of "affective reading," 14–15; in relation to "Romantic penmanship," 153; story of *The Amazon*, in relation to Cupid and Psyche, 84–85; in relation to Almodóvar's *Hable con ella*, 131–32; in relation to Freud's "Taboo of Virginity," 86–87, 95–96; in relation to ancient Amazons, 86–87; in relation to Hitchcock's *Rear Window*, 134, 135; and *Rebecca*, 98–99; and *Spellbound*, 87–96; and *Vertigo*, 107, 112; and Poe's "Morella," 99–102; and "Maelzel's Chess-Player," 110–12; in reference to Cabrera Infante's "La muerte de un autómata," 149, 150; in reference to breast mutilation among Amazons and split of primal androgyne in Plato's *Symposium*, 105–7; and Petronius's *Satyricon* and Sybil's plight in, 9–10; and Virgil's *Aeneid*'s underworld, 10; and *Great Gatsby*, 10; and Ulysses's role in contested authorship with his women lovers, 62–63; and Ulysses in exile in relation to Che Guevara, 70; and tenement life in reference to De Quincey and Fourier and Benjamin's *Arcades Project*, 71–74; and sexual activity at cinema, 74, 75; related to Lévi-Strauss and Amazonian myth, 75–77; and story of Pablo Efesio, 77–80; and story of Gerardito the barber and his ugly wife, 80–82;

and ugly wife related to Massys's *Portrait of a Grotesque Woman*, 80–81; related to "Ugly Duchess" in *Alice in Wonderland*, 82; Hotel Pasaje ruin related to Benjamin's *Das Passagen-Werk*, 83; in relation to Sorcerer-Clown in *Los palacios distantes* (Abilio Estévez), 83; *Mea Cuba*, punning in, 141; *Un oficio del siglo XX*, Garbo's looks examined in, 32; on Garbo's voice, 33; and review of *Vertigo* in November 1959 in relation to Orpheus and Eurydice, 97–98, 119, 122; and review of *Más allá del olvido* in relation to *Vertigo*, 120; *Tres Tristes Tigres (Three Trapped Tigers)*, related to *La Habana Para un Infante Difunto* as erotic labyrinth, 10; related to lampoon parodies of Trotsky's assassination, 138–39, 146; related to Lot's dream, 217 (n. 6); "La voz de la tortuga," 16–26; plot summary analyzed, 16–18; and Sybil in *Satyricon*, 9; and tortoise copulating behavior examined, 18–19; and Mock Turtle in *Alice in Wonderland*, 18–20, 24; and tortoise tale considered in reference to fiction and myth, 21; in reference to *zoemes* in Lévi-Strauss's study of myth, 21–22; in reference to myth of Prometheus and Pandora, 22–23; in relation to Ortiz's study of hurricane sacred symbols, 24–25; in relation to hunger, 23–24, 27

Caguama (sea tortoise), 18, 20–21; and wordplay with *caguamo*, 21, 210 (n. 3)

Cain (biblical), 6, 118, 123, 137, 139–41

Caín (Cabrera Infante's pen name), 32, 70, 97, 112, 113, 141

Calasso, Roberto: *Ka: Stories of the Mind and Gods of India*, 193; and Buddha, 201

Needham, Rodney: *Primordial Characters*, on myths and the impossible, 18

Nietzsche, Friedrich: on his life as portrayed in *Ecce Homo*, 155–56; health at time of writing *Human, All Too Human* compared with Martí's when he wrote *Versos sencillos*, 155–56; his life and Martí's contrasted, 157–58; authorship of *Thus Spoke Zarathustra: A Book for Everyone and No One* in relation to Martí's career, 157–58; Derrida's notion of "spectrality" in relation to Martí's Nietzschean afterlife, 160; on Wagner translated into German in reference to Martí cult, 162–63; on Zarathustra and friendship, 164–65; on Zarathustra as pariah, 165–66; on socialism, 168

Novás Calvo, Lino: *Pedro Blanco, el negrero,* and Byron's *Don Juan,* 67; as Caliban figure, 68; as Romantic Machiavel, 68

Ortiz, Fernando: *Contrapunteo cubano del tabaco y el azúcar (Cuban Counterpoint: Tobacco and Sugar),* on Arawak stories of flood and exodus, 46–47; *Ensayos etnográficos,* on feast of *Día de Reyes,* 222–23 (n. 18); *El huracán: su mitología y sus símbolos,* on Arawak beliefs about hurricane, 24–26; *Los negros brujos,* on twin brotherhood of *jimaguas,* 206–7; and scapegoating of black healers, 207, 224 (n. 34)

Padura Fuentes, Leonardo, 3, 5, 170; relation to character Conde, 153; relation to Conde's status as Romantic avatar, 168–69; use of casuistry in authorship disclaimer in *Pasado perfecto,* 171; and altered calendar in *Las cuatro estaciones,* 172–73; and "obstinate effect of reality" claim and Lacan's notion of traumatic cause, 174; publication of *La novela de mi vida,* 178; and chronology of Heredia's life, 178; comments on Heredia's ideas on independence, 178; dedicates *La novela de mi vida* to father, 184; and "Leonardo" signature in *Máscaras,* 192; relation of Magus figure Forcade to Coleridge's Old Man in "Limbo," 203; relation of *jimagua* (twin) brotherhood to Ortiz, 206; *Las cuatro estaciones,* 1989 calendar altered in, 170–71, 174–77; related to Romantic historical novel, 172–74; on issue of generational trauma, 174, 176–77; *Pasado perfecto,* crime committed on *Día de Reyes* (Epiphany) in, 182–83; *Hamlet* quoted in, 185; *Vientos de Cuaresma,* Lent and Easter overlap in, 183–84; surveillance by CDRs in, 184; grave diggers' scene in *Hamlet* alluded to in, 185–86; political and religious dissidence related in, 186–87; *Máscaras,* crossdressing and multiple role playing in, 187–89; cross-dressing related to Christological lore and murder in, 187; symbolic parricide and political murder mixed in, 187; da Vinci's *Vitruvian Man* as murder clue in, 189; relevance of Freud's essay on da Vinci's homosexuality considered in, 191–92; plot relevance of Castro's birthday surmised in, 194–96; issue of "squalor" considered in reference to Salinger's fiction in, 196; *Paisaje de otoño,* homophobic machismo's role examined in reference to "whoreson" slur in *Hamlet* in, 196–97; *Hamlet*'s

envisioning cuba

Eduardo González, *Cuba and the Tempest: Literature and Cinema in the Time of Diaspora* (2006).

Samuel Farber, *The Origins of the Cuban Revolution Reconsidered* (2006).

Lillian Guerra, *The Myth of José Martí: Conflicting Nationalisms in Early Twentieth-Century Cuba* (2005).

Rodrigo Lazo, *Writing to Cuba: Filibustering and Cuban Exiles in the United States* (2005).

Alejandra Bronfman, *Measures of Equality: Social Science, Citizenship, and Race in Cuba, 1902–1940* (2004).

Edna M. Rodríguez-Mangual, *Lydia Cabrera and the Construction of an Afro-Cuban Cultural Identity* (2004).

Gabino La Rosa Corzo, *Runaway Slave Settlements in Cuba: Resistance and Repression* (2003).

Piero Gleijeses, *Conflicting Missions: Havana, Washington, and Africa, 1959–1976* (2002).

Robert Whitney, *State and Revolution in Cuba: Mass Mobilization and Political Change, 1920–1940* (2001).

Alejandro de la Fuente, *A Nation for All: Race, Inequality, and Politics in Twentieth-Century Cuba* (2001).